Civil Rights and the Making of the Modern American State

Did the civil rights movement impact the development of the American state? Despite extensive accounts of civil rights mobilization and narratives of state building, there has been surprisingly little research that explicitly examines the importance and consequence that civil rights activism has had for the process of state building in American political and constitutional development. Through a sweeping archival analysis of the NAACP's battle against lynching and mob violence from 1909 to 1923, this book examines how the NAACP raised public awareness, won over U.S. presidents, and secured the support of Congress. In the NAACP's most far-reaching victory, the Supreme Court ruled that the constitutional rights of black defendants were violated by a white mob in the landmark criminal procedure decision *Moore v. Dempsey* – a decision that changed the relationship of state and local courts to the national state. This book establishes the importance of citizen agency in the making of new constitutional law in a period unexplored by previous scholarship.

Megan Ming Francis is Assistant Professor of Political Science at Pepperdine University. She completed her PhD in the Department of Politics at Princeton University in 2008 and served as a Postdoctoral Fellow at the University of Chicago in 2008–2009 and as a Jerome Hall Postdoctoral Fellow at the Center of Law, Society, and Culture at Indiana University Maurer School of Law in 2009–2010. Francis's research interests include American political development, race, crime, capitalism, and civil rights.

Civil Rights and the Making of the Modern American State

MEGAN MING FRANCIS

Pepperdine University

CAMBRIDGE
UNIVERSITY PRESS

CAMBRIDGE
UNIVERSITY PRESS

32 Avenue of the Americas, New York NY 10013-2473, USA

Cambridge University Press is part of the University of Cambridge.

It furthers the University's mission by disseminating knowledge in the pursuit of education, learning and research at the highest international levels of excellence.

www.cambridge.org
Information on this title: www.cambridge.org/9781107697973

© Megan Ming Francis 2014

First published 2014

A catalogue record for this publication is available from the British Library

Library of Congress Cataloguing in Publication data
Francis, Megan Ming, 1981–
Civil rights and the making of the modern American state / Megan Ming Francis, Pepperdine University.
    p.   cm.
Includes bibliographical references and index.
ISBN 978-1-107-03710-6 (hardback) – ISBN 978-1-107-69797-3 (paperback)
1. Civil rights – United States   2. National Association for the Advancement of Colored People.   3. African Americans – Civil rights – History – 20th century.   4. African Americans – Legal status, laws, etc.   5. Civil rights movements – United States – History – 20th century.   6. United States. Supreme Court.   7. Lynching – Law and legislation – United States   8. Constitutional law – United States.   I. Title.
JC599.U5F73   2014
323.0973–dc23   2013046192

ISBN 978-1-107-03710-6 Hardback
ISBN 978-1-107-69797-3 Paperback

To my parents, Horace and Annette Francis, who taught me how to be courageous in fighting for the things I believe in, but most of all taught me how to love.

Contents

Figures and Table

Figures

Table

Illustrations

Acknowledgments

This book was not supposed to happen. Eight years ago, I was at the precipice of leaving the academy. It was the spring of 2005, and I stood on the stairs looking up at the building that housed the Department of Politics at Princeton University and vowed never to return. I was near the end of my second year in graduate school, three weeks away from PhD qualifying exams, and five weeks away from final exams in my last year of coursework, and I did not feel like I wanted anything to do with political science. I felt that the area of research I cared about most – the intersection of law, race, and American political development – was marginalized in the discipline and I was tired of fighting others to care. Unfortunately for my hasty vow and fortunately for my career, I turned around and at that moment ran into Paul Frymer, my thesis advisor, who saw the look of distress on my face and talked me off the proverbial ledge. His ability to wear down my resolve that day changed a lot of things and set me on the course that I am still currently on. I would continue on at Princeton and write a dissertation that I was proud of under the tutelage of a brilliant group of scholars. Indeed, if there has been one lesson that stands out to me over the course of this book project, it is that writing and research comprise a journey that takes one down many unexpected but fascinating roads. I am blessed and humbled that this is part of what I do for a living.

This book has been written because of an incredible network of support from family, friends, colleagues, and mentors to whom I am forever indebted. Firstly, to my dissertation committee: To Melissa Harris-Perry for being a courageous and inspiring mentor and friend. My sincerest thanks to Melissa for always finding time in her life for me and my work. Melissa's blunt honesty about my scholarship has always pushed me to do better (and to rewrite whole chapters!), and her contagious laughter lifted me during some of my most trying times at Princeton. To Paul Frymer, without whom I likely would never have finished Princeton. My thanks to Paul for shepherding me through graduate school – on the west and the east coasts. Paul's scholarship has influenced my own immensely. Tali Mendelberg saw something in me at a very early stage and encouraged me to pursue graduate studies at Princeton. Her genuine support of my interests from 2003 until now has been deeply humbling. From Mahalia Jackson, to W. E. B. Du Bois, to E. Franklin Frazier, no one can wax poetic the religious, music, and class dimensions of African Americans quite like Cornel West. Everyone should be so fortunate to learn from four scholars with such incisive intellect. I only hope that I have made them proud.

Edward Cox and Alexander Byrd were my undergraduate professor exemplars at Rice University. Through their teaching they exhibited a portrait of something that I hoped I might someday become. Both Ed and Alex took time out of their busy schedules to help me become a better student, an avid reader, a probing questioner, and, most importantly, a more adept writer. From "Caribbean Nation Building" to "Blacks in Reagan's America," I was taught to think independently, and that the answers to big questions often lay outside of the parameters in which we are traditionally taught to think about things. My thanks to Ryan Hall for encouraging me to attend my first political science class. Evan Pankey was the critic I never wanted, but he made this book better. Uri McMillan has been my rock since our all-nighter days while undergrads at Rice University. I'm not quite sure what I would have done without him (or his snark, or his style) on this academic journey. Vasco Bridges and I have shared a long friendship from Houston to Brooklyn to yearly barbeques. Somewhere along the way, he helped make the most difficult period of graduate school bearable by nursing me through it on a diet of turkey burgers and margaritas – and sometimes just margaritas. I am forever grateful.

There is little doubt that graduate school was tough but there were a number of people that helped to make it better. To my Princeton comrades who kept me sane: Christina Azene, Justin Crowe, Michael Cutrone, Diana Hill, Tehama Lopez, and Cristina Mora, who each in their own individual way stayed attuned to their personal compass and chartered their own paths during and in the years after Princeton. The courageousness of this group was inspiring in countless ways. Leah Wright has been my kindred soul in the academy ever since graduate prospect weekend in 2003, and her friendship and brilliance have allowed me to weather many a storm unscathed. A tremendous intellectual debt is owed to Emily Zackin who often knew what I was trying to argue better than I did in grad school. Her heart and intellect are boundless. Associate Dean Karen Jackson-Weaver was a godsend and provided much-needed support and encouragement.

I'm always surprised and humbled when scholars who have provided an inspiration for my own scholarship take an interest in my work. In particular, I thank Charles Epp, Lisa Miller, Mark Tushnet, and Rick Valelly for reading different chapters in this book and providing constructive suggestions over the years. When there was no time, somehow Cathy Cohen made time to read my work and guide me during my postdoc at the University of Chicago.

I feel especially grateful, as Cathy's important scholarship has left an enduring mark on my own research. Dennis Hutchinson gave me some of the harshest yet most useful feedback – this book is better because of it. My thanks to Michael Dawson for being so very generous with his time and for going above and beyond the call of duty in providing feedback and helping me to shape the dimensions of my book project. If we had more people with the type of activist commitments that Michael has, the academy would be a better place. I am grateful to Alvin Tillery, without whom I might never have had the gumption to approach Cambridge at a fateful APSA in Toronto. Al has been an amazing mentor and an even better friend. My deepest thanks to him for doing the impossible: making political science fun. Jane Junn has been the best coach on how to "hit something out of the ballpark." After a grueling conference, she sacrificed sleep on a plane to help fine-tune my book argument on a scrap piece of paper. Jane's sense of humanity and integrity continues to inspire me.

I was fortunate to be at Indiana University Maurer School of Law during the first year of the Center of Law, Society, and Culture's postdoctoral program, where Michael Grossberg and Ajay Mehrotra were the codirectors. Both Mike and Ajay took an immense amount of time to read and provide feedback when they didn't have to. Also thanks to Kevin Brown, Khalil Gibran Muhammad, and Ryan Scott for helpful suggestions and mentorship.

At Pepperdine University I am surrounded by a breathtaking view of the Pacific but more importantly a wonderful array of junior and senior colleagues and friends. All junior scholars should be so fortunate. Dan Caldwell, Joel Fetzer, Nate Klemp, Brian Newman, Candice Ortbals, Steve Rouse, Chris Soper, and Robert Williams have been particularly supportive of this book. Every day, I count myself lucky to have Elizabeth Essary in my life as a colleague and a friend.

I would have never survived the multiyear revision process necessary to make this book stronger if it wasn't for the help of very important people along the way. Much of this book is done because of the support and encouragement of Bing Howell, my only fan club member, during the roughest moments of this project. I owe him an enormous debt for finding joy for me when I couldn't find it myself. Lee Ann Wang, my soul's counterpoint, has always been just a phone call away. Thank you for more than eighteen years of friendship filled with laughter and ballads we have no business singing. Michael Ralph's searing criticism pushed me to make this book stronger. My thanks to Ramzi Kassem for expert advice around some thorny habeas law questions and an inspiring commitment to unmasking inequalities in our legal system. Deepthy Kishore is one of my dearest friends; she lent her legal expertise to my court chapter amid a horrible power outage in DC. Alzo Slade provided shelter and turkey bacon, and made me laugh until my sides hurt during many research trips to New York. And to my CPC family (Uri, Leah, Mike, Laurence Ralph, and Eva Haldane) – our little community of like-minded scholars has been immensely fulfilling in an often lonely line of work.

Lewis Bateman, my editor at Cambridge, saw the promise in this project at a very early stage. My thanks to him for patiently waiting. There never was a doubt in my mind that I wanted this book to go with Cambridge, as he "got" this project far before many did, and I am grateful. Many thanks to Shaun Vigil for his patience in answering my frantic emails. And my gratitude to the excellent anonymous reviewers of this manuscript for many helpful suggestions.

Libraries are the unsung heroes of academic research, and I am proud of my library card collection. I have visited many to write this book. My deepest gratitude to the following libraries and the librarians and archivists that fill them: Library of Congress (Manuscript Reading Room, Prints and Photographs Reading Room), Wisconsin Historical Society Library, Widener Library at Harvard University, Houghton Library at Harvard University, Firestone Library at Princeton University, New York Public Library (Rare Books and Manuscripts Division), The Regenstein Library at the University of Chicago, and Payson Library at Pepperdine University.

Critical institutional support that has aided me in completing this book has been graciously provided by Princeton Graduate School; Center for Law, Society, and Culture at Indiana University Maurer School of Law; the Political Science Department at University of Chicago; Pepperdine University, Dean's Office at Seaver; and the Ford Foundation. A portion of Chapter 2 is drawn from my article "The Battle for the Hearts and Minds of America," which was published in *Souls* 13, no. 1 (2011), reprinted with permission from Taylor and Francis Ltd.

My life outside of the academy is just as important as my life inside the academy. In this area, there are certain people who have shaped my life in ways that the words "thank you" will never seem sufficient: To my sister/cousin Camille Walker for digging me out of many a deep dark academic hole and often reminding me that there was life outside of research and writing. She was the balance I didn't know I needed but don't know what I'd do without. I am particularly indebted to the following supportive voices in my life: Tiana Allen, Michelle Antwi, Alexandria Carroll, Jessica Carter, Stan Chen, Christopher Coes, Jeff Dess, Anthony Francis, Hollins Gause, Jaira Harrington, Eddie Lincoln, Stephanie McDuffie, Julie Merseth, Mike Mitchell, Adrienne Packard, Shana Pearson, Philip Rigueur, Samijo, Tia Silas, Sara Stewart, Matt Story, and Marvin Wilmoth. Thanks to a cat named Meebo and a corgi named President Bartlet for all the distractions. FWMJ has been incredibly supportive and allowed me to pour time into finishing this book project (albeit with time wasted on funny Facebook posts). My sincerest thanks to him for moving across the country and providing me with the exact kind of balance I need. He makes me laugh harder and smile bigger. When I'm done writing, let's go get some xiao long bao!

My deepest debt of gratitude is reserved for the memories of the people that fill this book and give it life – those who put their lives on the line so that true American democracy could actually appear within reach. Sometimes when I did not feel like completing this manuscript, their writings on tattered papers inspired me to keep going. From their work on fighting lynchings to their symbolic gains in the Wilson and Harding administrations and then to legal strategizing sessions that culminated in the landmark victory in front of the Supreme Court, this group of women and men forced the federal government to pay attention to their struggle. Today, we stand on the shoulders of greats, and my small hope in writing this book is that we not forget important accounts of how people on the margins of our society helped to close the vast gulf that existed between democratic rhetoric and reality. Nor that we forget how much power we still possess in working collectively toward a more just political and legal system.

Abbreviations

ACLU	American Civil Liberties Union
AFPS	American Fund for Public Service (The Garland Fund)
AL	Arthur Link
APD	American Political Development
BOD	Board of Director
CCR	Center for Constitutional Rights
CPR	Communities United for Police Reform
KKK	Ku Klux Klan
LOC	Library of Congress
NAACP	National Association for the Advancement of Colored People
NACW	National Association of Colored Women
NUL	National Urban League
PFHUA	Progressive Farmers and Household Union of America
UL	Urban League
UNIA	United Negro Improvement Association
Waskow	Waskow Papers

Rethinking Civil Rights and American Political Development

What's past is prologue.

– *William Shakespeare*

This is the sort of work which the National Association for the Advancement of Colored People is doing. It is a broader question than that of obtaining justice for Negroes. It is a fight for the high principles which we as Americans revere.

– *Walter White*[1]

It was a dreary night on September 30, 1919, when a small group of African American tenant farmers peacefully gathered in a church in Phillips County, Arkansas, to organize in seeking relief from the sharecropping system that kept them as virtual slaves to their white landlords. However, the meeting would not end in success. Aware of the union of African Americans, a small band of white law enforcement officials disrupted the gathering by firing shots into the church, first shattering the ceiling lights and then aiming at the frightened men, women, and children trapped in the darkened building. Their fire was returned with fire from inside the church, and one white man was killed. Declaring that the African Americans were forming a plot to kill the "good whites" of Phillips County, prominent whites called on the Ku Klux Klan and other white vigilante organizations from neighboring states such as Mississippi and Tennessee to quell the fabricated insurrection by African Americans. What ensued in Phillips County would become the worst display of racial violence up to that point in the twentieth century: more than 200 African American men, women, and children were indiscriminately hunted and shot down over the course of three days. Thousands were driven from their homes, and the African

---

[1] Walter White to George Wickersham (former Attorney General in President William Howard Taft's administration) in reference to the NAACP victory in *Moore v. Dempsey*, Letter, March 9, 1923, NAACP Papers, Manuscript Division, Library of Congress, Washington, DC.

American section of town was looted and destroyed. When the dust cleared, seventy-two African American men had been arrested. After swift trials dominated by a bloodthirsty mob, all seventy-two were found guilty, and twelve were sentenced to death by the electric chair.

The Phillips County massacre was not an anomaly; the summer of 1919 had been marked by a series of horrifying race riots across the country.[2] Still, it stood out as the incident with the most devastating consequences and clearly displayed the power of white supremacy and the inadequacy of the American justice system. Twelve African American men faced what the National Association for the Advancement of Colored People's (NAACP) founder William English Walling called "lynching by law." These men, sharecroppers by profession, had been harassed in the first place because they sought to organize against exploitive white landowners who refused to pay them the market price for their cotton. Each member of the Phillips County 12 received a trial that was no longer than an hour. In the courtroom was a bloodthirsty mob that had agreed to let the legal proceedings take place only after the courts had promised that the accused would be found guilty and executed.[3]

The trial was just the latest example of the vulnerability of African American citizenship in postbellum America. At the time this incident occurred, Jim Crow justice was only an inch away from Judge Lynch. It was 1919, and mob-dominated trials and coercive methods of dealing with African American defendants in southern courtrooms were far from abnormal. The national government did not interfere in state criminal proceedings, and no uniform criminal procedure code existed. Individual states were responsible for the handling of their own criminal proceedings.

Despite not having a formal legal arm, the NAACP took as a serious affront the idea that twelve innocent African American men could be sentenced to die in an American courtroom. The sham trial threatened to undermine everything the organization had worked so hard to accomplish. The aspirations to effect equality in education, voting, and labor were doomed if brutal violence against African Americans could continue without punishment. Thus, legal support of the Phillips County 12 seemed like a necessary step for the NAACP. The circumstances surrounding the case were daunting; still, it chose to get involved. More than three years later, the NAACP's work would culminate in the precedent-setting Supreme Court criminal procedure decision, *Moore v. Dempsey* 261 U.S. 86 (1923), which would mark the first time the federal government interfered in state criminal court proceedings. The question before the Supreme Court was whether the presence of a mob in a courtroom violated the due process clause of the Fourteenth Amendment. In a decision written by Justice Oliver Wendell Holmes, the Supreme Court ruled in favor of the

---

[2] Arthur Waskow, *From Race Riot to Sit-In, 1919 and the 1960s: A Study in the Connections Between Conflict and Violence*, Garden City, NY: Anchor Books, 1967.

[3] Walter White, "'Massacring Whites' in Arkansas," *The Nation*, December 6, 1919, Waskow.

African American defendants and declared that a fair trial must be free from mob domination.

The initial incident that led to *Moore v. Dempsey* coincided with the apex of the NAACP's anti-lynching crusade. The issue of racial violence was foremost on the agenda of the NAACP because unchecked lynching and mob violence were some of the greatest impediments to equality for African Americans at the time of the NAACP's founding in 1909. After the brief period known as Reconstruction came to a close, state governments across the South sought to construct a system of racial and economic domination reminiscent of slavery. They set out to accomplish this goal through unrestricted racial violence. During the post-Reconstruction period, white mobs were free to inflict violence upon African Americans; they could easily, for instance, lynch an African American without punishment.[4] Numerous examples exist in which African Americans were lynched because they were in the wrong place at the wrong time, or when there were new challenges to southern political authority, and especially when the economic standing of southern whites was threatened.[5] Against such injustice African Americans had no recourse. Law enforcement and government officials looked the other way and thus played a complicit role in the violence.

The NAACP was established in the aftermath of a race riot in Springfield, Illinois, that occurred on August 14, 1908. During the riot, white mobs stormed through the African American district, burning homes and destroying business establishments. It took more than 4,000 militiamen two days to restore order. By this time, two people had already been lynched, and 2,000 African Americans had fled the city. Shock waves reverberated throughout the nation that such violence could occur in the North. The racist violence evidenced in the Springfield riot heightened the need for action and mobilized reformers to act. As a result, a biracial coalition of activists, clergy, and scholars was formed in 1909 as a watchdog of liberties for African Americans. The coalition members sought to create a unified front against future racial injustice and committed themselves to improving the fragile citizenship rights of African Americans.[6]

---

[4] Walter Francis White, *Rope & Faggot: A Biography of Judge Lynch*, New York and London: A. A. Knopf, 1929; Ida B. Wells, *Crusade for Justice: The Autobiography of Ida B. Wells*, Chicago: The University of Chicago Press, 1970; A. Arthur Raper, *The Tragedy of Lynching*, Chapel Hill: University of North Carolina Press, 1933; W. E. B. Du Bois, *Black Reconstruction in America*, New York: Atheneum, 1935; Leon Litwack, *Trouble in Mind: Black Southerners in the Age of Jim Crow*, New York: Vintage Books, 1998.

[5] Susan Olzak, "The Political Context of Competition: Lynching and Urban Racial Violence, 1882–1914," *Social Forces* 69, no. 2 (1990): 395–421; Stewart Tolnay, E. M. Beck, and James Massey, "Black Competition and White Vengeance: Legal Execution of Blacks as Social Control in the Cotton South, 1890 to 1929," *Social Science Quarterly* 73 (1992): 627–644; Stewart Tolnay and E. M. Beck, *A Festival of Violence: An Analysis of Southern Lynchings, 1882–1930*, Urbana: University of Illinois Press, 1995.

[6] For accounts of the development of the NAACP, see the following: Langston Hughes, *Fight for Freedom*, New York: W. W. Norton, 1962; Charles Flint Kellogg, *NAACP: A History of*

From the beginning, the NAACP remained committed to raising national awareness to the injustice of racial violence. Particularly notable was the development of its anti-lynching and mob-violence-reduction campaign. To conduct this campaign, the NAACP began by implementing a strategy to place the issue of racial violence in mainstream discourse. The first task undertaken by the anti-lynching campaign was to raise public awareness among whites of lynching and mob violence. Lynching persisted, and the NAACP believed this was because most white Americans knew very little about the terrorism lynching and mob violence inflicted upon African American communities.[7] If they were aware of the barbarism of lynching, the NAACP reasoned, white Americans would be appalled, and steps would be taken "to end this miserable disgrace and foul blot upon the fair name of America."[8] To this end, the NAACP concentrated on investigating lynchings and developed a three-pronged media strategy focused on writing articles, producing anti-lynching pamphlets, and utilizing its own organizational magazine, *The Crisis*, to reach white Americans. By articulating the terror of lynching and broadcasting it to a wider audience through these different channels, the NAACP hoped the normalized attitudes toward lynchings – acceptability in the South and indifference in the North – would change and turn decidedly against lynching.[9]

The battery of NAACP activities focused on changing public opinion about lynching provided a necessary shock to a society that was at best ambivalent over the lynching of African Americans. Aided by resources, contacts, and well-placed board members, the NAACP was able to get the word out about lynching. The infusion of an alternative perspective into the public domain provided white Americans with another way to interpret lynchings. Nevertheless, despite the greater presence of lynching and mob violence in mainstream discourse, the NAACP's publicity activities did not completely end lynching. Even more frustrating, it became apparent that many whites were aware of the racist violence African Americans endured but did nothing to stop the injustice.

It was not enough for the NAACP to raise the public's awareness about mob violence and lynchings; the organization knew a lot of power lay in politics and felt it necessary to supplement publicity with work in the legislative

---

the *National Association for the Advancement of Colored People*, Baltimore: Johns Hopkins University Press, 1967; B. Joyce Ross, *J. E. Spingarn and the Rise of NAACP, 1911–1929*, New York: Atheneum, 1972; Minnie Finch, *The NAACP: Its Fight for Justice*, London: The Scarecrow Press, 1981; Patricia Sullivan, *Lift Every Voice: The NAACP and the Making of the Civil Rights Movement*, New York: New Press, 2009.

[7] "The world does not know, it does not realize evil or its significance in nine cases out of ten. This is particularly true of the situation of American Negroes." In Seventh Annual Report for the Year 1916, NAACP Papers, Manuscript Division, Library of Congress, Washington, DC.

[8] Tenth Annual Report for the Year 1919, p. 17, NAACP Papers, Manuscript Division, Library of Congress, Washington, DC.

[9] August Meier, *Negro Thought in America, 1880–1915: Radical Ideologies in the Age of Booker T. Washington*, Ann Arbor: The University of Michigan Press, 1963, p. 161.

arena where it sponsored an anti-lynching bill and began a historic drive in Congress in 1921. In a very short time, the NAACP remade itself into an anti-lynching lobbying organization, and, through direct lobbying to individual Congressmen and an expansive grassroots effort, pressured lawmakers in the House of Representatives to pass the anti-lynching bill. In less than a year, leading House Republicans went from a hands-off approach to anti-lynching legislation to actively advocating on its behalf and defending the necessity for such legislation against a determined coalition of southern Democrats. The NAACP-supported anti-lynching bill passed the House of Representatives by a commanding two-thirds vote. However, the bill was filibustered in the Senate and never made into a law.

The NAACP also trained its eyes on the Oval Office where, after much persuasion, the organization succeeded in placing racial violence on the presidential agenda. Through a relentless barrage of appeals, the NAACP was able to convince President Woodrow Wilson and President Warren G. Harding to publicly denounce lynching and mob violence. After mounting pressure, Wilson conceded to NAACP demands during his second term, and Harding complied with NAACP requests for a strong statement against lynching as soon as he assumed office. The public statements made by Wilson and Harding against lynchings are particularly remarkable because both men initially expressed an unwillingness to address the issue. Private correspondence also reveals other significant areas where Wilson and Harding directly responded to NAACP requests: Wilson halted the killings of an African American army battalion that came under court marshal, and Harding supported the NAACP-sponsored anti-lynching bill. Nevertheless, similar to its efforts in Congress, the NAACP did not ultimately get what it wanted: the presidential denouncements did not end lynching, nor were the presidents willing to actively push for anti-lynching legislation.

The marked increase in the NAACP's involvement at the political level can be traced to the additions of James Weldon Johnson as NAACP secretary and Walter White as assistant secretary in 1916 and 1918, respectively. Together they put renewed pressure on the political branches and aggressively pushed for a greater NAACP presence in national politics. By awakening the public and political consciousness to lynching and mob violence, the NAACP played a major role in creating an environment that was receptive to the need for more safeguards in the criminal justice process. Nevertheless, despite this work, the number of lynchings continued to increase. Exasperated with the pace of progress in the social and political contexts and aware that a lot of power lay in the law, the NAACP turned its attention to the legal arena, where the organization was able to challenge the boundaries of constitutional doctrine in the area of criminal procedure.

The NAACP's influence was displayed most prominently in the landmark decision *Moore v. Dempsey*. Through this ruling, the Supreme Court made history by breaking from an established tradition of federalism and changed the federal government's position on racial violence. With this case, the Supreme Court finally moved the federal government from a rut of frustrating symbolic rhetoric to substantive legal guarantees.

Once the NAACP secured this decision from the Supreme Court, new precedent was established, and the Supreme Court entered a new era of jurisprudence no longer bound by strict deference to state courts. After *Moore v. Dempsey*, the Supreme Court made clear it was no longer willing to ignore the blatant racism that existed in southern courtrooms. Subsequently, the Supreme Court displayed its willingness to intervene on behalf of helpless African American defendants in a number of precedent-setting cases in the 1930s and 1940s, such as *Powell v. Alabama* (establishing that defendants in capital cases have a right to state-appointed counsel),[10] *Hollins v. Oklahoma* (the first of many decisions declaring exclusion of African American jurors unconstitutional),[11] *Brown v. Mississippi* (ruling that confessions exacted through torture violated the due process clause),[12] and *Chambers v. Florida* (establishing that confessions obtained under duress were illegal).[13] Beginning with these cases in the first half of the twentieth century, the power of federal courts vis-à-vis state courts in the area of criminal law began to expand. The Supreme Court decisions during this period sent a message to state governments that a criminal trial had to have more than simply the appearance of being conducted in a lawful manner – it had to have substance as well. By doing so, the Supreme Court positioned itself as a major institutional player in the politics of race in Jim Crow America.

Moore v. Dempsey is known for the legal precedent it helped establish, yet the Supreme Court's complicated journey to a final outcome has been obscured in the existing literature. In line with public law scholars who have linked expansions in court power to elected officials as well as public opinion, the leading view explains the federalization of power in criminal law as a product of the changing political and social environment.[14] It is often

[10] 287 U.S. 45 (1932): One of the notorious Scottsboro cases where nine young black men were accused of raping two white women on a train. The young men barely escaped a lynch mob and were swiftly sentenced to death. On appeal, the Supreme Court reversed the convictions based on the due process clause of the Fourteenth Amendment and stated that fundamental fairness required that counsel be appointed.

[11] 295 U.S. 394 (1935): An African-American man convicted of a rape in Oklahoma charged that blacks had systematically been excluded from jury service based solely on account of their race.

[12] 297 U.S. 278 (1936): A case where three African American Mississippi men were stripped naked and beaten with leather straps with buckles and tortured by pseudo-lynching until they confessed to murdering their white plantation owner. The court's majority opinion cited *Moore v. Dempsey*.

[13] 309 U.S. 227 (1940): A situation arose when more than thirty black men were rounded up without warrants and brought to the county jail whereupon they faced persistent and repeated questioning that went on for several days.

[14] Mark Graber, "The Nonmajoritarian Difficulty: Legislative Deference to the Judiciary," *Studies in American Political Development* 7 (1993): 35–73; Paul Frymer, "Acting When Elected

assumed, as Michael Klarman argues, that this was a fairly straightforward and easy decision. Klarman correctly stresses that, by the time *Moore v. Dempsey* appeared before the nation's highest court, the public (including national politicians) had become more concerned about the "problems of interracial violence and lawlessness."[15] Yet his analysis does not explain how political and social conditions change so as to permit a case like *Moore v. Dempsey* to be decided the way it was. Nor does it take into account the independent role of the litigation process on the Supreme Court's decision in *Moore*. To be clear, this book does not mean to suggest that the established theories are completely without merit; they do tell the truth, but they are incomplete. As a result, other significant factors that contributed to the beginning of federal involvement in state criminal trials are sidelined in favor of a direct link between political-social transformations and the construction of a stronger national judiciary. Warning political scientists about this kind of reductionism in our theorizing about institutions, Robert Lieberman writes:

To explain a change in some familiar state of affairs, we must assume an antecedent change in one or more causal factors that were previously part of a stable system. But after making this move we are left with the same problem: What caused this antecedent change, if not some change farther back in the causal chain? At some point in this sequence, the source of change must come from outside the system.[16]

This book endeavors to reorient how we think about American political and constitutional development, away from a narrow focus on institutions and elite state actors to a broader study that encompasses bottom-up change from organized citizens on the ground. Unlike previous research, this book demonstrates the role of the NAACP in shaping the path of development. Indeed, path dependence research has highlighted the significance of the early stages of institutional development in the shaping of future outcomes.[17] My own research reveals that by taking a step back and examining the antecedents to change in the political and social environment, we will see the critical role

---

Officials Won't: Federal Courts and Civil Rights Enforcement in U.S. Labor Union, 1935–85," *American Political Science Review* 97, no. 3 (2003): 483–499; Barry Friedman, *The Will of the People: How Public Opinion has Influenced the Supreme Court and Shaped the Meaning of the Constitution*, New York: Farrar, Straus and Giroux, 2009.

[15] Michael Klarman, "*The Racial Origins of Modern Criminal Procedure*," *Michigan Law Review* 99, no. 1 (October 2000), p. 60; Michael Klarman, *From Jim Crow to Civil Rights: The Supreme Court and the Struggle for Racial Equality*, Oxford: Oxford University Press, 2004; Malcolm Feely, "The Black Basis of Constitutional Development" in *Earl Warren and the Warren Court: The Legacy in American and Foreign Law*, edited by Harry N. Scheiber, Lanham, MD: Lexington Books/Rowman & Littlefield Publishers, 2007, pp. 66–67.

[16] Robert Lieberman, "Ideas, Institutions, and Political Order: Explaining Political Change," *The American Political Science Review* 96, no. 4 (December 2002), p. 698.

[17] Paul Pierson, *Politics in Time: History, Institutions, and Social Analysis*, Princeton, NJ: Princeton University Press, 2004.

the NAACP played in this case and by extension, in the construction of the national judiciary and civil rights.

Civil Rights–Centered Approach

This book places the NAACP at the crux of understanding the building of the twentieth-century American state. Using the NAACP's anti-lynching campaign, I determine the NAACP influenced the reshaping of institutions and the actions of individuals in a period critical to state development. First, I argue that the NAACP played a pivotal role in the growth of federal court power in criminal procedure and subsequently in civil rights by helping the Supreme Court wrestle away jurisdiction from state courts in the first quarter of the twentieth century. The importance of understanding the foundation of the Supreme Court's criminal procedure jurisprudence is magnified by its relation to the development of civil rights in the United States. *Moore v. Dempsey* marked a critical moment that helped federal courts see that the states were too weak to protect the most basic right to citizenship – the right to live – and thus the responsibility was up to the Supreme Court. Subsequently, the Supreme Court began a long tradition, climaxing in the 1950s and 1960s, of using the unequal treatment of African Americans as justification to power-grab from state courts.

In contemporary scholarship, we accept that the Supreme Court was an important institutional player in the furthering of a federal civil rights agenda in the twentieth century, but we do not trace it back to this path-dependent fork in the road. Part of this negligence is attributable to the oversaturation of *Brown v. Board of Education* 347 U.S. 483 (1954) in the literature. However, the starting point of civil rights was not born out of struggles around gaining equal access to education; that famous struggle built on the battle to have the right to live protected. In other words, the starting point of a more expansive federal civil rights agenda can be traced to the state's response to anti-lynching crusades. Without the NAACP, *Moore* would have never reached the Supreme Court, and the expansion of the Court in the areas of criminal procedure and civil rights would have come later or not at all. This is so because *both* the NAACP's focus on education desegregation litigation and the funding structure that birthed the storied NAACP Legal Defense Fund (NAACP-LDF) originated from a generous grant from the American Fund for Public Service (AFPS) in 1930. However, as evident in the AFPS archives, the NAACP's anti-lynching campaign first attracted the attention of the funder in 1922 and provided the basis of an invaluable relationship between the two organizations.[18] In this

---

[18] Appropriation of $2,500 for an educational campaign in connection with the Federal Anti-Lynching Campaign was voted into effect on October 11, 1922. An additional appropriation of $865.50 was voted on and approved on January 24, 1923. Reel 10, Box 15, American Fund for Public Service Records, Rare Books and Manuscripts Division, Schwarzman Building, New York Public Library.

way, the NAACP's campaign against racial violence and the subsequent victory in *Moore v. Dempsey* can be thought of as a critical juncture—a moment when the organizing logic of civil rights was established and new possibilities for political change were opened up.[19] We miss a crucial part of the development of the twentieth-century civil rights state by not systematically analyzing this earlier period.

Second, the NAACP's anti-lynching struggle influenced the strategies that African American political actors viewed as viable. Fighting for equal rights in American courtrooms was not the primary objective of the NAACP when it was founded. In 1909, the NAACP began a struggle for African Americans to gain the right to citizenship. And by 1919, the fledgling NAACP was making its presence known at the legislative, executive, and judicial levels of the federal government at the same time. Most existing scholarship focuses on the deployment of different strategies civil rights groups used to fight for equal rights, often comparing which was the most effective, but I remain unconvinced that we sufficiently understand how these strategies become identified as reasonable and prominent in social movement organizations. In other words: in the period before there was a canon of known civil rights strategies, how did litigation become recognized as part of this canon? Specifically, why was the NAACP's main site of contestation over civil rights in American courtrooms instead of in the American political process or in the streets? Available accounts on the NAACP and civil rights often treat it as an inevitable that the NAACP pursued a litigation-centered strategy – but this was not a foregone conclusion.

This book proposes that the NAACP's focus on a litigation strategy to fight for equal citizenship in the twentieth century was a strategic decision, constructed through a series of wins and losses during the formative years of movement activism.[20] I argue that to understand this choice of movement strategy, it

---

[19] In making this claim, I am applying historical institutionalist ideas about critical junctures and path dependence to non-state institutions. There is, of course, an impressive literature; see for example: Rogers Smith, "If Politics Matters: Implications for a 'New Institutionalism,'" *Studies in American Political Development* 6, Spring (1992): 1–36; G. John Ikenberry, "History's Heavy Hand: Institutions and the Politics of the State," unpublished manuscript, 1994; Karen Orren and Stephen Skowronek, "Beyond the Iconography of Order: Notes for a 'New Institutionalism,'" in *The Dynamics of American Politics: Approaches and Interpretations*, edited by Lawrence Dodd and Calvin Jillson, Boulder, CO: Westview Press, 1994; Paul Pierson, "The Path to European Integration: A Historical Institutionalist Approach," *Comparative Political Studies* 29, no. 2: 123–163; Kathleen Thelen, "Historical Institutionalism in Comparative Politics," *Annual Review of Political Science* 2, no. 1 369–404. David Broockman was particularly useful in thinking through this point.

[20] For scholarship that calls attention to the need to focus on the internal processes of social movements and decision making of movement actors, see: Clayborne Carson, "Civil Rights Reform and the Black Freedom Struggle" in *The Civil Rights Movement in America*, edited by Charles Eagles, Jackson: University Press of Mississippi, 1986, pp. 19–32; Lee Ann Banaszak, *Why Movements Succeed or Fail: Opportunity, Culture, and the Struggle for Woman Suffrage*, Princeton: Princeton University Press, 1996; Sarah Soule, *Contention and Corporate Social Responsibility*, New York: Cambridge University Press, 2009; Holly McCammon, *The U.S.*

is necessary to view the NAACP's campaign against racist violence as a site of civil rights strategy production. In doing so, this book deviates from the main thrust of social movement scholarship, which points to a receptive political climate or "political opportunity structure" to help explain huge civil rights breakthroughs.[21] A political opportunity theoretical framework suggests that there are institutional circumstances ripe for change or political allies that are sympathetic – neither of which was in place for the NAACP in 1909. Instead of a retrospective focus on what political conditions allow movement victories, I address an area wherein researchers have spilled far less ink: What decisions do movement actors make that help bring about success?

The historical overview of the NAACP's early fight to rid the nation of lynching and mob violence demonstrates that the litigation strategy took precedence because of prior setbacks using political and public opinion tactics as well as fundraiser imperatives. The NAACP's public opinion and political lobbying campaigns did not fail – they produced valuable gains in terms of bringing more people into the movement, demonstrating the power of collective action, and building up financial resources. However, when it came to substantive political gains – in terms of a new federal law granting protection against racist violence – the door seemed to be stubbornly closed in the executive and legislative branches.

The judicial branch was different; it appeared as if the NAACP could push open the door to constitutional litigation. In 1919, when the incident leading to *Moore v. Dempsey* occurred, the NAACP perceived litigation to be burdensome and financially straining, but after the Supreme Court's decision in *Moore*, the NAACP was singing a different tune, praising the virtues of litigation as the organization viewed the judiciary as permeable.[22] NAACP financial reports make clear the changing organizational priorities, showing that during 1919, the NAACP spent $1,000 on legal defense and $15,793 on publicity

Women's Jury Movements and Strategic Adaptation, New York: Cambridge University Press, 2012. For scholarship that focuses on the necessity of building up an organizational support structure that will initially face setbacks, see: Michael McCann, *Rights at Work: Pay Equity Reform and the Politics of Legal Mobilization*, Chicago: University of Chicago Press, 1994; Charles Epp, *The Rights Revolution: Lawyers, Activists, and Supreme Courts in Comparative Perspective*, Chicago: University of Chicago Press, 1998; Eve Weinbaum, *To Move a Mountain: Fighting the Global Economy in Appalachia*, New York: The New Press, 2004; Steven Teles, *The Rise of the Conservative Legal Movement: The Battle for Control of the Law*, Princeton: Princeton University Press, 2008; Blair Kelley, *Right to Ride: Streetcar Boycotts and African American Citizenship in the Era of Plessy v. Ferguson*, Chapel Hill: The University of North Carolina Press, 2010.

[21] Doug McAdam, *Political Process and the Development of Black Insurgency, 1930–1970*, Chicago: University of Chicago Press, 1982.

[22] Tenth Annual Report for the National Association for the Advancement of Colored People, 1920, p. 50. NAACP Papers, Manuscript Division, Library of Congress, Washington DC; Fourteenth Annual Report for the National Association for the Advancement of Colored People, 1925. NAACP Papers, Manuscript Division, Library of Congress, Washington, DC.

and political work related to the fight against lynching.[23] However, in 1925, the year after the last man connected to the Supreme Court decision in *Moore v. Dempsey* was released, the NAACP expended $18,423 on legal defense and $2,600 on publicity and political work. In six years, the NAACP made a dramatic reversal in its approach to racial injustice, and in subsequent years the organization focused the majority of its resources on litigation.[24] Of course the NAACP did not abandon politics altogether after *Moore v. Dempsey*, but with limited resources, the NAACP had to make critical cost-benefit decisions about where best to spend its money, and it seemed a litigation strategy might improve its chances of success. In the succeeding decades, a formal legal arm was established, and the long tradition of pathbreaking legal victories secured by Charles Hamilton Houston, Thurgood Marshall, and the rest of the NAACP-LDF attorneys evolved.

Blind Spots in Two Literatures

The ruptures in the dominant narratives of constitutional development and African American politics that this book proposes deserve some explanation. I begin by examining the subfield of American political development (APD), which reveals two important features often overlooked by scholars in this area. First, it highlights the under-theorizing of civil rights organizations and in particular the NAACP on state development. Second, it points to the fixation of the scholarship on locating the origins of civil rights in the New Deal era, resulting in the neglect of other possible areas of inquiry. I then move to a discussion of how African American politics have supported this APD narrative by anchoring the birth of the modern-day civil-rights movement post 1940.[25] Even scholarship that focuses on the rise of civil rights before this widely recognized "classical phase" of movement activism has focused largely on social history, rarely addressing the links between political activism and state policy making.[26]

---

[23] Tenth Annual Report for the National Association of Colored People, 1920, NAACP Papers, Library of Congress, p. 81.

[24] Mark Tushnet has detailed the building of the NAACP's litigation campaign beginning in 1925. For more see: *The NAACP's Legal Strategy Against Segregated Education, 1925–1950*, Chapel Hill: University of North Carolina Press, 1987.

[25] Notable exceptions to this long-standing trend in the scholarship include: Martha Biondi, *To Stand and Fight*, Cambridge, MA: Harvard University Press, 2006; Glenda Gilmore, *Defying Dixie: The Radical Roots of Civil Rights, 1919–1950*, New York: W. W. Norton & Co., 2008; Thomas Sugrue, *Sweet Land of Liberty: The Forgotten Struggle for Civil Rights in the North*, New York: Random House, 2008.

[26] William Chafe, *Civilities and Civil Rights: Greensboro, North Carolina, and the Black Struggle for Freedom*, New York: Oxford University Press, 1980; Aldon Morris, *The Origins of the Civil Rights Movement: Black Communities Organizing for Change*, New York: The Free Press, 1984; Charles Payne, *I've Got the Light of Freedom: The Organizing Tradition and the Mississippi Freedom Struggle*, Berkeley: University of California Press, 1995; Robert Norrell,

Scholarship focused on the historical development of the American state lies primarily in the subfield of American political development.[27] APD scholars situate their analyses in a much longer time period than most political scientists. Through this focus, they are able to piece together informative accounts of the institutions that govern America. Important works by APD scholars have produced studies linking institutional development to the processes of American industrialization, bureaucratization, party development, capitalism, and social-policy formation.[28] APD scholars are not simply interested in explaining a particular moment in time; their inquiry is about asking big questions concerning how institutions form and in identifying reasons for stability and change. APD's emphasis on treating conditions as if they are in constant transition (with politics never in equilibrium) sets its research apart from other scholarly political science undertakings.

Of particular focus is the "American state," which is often the unit of analysis. Early scholarship in American politics dismissed the notion that a strong state akin to the modern nation states of Europe existed in the United States, instead attributing responsibility for the seemingly decentralized governing arrangement to a political culture dominated by Tocquevillian liberalism.[29] Work in APD led the charge in rejecting first the statelessness presumption, and second the restricting weak/strong dichotomy that typified much of the American politics literature, revealing that a nation state does indeed exist in the United States today – it's just different than the European model.[30] While this earlier research

Reaping the Whirlwind: The Civil Rights Movement in Tuskegee, Chapel Hill: The University of North Carolina Press, 1998.

[27] Karen Orren and Stephen Skowronek, *The Search for American Political Development*, New York: Cambridge University Press, 2004.

[28] See Stephen Skowronek, *Building a New American State: The Expansion of National Administrative Capacities, 1877–1920*, New York: Cambridge University Press, 1982; Martin Sklar, *The Corporate Reconstruction of American Capitalism, 1890–1916: The Market, the Law, and American Politics*, New York: Cambridge University Press, 1988; Theda Skocpol, *Protecting Soldiers and Mothers: The Political Origins of Social Policy in the United States*, Cambridge: Harvard University Press, 1992; Richard Bensel, *The Political Economy of American Industrialization, 1877–1900*, New York: Cambridge University Press, 2000; Scott James, *President, Parties, and the State: A Party System Perspective on Democratic Regulatory Choice, 1884–1936*, New York: Cambridge University Press, 2000; Daniel Carpenter, *The Forgoing of Bureaucratic Autonomy: Reputations, Networks, and Policy Innovation in Executive Agencies, 1862–1928*, Princeton: Princeton University Press, 2001.

[29] Gunnar Myrdal, *An American Dilemma: The Negro Problem and Modern Democracy*, New York: Harper and Row, 1944 [1962]; Louis Hartz, *The Liberal Tradition in America: An Interpretation of American Political Thought Since the Revolution*, New York: Harcourt, 1955; Alexis de Tocqueville (ed. J. P. Mayer). *Democracy in America*, Garden City, NY: Doubleday, 1969.

[30] For the former, see: Stephen Skowronek, *Building a New American State: The Expansion of National Administrative Capacities, 1877–1920*, New York: Cambridge University Press, 1982; Peter Evans, Dietrich Rueschemeyer, and Theda Skocpol, eds., *Bringing the State Back In*, New York: Cambridge University Press, 1985; Daniel Carpenter, *The Forging of Bureaucratic Autonomy: Reputations, Networks, and Policy Innovation in Executive Agencies, 1862–1928*,

relied on a focus on traditional institutional structures, recent work has pushed past this framework and revealed how different aspects, not widely understood as connected to state building, actually contributed to the creation of a modern American state.[31] For example, Jacob Hacker has reconceived the growth of the welfare state to include private actors (health insurance companies and private pension programs) and details how the demarcation line between the public and private sector in the American system of social provision was often blurred, which allowed for government regulation of benefits that were supposedly private.[32] Tracy Steffes examines public schooling during the Progressive Era and shows how the deepening role of the state in school reform – working through and with districts to build consensus around new policies rather than administering changes directly – was an important part of expanding the institutions and the authority of government during this period.[33] Continuing the focus on unconventional sources of state power but in the area of law, Sean Farhang convincingly argues that private enforcement litigation, incentivized by Congress, played a crucial role in the growth of America's regulatory state.[34] This revival of scholarship on the American state has expanded our purview of the range of possible factors that contribute to state building.

Despite these new research directions, there is an important understudied area that necessitates attention: APD scholars have not sufficiently examined how civil rights organizations have contested the boundaries of the American state.[35] This absence is especially striking considering pioneering work by

Princeton: Princeton University Press, 2001. For the latter, see: Peter Baldwin, "Beyond Weak and Strong: Rethinking the State in Comparative Policy History," *Journal of Policy History* 17 (2005): 12–33; Desmond King and Robert Lieberman, "Finding the American State: Transcending the 'Statelessness' Account," *Polity* 40, no. 3 (2008): 368–337; William Novak, "The Myth of a 'Weak' State," *The American Historical Review* 113, no. 3 (2008): 752–772.

[31] For an excellent review of comparative and domestic literature, see: Desmond King and Robert Lieberman, "Ironies of State Building: A Comparative Perspective on the American State," *World Politics* 61, no. 3 (2009): 547–588.

[32] Jacob Hacker, *The Divided Welfare State: The Battle over Public and Private Social Benefits in the United States*, New York: Cambridge University Press, 2002.

[33] Tracy Steffes, *School, Society, and State: A New Education to Govern Modern America, 1890–1940*, Chicago: University of Chicago Press, 2012.

[34] Sean Farhang, *The Litigation State: Public Regulation and Private Lawsuits in the United States*, Princeton: Princeton University Press, 2010. For other works that identify litigation as a source of state building, see: George Lovell, *Legislative Deferrals: Statutory Ambiguity, Judicial Power, and American Democracy*, New York: Cambridge University Press, 2003; Paul Frymer, "Acting When Elected Officials Won't: Federal Courts and Civil Rights Enforcement in U.S. Labor Unions, 1935–85," *American Political Science Review* 97 (2003): 483–499; John Skrentny, "Law and the American State," *Annual Review of Sociology* 32 (2006): 213–244; Desmond King, "The American State and Social Engineering: Policy Instruments in Affirmative Action," *Governance* 20 (2007): 109–126; Justin Crowe, *Building the Judiciary: Law, Courts, and the Politics of Institutional Development*, Princeton: Princeton University Press, 2012.

[35] While the civil rights movement has been understudied, there is a substantial APD literature that has detailed how the labor movement was significant for the modern state. See for example: Karen Orren, *Belated Feudalism: Labor, the Law, and Liberal Development in the*

Desmond King has revealed the significance of the federal government as an active participant in the process of fostering and maintaining a "segregationist order" that lasted until the Civil Rights Act of 1964.[36] Instead of civil rights organizations, however, most scholars of APD suggest that institutions and bureaucratic actors are critical for understanding the roots and dynamics of political and historical shifts and events.[37] Even scholars who are convinced that challenges to racial hierarchies are a persistent part of America's racial order have not focused much on how civil rights activists and organizations not only contributed to critical periods of American state building but were necessary for overcoming institutional stasis.[38]

Through a top-down focused narrative, APD scholars link the origins of statutes guaranteeing equal citizenship and representation to macro-institutional factors like the emergence of the Cold War in 1946 instead of what social movement scholars identify as the so-called watershed events such as Bloody Sunday in Selma, the bus boycotts in Montgomery, or Freedom Summer in Mississippi. It is not that scholars have so much ignored civil rights organizations – numerous APD scholars have investigated the role of community-level civil rights mobilization in impacting the development of the American state in the post–World War II era – but that these works ultimately place the determinative causal actors for changes in civil rights to be state elites motivated by exogenous issues such as foreign policy and party.[39] In particular, Mary Dudziak

United States, New York: Cambridge University Press, 1991; William Forbath, *Law and the Shaping of the American Labor Movement*, Cambridge: Harvard University Press, 1991; Theda Skocpol, *Protecting Soldiers and Mothers: The Political Origins of Social Policy in the United States*, Cambridge: Harvard University Press, 1992; Victoria Hattam, *Labor Visions and State Power: The Origins of Business Unionism in the United States*, Princeton: Princeton University Press, 1993; Elizabeth Sanders, *Roots of Reform: Farm Workers and the American State, 1877–1916*, Chicago: University of Chicago Press, 1999.

[36] King argues early on, "For Black Americans, the US Federal government was a defender of the constitutionality and legally sanctioned practice of segregation and its consequences." Desmond King, *Separate and Unequal: Black Americans and the US Federal Government*, New York: Oxford University Press, 1995, p. 5. See also: Desmond King and Robert Lieberman, "American State Building: The Theoretical Challenge" in *The Unsustainable American State*, edited by Lawrence Jacobs and Desmond King, Oxford: Oxford University Press, 2009.

[37] Karen Orren and Stephen Skowronek, *The Search for American Political Development*, New York: Cambridge University Press, 2004.

[38] Desmond King and Rogers Smith, *Racial Orders in American Political Development*, American Political Science Review 99, no. 1 (2005): 75–92. Deviating slightly from their earlier work, King and Smith propose that American racial politics have been structured by evolving systems of "racial policy alliances" defined as "coalitions of participants in social movements, civic organizations, political parties, and also officials in control of some governing institutions." See Desmond King and Rogers Smith, *Still a House Divided: Race and Politics in Obama's America*, Princeton: Princeton University Press, 2011. For a critique see Robert Gooding-Williams, "Autobiography, Political Hope, Racial Justice," *Du Bois Review*, Special Issue: Post-Racialism, forthcoming 2014.

[39] See Frances Fox Piven and Richard Cloward, *Poor Peoples Movement: Why They Succeed, How They Fail*, New York: Pantheon Books, 1977; Edward Carmines and James Stimson, *Issue Evolution: Race and the Transformation of American Politics*, Princeton: Princeton

argues that in the immediate post–World War II era, racial discrimination in the United States received increasingly negative attention from other countries, which were quick to point out the contradictions between American political ideology and American practice. Philip Klinker and Rogers Smith agree with this relationship between the Cold War imperative and civil rights breakthroughs, explaining, "never before had U.S. leaders given so much weight to international considerations; and never before had a war that triggered racial reforms been followed by an international context generating such strong imperatives to sustain and extend those reforms."[40] In other words, the need to fend off international criticism, not community-level civil rights mobilization, gave the federal government an incentive to promote social change at home. This research tradition has helped to produce richer narratives about the modernization and the development of U.S. institutions; however, it has stumbled in conceptualizing civil rights groups as a component of the narrative, but ultimately not integral to policy changes and transformations in the American state.

The problem with these top-down accounts of political change is that they privilege institutions over citizen agency and thus understate the role of civil society and different forms of civic activity. This is unfortunate because civil society, by making the exercise of state power more accountable to the public, can help to make state institutions more democratic.[41] Just as it is important to consider the way institutions shape the development of the American political system, it is just as necessary to take seriously the role that black civil society via civil rights organizations plays in state formation. Serious questions that have been overlooked include: What role did civil rights groups play in enlarging the capacity of the American state in the period before the peak of civil rights legislation in the 1960s? In what ways did black protest develop independently from white state definition? How did the emergence of African American protest shape the direction of the national policymaking agenda? In

University Press, 1989; Mary Dudziak, *Cold War Civil Rights : Race and the Image of American Democracy*, Princeton: Princeton University Press, 2000; Daniel Kryder, *Divided Arsenal: Race and the American State during World War II*, New York: Cambridge University Press, 2000; John Skrentny, *The Minority Rights Revolution*, Cambridge: Belknap Press of Harvard University Press, 2002.

[40] Philip Klinkner and Rogers Smith, *The Unsteady March: The Rise and Decline of Racial Equality in America*, Chicago: University of Chicago Press, 1999, p. 205.

[41] Iris Marion Young, *Inclusion and Democracy*, New York: Oxford University Press, 2000. For a brilliant discussion on civil society and its limits, see chapter 6. She argues on page 156: "Though civil society stands in tension with state institutions, a strengthening of both is necessary to deepen democracy and undermine injustice, especially that deriving from private economic power. Each social aspect – state, economy, and civil society – can both limit and support the others. Thus, social movements seeking greater justice and well-being should work on these fronts, and aim to multiply the links between civil society and states." See also: Robert Putnam, *Making Democracy Work: Civic Traditions in Modern Italy*, Princeton: Princeton University Press, 1993.

what ways was the process of racial change in the United States dynamic? This book does not deny large-scale wars and federal policy impacted civil rights mobilization, but it argues the process is more nuanced than APD scholars have thus far revealed in their accounts. Most obviously, through arguing that civil rights organizations mediate between black civil society and the state, this book offers an example of successful African American protest that does not fit neatly into the available APD theories of racial change.

A connected factor leading to the absence of racial groups in APD is the overemphasis on particular historical moments. Much of the APD scholarship centers on four periods: the founding, Civil War/Reconstruction, the Gilded Age and Progressive periods, and the emergence of the New Deal. In part, shaped by the canonical works that undergird this subfield, these are presumed to be the major periods in which the governing institutions of the United States were constructed and transformed. However, in the familiar APD account of the New Deal era, race is often submerged. In particular, a considerable amount of scholarship focuses on the building of the social welfare state, which has directly led to a minimization of race in APD since it was explicitly silent on race.[42] In a compromise necessary to gain the support of pivotal southern Democrats in Congress, the Social Security Act institutionalized racial inequality by excluding African Americans from receiving benefits. Thus, for scholars who have sought to explain how America developed into a welfare state, race is part of the analysis only as a factor to explain the strategy to get the South on board.[43]

Still, other New Deal scholars have hitched the emergence of a federal civil rights agenda directly to Franklin Delano Roosevelt's administration, but this work has followed a familiar APD orientation by placing the responsibility for this shift in civil rights squarely on the shoulders of prominent political actors.[44] Kevin McMahon focuses on the Roosevelt administration's influence on the Supreme Court in erecting a framework for civil rights and argues that the court's civil rights decisions are the by-products of an institutional mission

[42] Jill Quandagno, *The Transformation of Old Age Security: Class and Politics in the American Welfare State,* Chicago: University of Chicago Press, 1988; Robert Liberman, *Shifting the Color Line: Race and the American Welfare State,* Cambridge: Harvard University Press, 1998; Suzanne Mettler, *Dividing Citizens: Gender and Federalism in New Deal Policy,* Ithaca: Cornell University Press, 1998; Michael Brown, *Race, Money, and the American Welfare State,* Ithaca: Cornell University Press, 1999; Ira Katznelson, *When Affirmative Action Was White: An Untold History of Racial Inequality in Twentieth-Century America,* New York: W. W. Norton, 2005.

[43] For treatises on the former see: Theda Skocpol, *Protecting Soldiers and Mothers: The Political Origins of Social Policy in the United States,* Cambridge: Harvard University Press, 1992; Gareth Davies and Martha Derthick, *Race and Social Welfare Policy: The Social Security Act of 1935, Political Science Quarterly* 112, (1997), 217–235.

[44] Harvard Sitkoff, *A New Deal for Blacks: The Emergence of Civil Rights as a National Issue,* New York: Oxford University Press, 1978; Garth Pauley, *The Modern Presidency and Civil Rights: Rhetoric on Race from Roosevelt to Nixon,* College Station, Texas A&M University Press, 2001.

that was shaped by Roosevelt. McMahon assigns great responsibility to the Roosevelt court in paving the way to *Brown v. Board of Education*: Roosevelt's "nominees' adherence to rights-centered liberalism combined with their devotion to defer to the executive branch ensured that the NAACP would find fertile ground to lay its antisegregation precedential seeds, seeds that would one day – nourished in part by the Justice Department – sprout into *Brown v. Board*."[45] However, this reading overstates the role of federal institutions in *Brown v. Board of Education*; the decision was the continuation of the transformation in American politics that was initiated during the NAACP's national political campaign against racist violence.

Sidney Milkis, in a masterful account of the decoupling of the executive branch and political parties, extends the focus on the New Deal coalition under the presidency of Roosevelt's successor, President Harry Truman. Writing about civil rights inroads in the Truman era, Milkis argues, "The president's decision to move forward on this issue by administrative action strengthened the liberal commitment of the New Deal by emphasizing the executive branch rather than the Democratic party, as the agent of civil rights reform."[46] Although it acknowledges that the torch for igniting civil rights reform in the federal government might be better placed with Truman than with Roosevelt, Milkis's analysis still relies largely on political elites to explain shifts in governmental authority concerning civil rights.

This rendering of individual agency as insignificant to political and constitutional development should not be a surprise. As a result of the traditional APD periodization, the arrow of influence in most of these accounts points one way: institutions and political elites influence the actions of individuals.[47] So while the practices for understanding political development in political science

---

[45] Kevin McMahon, *Reconsidering Roosevelt on Race: How the Presidency Paved the Road to Brown*, Chicago: University of Chicago Press, 2004, p. 142.

[46] Sidney Milkis, *The President and the Parties: The Transformation of the American Party System Since the New Deal*, New York: Oxford University Press, 1993, p. 157.

[47] A notable exception to this long-standing trend is George Lovell's study of civil rights legal claims by citizens not organized in movements. Lovell writes, "Ordinary people can be savvy participants in dynamic processes in which both citizens and government officials articulate, evaluate, and dispute competing visions of law." For more see "Justice Excused: The Deployment of Law in Everyday Political Encounters," *Law & Society Review* 40, no. 2 (2006): 283–324; *This is Not Civil Rights: Discovering Rights Talk in 1939 America*, Chicago: University of Chicago Press, 2012. For other accounts that focus on the role of citizens in institutional development; see: Elizabeth Clemens, *The People's Lobby: Organizational Innovation and the Rise of Interest Group Politics in the United States, 1890–1925*, Chicago: University of Chicago Press, 1997; Elizabeth Sanders, *Roots of Reform: Farm Workers and the American State, 1877–1916*, Chicago: University of Chicago Press, 1999; Marie Gottshalk, *The Prison and the Gallows: The Politics of Mass Incarceration in America*, New York: Cambridge University Press, 2006; Paul Frymer, *Black and Blue: African Americans, the Labor Movement, and the Decline of the Democratic Party*, Princeton: Princeton University Press, 2008; Christopher Parker, *Fighting for Democracy: Black Veterans and the Struggle Against White Supremacy in the Postwar South*, Princeton: Princeton University Press, 2009; Kimberley Johnson, *Reforming Jim Crow: Southern Politics and State in the Age Before Brown*, New York: Oxford University Press, 2010.

have evolved, the general focus has remained relatively unchanged. Top-down scholarship on these four epochs begets more top-down scholarship. Rarely accounted for is how marginalized citizens can influence institutional structures. And herein lies an unintentional consequence of our fidelity to these four stages of development: APD scholars have overlooked ways in which the political and constitutional order is shaped during the intervening periods. Indeed, scholars have largely cast the periods in the middle that bind these four "big" moments of APD as inconsequential to understanding the construction of the American state.[48] In the case of a federal civil rights agenda, a neglect of the intervening periods has led to APD scholars misstating causal explanations.

But what about the impact of civil rights groups on the period of American political and constitutional development before the New Deal? On this question, the response from American politics is largely silence. This silence is supported by scholarship in African American politics and history that provides a narrative of African American political activism in national politics that exists within the bounds of Reconstruction and after 1930. The period in between, the time span that this book is concerned with, is considered to be a time of African American inaction on the national political scene.[49]

The traditional account of the African American struggle for equal rights follows roughly these lines: after the abolition of slavery, the brief period known as Reconstruction came about, and African Americans enjoyed an unprecedented level of equality and were active participants in the political life of the nation.[50] However, Redeemer Democrats soon overtook southern governments as Republicans withdrew troops and stripped African Americans of their political, economic, and social rights. Through the use of a number of harmful legal mechanisms (poll tax, grandfather clause, literacy test) and unrestrained violence, white supremacy reigned in the South and kept African Americans silent and subordinated for the first half of the twentieth century. Finally, as

---

[48] For an alternate perspective, see: Kimberley Johnson, *Governing the American State: Congress and the New Federalism, 1877–1929*, Princeton: Princeton University Press, 2006. In this study of federalism between 1877 and 1929, Johnson reveals that intergovernmental policy making between the federal and state governments did not always have the effect of constraining the nation state but often enhanced its capacity. Johnson's work is important for it demonstrates that in the period before the New Deal, the state was already being built.

[49] For further elaboration on this point about the silences of certain voices in historical narratives, see Michel-Rolph Trouillot, *Silencing the Past: Power and the Production of History*, Boston: Beacon Press, 1995. Trouillot's thoughtful analysis is especially useful in thinking about how history is created by the unconscious use of power by scholars. His work helps to rethink why the *Brown*-era narrative of civil rights has gained such wide acceptance and why the earlier struggle against racial violence has been largely ignored. But mostly, Trouillot's work challenges those of us who retell history to be attendant to the power dynamics that are ever present in our craft.

[50] W. E. B. DuBois, *Black Reconstruction in America, 1860–1880*, New York: The Free Press, 1935 [1992]; Eric Foner, *Reconstruction: America's Unfinished Revolution 1863–1877*, New York: Harper and Row, 1988.

the dominant narrative continues, unable to bear the oppression any longer, frustrated about their surrounding conditions, and propelled by the legal effort to overturn *Plessy v. Ferguson*,[51] African Americans in the South took to the streets and lunch counters in protest and finally forced the national government to pay attention to their plight.

Indeed, most mainstream accounts view the post-Reconstruction period as a time of growing African American disillusionment with national politics as African Americans begrudgingly accepted the undermining of their citizenship.[52] African Americans were completely shut out from the political process, their citizenship rights were wantonly denied in the South, and the legal process did not provide them with full equal protection.

Though a number of notable historical studies have broken from the traditional account by documenting a budding African American civil society, there is only a smattering of accounts that demonstrate how local African American political activism impacted politics at the national level during this period.[53] To explain this state of affairs, Earl Lewis argues that in the aftermath of Reconstruction, African Americans had to restructure their lives and turned inward whereby they "used Jim Crow's formative years to develop their institutional infrastructure further" and for a short time "remained committed to pursuing improvements in the home sphere."[54] It was thought that in order for African Americans to have any kind of substantial impact on the Jim Crow political establishment, they needed to first obtain the "ability to promote their own interests" through African American institutions such as the church and other benevolent organizations.[55] Other accounts of African American activism

[51] 163 U.S. 537 (1896).

[52] J. Morgan Kousser, *The Shaping of Southern Politics: Suffrage Restriction and the Establishment of the One-Party South, 1880–1910*, New Haven: Yale University Press, 1974; Leon Litwack, *Been in the Storm So Long: The Aftermath of Slavery*, New York: Vintage Books, 1980; Paul Frymer, *Uneasy Alliances: Race and Party Competition In America*, Princeton: Princeton University Press, 1999, pp. 49–86; Philip Klinkner and Rogers Smith, *The Unsteady March: The Rise and Decline of Racial Equality in America*, Chicago, The University of Chicago Press, 1999, pp. 72–105; Richard Valelly, *The Two Reconstructions: The Struggle for Black Enfranchisement*, Chicago: University of Chicago Press, 2004.

[53] John Hope Franklin, *From Slavery to Freedom: A History of African Americans*, 8th ed., New York : A. A. Knopf, 2000, p. 438; David Levering Lewis, *W.E.B. Du Bois: Biography of a Race, 1868–1919*, New York: H. Holt, 1993; Wilson Jeremiah Moses, *Creative Conflict in African American Thought: Frederick Douglass, Alexander Crummell, Booker T. Washington, W.E.B. Du Bois, and Marcus Garvey*, New York: Cambridge University Press, 2004; Deborah Gray White, *Too Heavy A Load: Black Women in Defense of Themselves, 1894–1994*, New York: W. W. Norton, 1999.

[54] Earl Lewis, *In Their Own Interests: Race, Class, and Power in Twentieth-Century Norfolk, Virginia*, Berkeley: University of California Press, 1990, pp. 23 and 29. See also Deborah Gray White, *Too Heavy A Load: Black Women In Defense of Themselves*, New York: W. W. Norton, 1999, p. 26.

[55] Earl Lewis, *In Their Own Interests: Race, Class, and Power in Twentieth-Century Norfolk, Virginia*, Berkeley: University of California Press, 1990, p. 67.

during this period provide further support that African Americans were largely sidelined in national politics. For example, Evelyn Brooks Higginbotham focuses on the way in which African American women engaged politically through the Baptist church in the period after Reconstruction because "segregation and pervasive violence" restricted their involvement in traditional mainstream political institutions.[56] In the seminal publication *The Negro in American Life and Thought: The Nadir, 1877–1901*, Rayford Logan argued that the time period in his book title marked the most dismal period of race relations in postbellum America.[57] In 1961, the eminent historian John Hope Franklin stated that "the long dark night" continued beyond 1901, until 1923.[58] And after surveying civil rights organizations of the early twentieth century, Harvard Sitkoff concluded, "White indifference and black weakness stymied the hope for any viable program of Negro advancement in the twenties."[59] These observations appear to be substantiated by the absence of civil rights organizations agitating at the national level in the first quarter of the twentieth century.

Political scientists, for the most part, have accepted this narrative of African American history without reservation as it seamlessly collapses into their own theories of state development. The different fields of research support the assumptions of the other and effectively tell us that African Americans were sidelined in national politics in the first half of the twentieth century and turned inward; so of course they had no role in shaping the American state during this period. As compelling and coherent as this dominant narrative might seem, it's incorrect and obscures a very important moment in the construction of the American state. A closer examination of the intersection between black political activism and early state building in American politics has been missing.

And this is what my research confronts. Using archival materials – much of which has not been used by other researchers – I conceptualize a new framework for the interaction between African American politics and American political and constitutional development: one that de-centers the role of political institutions and elite actors and that takes seriously the role of organized citizen agency in shaping the structural setting of political and constitutional change. Contrary to extant studies, the evidence presented in this book demonstrates that the period was not one of accommodation in national politics. It also explains how the NAACP impacted the national political scene and helped to enlarge state capacity in the first decades of the twentieth century, with implications for the following few decades. This book reveals that the foundation of the emerging civil rights state was already being built decades

---

[56] Evelyn Brooks Higginbotham, *Righteous Discontent: The Women's Movement in the Black Baptist Church, 1880–1920*, Cambridge: Harvard University Press, 1993, p. 89.

[57] Rayford Logan, *The Negro in American Life and Thought: The Nadir, 1877–1901*, New York: Dial Press, 1954.

[58] Sidney Hillman Lectures at Howard University, 1961.

[59] Harvard Sitkoff, *A New Deal for Blacks: The Emergence of Civil Rights as a National Issue*, New York: Oxford University Press, 1978, p. 26.

before *Brown*, the Civil Rights Act of 1964, and the Voting Rights Act of 1965, paving the way for those later landmark events.

Social Movements, Durable Changes, and Periodization

The understanding of the NAACP as a significant force in American state development owes partial credit to the vast scholarship on social movements in the field of political sociology. In particular, the area of outcomes and consequences provide strong reason to believe that social movement organizations are integral to policy and societal changes. In an analysis of the political and legal impact of the Mississippi civil rights movement, Kenneth Andrews argues that local movement organizations in the early 1960s contributed to the passage of the Voting Rights Act and that the sustained mobilization of activists in the 1970s and 1980s was instrumental in desegregating public schools and in the introduction of economic policy favorable to the poor.[60] In a study that included five of the big social movements in the post–World War II era, including civil rights, Frank Baumgartner and Christine Mahoney determine that these movements were successful in getting their concerns on the congressional agenda.[61] The recent work of Daniel Gillion builds on this critical area of research by examining the impact of minority protest on all three of the branches of government between the 1960s and 1990s. Gillion shows that in the area of the Supreme Court, minority protest helped to indirectly promote a climate of acceptability and at times generated public support for certain contentious race-related cases.[62] Considered together, the work of these scholars and numerous others have demonstrated the meaningful role of social protest to changes in policy.[63]

Yet, while this social movement scholarship provides a necessary and important corrective to literature in political science that often ignores the role of groups, there are still two gaps: first, previous research does not connect civil

[60] Kenneth Andrews, *Freedom is a Constant Struggle: The Mississippi Civil Rights Movement and Its Legacy*, Chicago: University of Chicago Press, 2004.

[61] Frank Baumgartner and Christine Mahoney, *Social Movements, the Rise of New Issues, and the Public Agenda*, In David S. Meyer, Valerie Jenness, and Helen Ingram, eds., *Routing the Opposition: Social Movements, Public Policy, and Democracy*, Minneapolis: University of Minnesota Press, 2005, pp. 65–86.

[62] Daniel Gillion, *The Political Power of Protest: Minority Activism and Shifts in Public Policy*, New York: Cambridge University Press, 2013.

[63] Sidney Tarrow, *Power in Movement. Social Movements, Collective Action and Politics*, New York: Cambridge University Press, 1994; Doug McAdam and Yang Su, *The War At Home: Anti-War Protests and Congressional Voting, 1965–1973*, American Sociology Review 67 (2002): 696–721; John Skrentny, *The Minority Rights Revolution*, Cambridge: Harvard University Press, 2002; Sarah Soule and Brayden King, *The Stages of the Policy Process and the Equal Rights Amendment, 1972–1982*, American Journal of Sociology 111 (2006): 1871–1909; Edwin Amenta, *When Movements Matter: The Townsend Plan and the Rise of Social Security*, Princeton: Princeton University Press, 2006.

rights movement activism to institutional changes in political and constitutional development. Winning a Supreme Court case or being mentioned in congressional hearings does not amount to a durable change in the national governing establishment.[64] Indeed, in a comprehensive review of the most high-profile movement articles in sociology from 2001 to 2009, Edwin Amenta et al. admitted that while informative, the studies did not fully address the question of whether movements are influential. To explain this state of affairs, Amenta and his colleagues conceded, "Almost all of the research is on policy, with only three instances of movements seeking structural influence."[65] Future work needs to focus more explicitly on the link between social movements and shifts in political institutions if we are to understand more conclusively how social movements matter to political change.

Second, much of the social movement literature on African American civil rights in sociology has coalesced around the pivotal political shift in the 1950s and 1960s. Doug McAdam widens the timeframe of his analysis, focusing on the period before the 1960s in explaining African American mobilization. However, his work also misses the role of the NAACP and the importance of *Moore* in creating new constitutional law:

> Between 1876 and 1930, the thrust of Supreme Court decisions in cases involving blacks had the effect of further limiting the opportunities for black political action by gradually eroding earlier constitutional provisions safeguarding civil rights. Of principal importance was the court's progressively narrow interpretation of the constitutional principles embodied in the Fourteenth Amendment.[66]

The consideration of the NAACP's role in litigating *Moore* and the resulting expansion in the protection of African American defendants through the due process clause of the Fourteenth Amendment weakens this conclusion. The first notice McAdam gives to significant NAACP action was in the period 1931–1954. He points to this timespan as being the critical years of NAACP activism, which led to a rise in black insurgency in the civil rights movement.[67] This book argues that the critical period started before the 1930s. That earlier period, even if it sometimes lacked tangible successes, was important to later events. Sociology research linking civil rights movement activism to changes

---

[64] Karen Orren and Stephen Skowronek, *The Search for American Political Development*, Cambridge: Cambridge University Press, 2004. On page 123, Orren and Skowronek define political development as "a durable shift in governing authority."

[65] Edwin Amenta, Neal Caren, Elizabeth Chiarello, and Yang Su, 2010, *The Political Consequences of Social Movements*, Annual Review of Sociology 36:287–307, p. 294. Study considered forty-five articles encompassing the analysis of fifty-four movement organizations in the top four sociology journals and *Mobilization*.

[66] Doug McAdam, *Political Process and the Development of Black Insurgency, 1930–1970*, Chicago: University of Chicago Press, 1982, p. 71.

[67] Doug McAdam, *Political Process and the Development of Black Insurgency, 1930–1970*, Chicago: University of Chicago Press, 1982. For more on the inability of the NAACP to have an impact see pp. 93–94 and for more on its mobilization from 1931–1954 see pp. 103–106.

in American politics often starts too late and falls almost exclusively in the post-1930s era, and as a result, there is insufficient research on the ways in which civil rights organizations before the 1930s might matter to the national political establishment.

Reimagining the Civil Rights Movement

This is a political science book, which is comfortably nestled between the two subfields of American political development and race and politics. However, this is clearly a book that takes historical methods seriously. Instead of drawing unnecessary distance from history as many political scientists do, I embrace what is quite obviously a study that has important lessons for political scientists *and* scholars of twentieth-century U.S. history. I believe both fields are valuable and that some of the best (and most exciting) scholarship occurs when disciplinary boundaries are breached. Since this is also a historical study, I want to turn now to address, explicitly, what I have thus far been stating implicitly about civil rights historiography: the origins of the civil rights movement and the role of the NAACP in this movement need to be reframed. Existing work on social movements, specifically the numerous accounts of the NAACP's litigation activities, have left the NAACP's fight against racial violence completely off of the radar.[68] Emblematic of this oversight is the work of Sitkoff, who casts aside the idea that the NAACP had any significant impact in the first quarter of the twentieth century. Similar to other civil rights historians, he completely ignores *Moore* while acknowledging two Supreme Court victories in whose litigation effort the NAACP played a minimal role. He goes even further to state that in the first quarter-century, "the NAACP could do nothing to affect the racial policies of southern governments or to compel the necessary corrective actions by the national government."[69] However, the NAACP's success in fighting against lynching and mob violence provides substantial counterevidence that it was able to impact the governing institutions on the local, state, and national levels. After the Supreme Court handed down its decision in *Moore v. Dempsey*, the case was sent back to the lower court where the sentences were reduced, and a short while afterward, the NAACP secured a

[68] Clement Vose, *Caucasians Only: The Supreme Court, the NAACP, and the Restrictive Covenant Cases*, Berkeley: University of California Press, 1959; Richard Kluger, *Simple Justice: The History of Brown v. Board of Education and Black America's Struggle for Equality*, New York: Knopf, 1975; Mark Tushnet, *The NAACP's Legal Strategy Against School Segregation, 1925–1950*, Chapel Hill: The University of North Carolina Press, 1987; Mark Tushnet *Making Constitutional Law: Thurgood Marshall and the Supreme Court, 1961–1991*, New York: Oxford University Press, 1997; Risa Goluboff, *The Lost Promise of Civil Rights*, Cambridge: Harvard University Press, 2007; Paul Frymer, *Black and Blue: African Americans, the Labor Movement, and the Decline of the Democratic Party*, Princeton: Princeton University Press, 2008.

[69] Harvard Sitkoff, *The Struggle for Black Equality 1954–1992*, New York: Hill and Wang, 1992, p. 8.

pardon for the men from the governor of Arkansas. Thus, the NAACP played a critical role in saving the lives of the Phillips County 12, which will be discussed in detail in Chapter 5. The inclusion of the NAACP's litigation struggle against the persistence of racial violence represents a significant cleavage in this dominant civil rights narrative about NAACP inaction during the earlier part of the twentieth century.

The ample amount of scholarship on the NAACP is the likely arena to find a corrective of the NAACP's role in the civil rights movement. However, much of this work has been dominated by a focus on the litigation campaign, which resulted in *Brown v. Board of Education* and in biographies of famous NAACP figures. There are a number of important new accounts that have explored the NAACP's activism before *Brown*, but even these do not go back far enough to chronicle the NAACP's fight against racial violence.[70] Most of this early research centers on the NAACP's litigation efforts on behalf of African American workers in the post–World War II years. For example, Risa Goluboff shows how the NAACP's labor discrimination litigation of the 1940s helped to shape the construction of "civil rights" in America.[71] Also focusing on labor, Paul Frymer finds that through the bringing of claims of union racism in courtrooms, the NAACP played a decisive role in integrating resistant labor unions.[72] Another area of NAACP scholarship explores the construction of the organization's litigation strategy and the world of African American lawyers in the period before *Brown* was constructed.[73] Most notably, Mark Tushnet locates the origins of the NAACP's education desegregation legal strategy in 1925 as initiating with a grant from the Garland Fund, but even this focus on litigation misses the impact of the NAACP's Supreme Court victory in *Moore*

---

[70] Clement Vose, *Caucasians Only: The Supreme Court, the NAACP, and the Restrictive Covenant Cases*, Berkeley: University of California Press, 1959; Mark Tushnet, *The NAACP's Legal Strategy Against Segregated Education, 1925–1950*, Chapel Hill: University of North Carolina Press, 1987; Kenneth Goings, *The NAACP Comes of Age: the Defeat of Judge John J. Parker*, Bloomington: Indiana University Press, 1990; Kenneth Mack, Rethinking Civil Rights Lawyering and Politics in the Era Before "Brown," *The Yale Law Journal* 115, no. 2 (2005): 256–354; Risa Goluboff, *The Lost Promise of Civil Rights*, Cambridge: Harvard University Press, 2007; Sophia Lee, "Hotspots in a Cold War: The NAACP's Postwar Workplace Constitutionalism, 1948–1964," *Law and History Review* 26 (2008): 327; Paul Frymer, *Black and Blue: African Americans, the Labor Movement, and the Decline of the Democratic Party*, Princeton: Princeton University Press, 2008.

[71] Risa Goluboff, *The Lost Promise of Civil Rights*, Cambridge: Harvard University Press, 2007.

[72] Paul Frymer, *Black and Blue: African Americans, the Labor Movement, and the Decline of the Democratic Party*, Princeton: Princeton University Press, 2008.

[73] Richard Kluger, *Simple Justice: The History of Brown v. Board of Education and Black America's Struggle for Equality*, New York: Knopf, 1975; Susan Carle, "Race, Class, and Legal Ethics in the Early NAACP (1910–1920)," *Law and History Review* 20, no. 1 (2002): pp. 97–146; Kenneth Mack, *Representing the Race: The Creation of the Civil Rights Lawyer*, Cambridge: Harvard University Press, 2012; Tomiko Brown-Nagin, *Courage to Dissent: Atlanta and the Long History of the Civil Rights Movement*, New York: Oxford University Press, 2012.

and the legal mobilization effort that produced the decision.[74] A few historical accounts of the NAACP give passing reference to the NAACP's fight against lynching, but *Civil Rights and the Making of the Modern American State* is the first book-length examination and the first in political science that connects American political and constitutional development, African American politics, and the criminal-procedure revolution.[75]

The NAACP's campaign against racial violence is critical to reframing the long civil rights movement.[76] Though a number of important figures and organizations came before the NAACP was established to champion the issue of racial violence (e.g., Ida B. Wells's Antilynching League, The Niagara Movement, Monroe Trotter's National Equal Rights League, T. Thomas Fortune, John Milholland's Constitution League), they were unable to penetrate any branch of the federal government. The NAACP, operating as a social movement organization at the beginning of the twentieth century, left an indelible mark on the American political system. Through a campaign against racial violence from 1909 to 1923, the NAACP was able to impact the legislative, executive, and judicial branches of the federal government in a way that America had never witnessed from a civil rights organization. Considering the hostile time period in which these changes took place, this was no small feat. In this way, the NAACP's struggle against lynching and mob violence can be seen as setting the stage for future civil rights battles.

Overview of the Analysis

The chapters that follow elaborate the story of the NAACP's campaign against racial violence. I focus on the different branches of the federal government where the NAACP waged its struggle and show how the organization worked around and directly within the executive branch, the legislature, and the judiciary. In

---

[74] Mark Tushnet, *The NAACP's Legal Strategy Against Segregated Education, 1925–1950*, Chapel Hill: University of North Carolina Press, 1987.

[75] There are two monographs that focus on different aspects of the NAACP's fight against racial violence: Robert Zangrando centers his analysis on the NAACP's anti-lynching legislation efforts in Congress in *The NAACP Crusade Against Lynching, 1909–1950*, Philadelphia: Temple University Press, 1980; and Richard Cortner has completed a detailed study of the NAACP's legal battle over *Moore v. Dempsey* in *A Mob Intent on Death: The NAACP and the Arkansas Riot Cases*, Middleton: Wesleyan University Press, 1988. However, no accounts exist that examine the full range of the NAACP's campaign against racial violence.

[76] Nikhil Pal Singh, *Black is a Country: Race and the Unfinished Struggle for Democracy*, Cambridge: Harvard University Press, 2004; Jacquelyn Dowd Hall, "The Long Civil Rights Movement and the Political Uses of the Past," *Journal of American History* (March 2005): 1233–1263; Glenda Gilmore, *Defying Dixie: The Radical Roots of Civil Rights, 1919–1950*, New York: W. W. Norton & Co., 2008; Thomas Sugrue, *Sweet Land of Liberty: The Forgotten Struggle for Civil Rights in the North*, New York: Random House, 2008; Patricia Sullivan, *Lift Every Voice: The NAACP and the Making of the Civil Rights Movement*, New York: New Press, 2009.

recounting the NAACP's mobilization in the federal government, I discuss the impact of citizen agency on political and constitutional development. My analysis reveals that the NAACP helped to push the Supreme Court in a direction it was not initially willing to go and by doing so, forever changed the path of civil rights and the Supreme Court's criminal procedure jurisprudence.

But before I account for the NAACP's agitation in the federal government, I discuss the organization's role in shifting the landscape of public opinion. Instead of beginning with the education desegregation litigation of the 1950s and 1960s, Chapter 2 traces a tradition in civil rights that begins with the NAACP's media campaign to fight unjust racial violence between 1909 and 1925. This chapter describes how the NAACP, in order to wage a battle against negative public perceptions, executed a three-pronged media strategy focused on writing newspaper articles, publishing pamphlets, and printing its own magazine, *The Crisis*. By articulating the terror of lynching and broadcasting it to a wider audience through these different channels, the NAACP achieved considerable success in reframing the debate concerning African American criminality and American justice. However, we learn in Chapter 2 that when lynchings did not end as a result of these opinion-shaping activities, the NAACP was left with the startling realization that it would have to adopt another strategy to battle racial violence. The chapter views the NAACP's inability to end racial violence solely through publicity activities as critical in the organization's decision to turn to politics and litigation in subsequent years.

Chapter 3 begins my focus on the federal government and describes how the NAACP viewed the executive office as a vehicle for civil rights change and worked to gain specific supports from President Woodrow Wilson and President Warren G. Harding. This chapter departs from standard treatments of Wilson and Harding and argues that we have not previously captured the complexity of their approach to civil rights. The critique is made empirically with untapped archival material from presidential libraries. Contrary to existing accounts, this chapter will reveal that during his second term, Wilson directly responded to demands from the NAACP in a way that complicates how previous scholars have understood Wilson's race agenda. In this chapter, I determine that Wilson increased his efforts to protect African Americans during his second term because the NAACP couched its claims of equality in terms of the right to live. This chapter also sheds light on Harding and reveals that he met numerous times with James Weldon Johnson and responded to the NAACP's request to speak out about lynching. Thus, the chapter allows a fuller understanding of how civil rights groups and their supporters were contesting the boundaries and laying the groundwork for future protest in the Oval Office.

Chapter 4 investigates the NAACP's efforts in the legislative arena where the organization supported the passage of an anti-lynching bill in Congress in 1921. In a very short time, the NAACP remade itself into an anti-lynching lobbying organization and, through direct lobbying to members of Congress and an expansive grassroots effort, pressured lawmakers in the House of

Representatives to pass the first-ever anti-lynching bill. In less than a year, leading House Republicans went from a hands-off approach to anti-lynching legislation to actively advocating on its behalf and defending the necessity for such legislation against a determined coalition of southern Democrats. The NAACP-sponsored anti-lynching bill passed the House of Representatives by a commanding two-thirds vote. However, not even one year after House passage, the bill died on the Senate floor as a coalition of southern Democrats and conservative northern Republicans filibustered it. The defeat of the anti-lynching bill was deeply frustrating to the NAACP's leadership, many of whom had devoted all of their energies to working on the bill's passage. The chapter argues that it is impossible to explain the arc of the NAACP's civil rights strategy without reckoning with the tremendous role the NAACP played in working for anti-lynching legislation. In the course of one year, the NAACP felt the joy of victory and the stinging blow of political defeat. This chapter views the campaign for anti-lynching legislation as an important turning point in the NAACP's battle against lynching. After this loss, the NAACP was forced to face the harsh reality that despite the federal government's previous support of African American rights (Civil War amendments and Reconstruction), the legislative process would no longer be the most productive venue to pursue an agenda focused on the protection of equal citizenship for African Americans.

Turning to the legal arena, Chapter 5 explores the role of the NAACP in *Moore v. Dempsey*, the case that sparked the modern revolution in criminal procedure doctrine. Through archival research of the events surrounding *Moore v. Dempsey*, this chapter uncovers the dominant role played by the NAACP. In fact, archival material reveals that this case would never have reached the Supreme Court without the tremendous organizational effort on behalf of the NAACP through three major ways: publicity used to raise awareness about the important issues and to galvanize public opinion, fundraising to finance the lengthy litigation, and experienced legal counsel who could expertly fight the case in the courtroom. The chapter follows the case during the arduous five-year litigation battle and demonstrates that the NAACP was present at every step and actively involved in the complicated legal struggle that finally led to the development of new constitutional law. Chapter 5 argues that the legal battle waged in *Moore v. Dempsey* changed the NAACP's strategic focus and the understanding among its supporters about how to successfully fight for racial justice in American society. By demonstrating that the fight against racist violence could be successfully carried out in American courtrooms, the NAACP showed the rest of the nation the power of litigation to alter the operation of racism in American society.

The sixth and final chapter draws together the findings from the previous empirical chapters and explores the trajectories of the NAACP and the anti-lynching struggle for the development of civil rights and American politics in the twentieth century. The chapter connects the NAACP's anti-lynching campaign directly to *Brown v. Board of Education* through the Garland Fund. The

NAACP's focus on education and the funding that birthed the Legal Defense Fund (NAACP-LDF) came from a $100,000 grant from the Garland Fund in 1930. However, before that now-famous grant, in 1922 the Garland Fund was interested in an organization working to bring about greater racial equality and was impressed with the NAACP's campaign to push its anti-lynching bill through Congress, so it supported the association's work with a small grant. In other words, without the attention garnered through its anti-lynching campaign, the NAACP might never have focused on education and certainly would not have had the funds to marshal an expansive litigation campaign against segregated education, which culminated in *Brown*. Thought about in this light, the NAACP's anti-lynching campaign marked a critical fork in the road in the civil rights state. I conclude that the autonomy of the state and political elites need to be questioned and that examining more closely the role of citizen agency will likely enrich analyses of political and constitutional development. Ultimately, my excavation of the NAACP's campaign against racial violence hopes to change the way we think about the development of civil rights and the role of citizens in constitutional development.

2

The Birth of the NAACP, Mob Violence, and the Challenge of Public Opinion

Our country's national crime is lynching.

– Ida B. Wells, 1900[1]

He who attacks lynching attacks one of the oldest, one of the most deeply rooted of the institutions peculiarly American, one eminently respectable in origin, which is regarded by its adherents, not as in opposition to the established laws, but rather as a supplement to them – a species of common law which is as old as the country.

– Roy Nash, 1916[2]

The National Association for the Advancement of Colored People (NAACP) boldly declared, "Lynching can be stopped when we reach the heart and conscience of the American people."[3] In the beginning, the NAACP viewed the fight against lynching as a moral struggle "of the brain and the soul and to the brain and the soul of America."[4] In order to wage a battle against negative public perceptions in the first quarter of the twentieth century, the NAACP launched an expansive public education media campaign where the organization investigated lynchings, wrote newspaper articles, published pamphlets, and printed its own magazine, *The Crisis*. The NAACP's initial exposure-focused strategy was predicated on the belief that white Americans would become so enraged that they would feel compelled to do something to end the tragedy of

---

[1] Ida B. Wells, "Lynch Law in America," *The Arena* 23, no. 1 (1900): 15–24.

[2] Box 2, "Memorandum for Mr. Philip Peabody on Lynch-Law and the Practicability of a Successful Attack Thereon, By Roy Nash," May 22, 1916, Moorfield Storey Papers, Manuscript Division, Library of Congress, Washington, DC.

[3] NAACP, Tenth Annual Report for the Year 1919, NAACP Papers, Manuscript Division, Library of Congress, Washington, DC.

[4] NAACP, Tenth Annual Report for the Year 1919, p. 89. NAACP Papers, Manuscript Division, Library of Congress, Washington, DC.

racial violence. Today, looking back, it seems unlikely that the NAACP would conceive that a solution to the deepest problems that Americans faced to equal citizenship would come about through trying to change public opinion alone. But they did, revealing that "public opinion is the main force upon which the Association relies for a victory of justice" not political or legal advances.[5] Even NAACP director of publicity and research W. E. B. Du Bois expressed his initial conviction that appealing to the hearts and minds of Americans would end lynching when he wrote, "I regarded it as axiomatic that the world wanted to learn the truth and if the truth was sought with even approximate accuracy and painstaking devotion, the world would gladly support the effort. This was, of course, but a young man's idealism, not by any means false, but also never universally true."[6] Indeed, Du Bois and the rest of the NAACP would soon realize the limits of a movement aimed at reaching the "soul of America" and the resulting need to engage the federal government in preventing racial injustices at the state level.

In this chapter, I will suggest that racial violence was the gateway issue for the NAACP and that addressing this issue in the sphere of public opinion was instructive to its understanding of how to strategically fight for civil rights in the United States. Arguing that racial violence was the NAACP's first big civil rights issue necessitates a discussion of Ida B. Wells. In the first section of this chapter, I wish to emphasize how Wells's fight to end lynching shaped the focus of the NAACP from the outset. The second section continues to address the antecedents to the NAACP, placing its emergence within the coming together of white progressives and African American radicals. The next section documents the formal establishment of the NAACP as an organization and the prominence of lynching and mob violence on its agenda. The fourth section discusses in detail the NAACP's three-pronged opinion-shaping strategy to stop the prevalence of lynching and mob violence. In particular, I contend that the NAACP used different types of publications to reach specific audiences. Finally, in the last section, I link the NAACP's eventual turn toward political protest in the federal government to its shortcomings in its public opinion campaign. The NAACP began to realize lynchings and mob violence were occurring, not because of whites who held ill-informed racial beliefs but because local and state governments condoned the violent spectacle.

NAACP Founding

To explain why the NAACP focused on the issue of racial violence and first adopted a media strategy, it will be helpful to focus on the events that preceded

---

[5] NAACP, Tenth Annual Report for the Year 1919, p. 91. NAACP Papers, Manuscript Division, Library of Congress, Washington, DC..

[6] W. E. B. Du Bois, *Dusk of Dawn: An Essay Toward an Autobiography of a Race Concept*, New York: Harcourt, Brace & Co., 1940, p. 68.

the organization's development. While the NAACP's strategy to fight racial injustice was certainly dependent on its internal board, the organization's decisions and understanding of the political environment was also mediated by the events that occurred before the organization was formed. Thus, to properly understand the beginnings of the NAACP, it is necessary to trace the historical patterns that set the stage for the NAACP. In particular, one may distinguish four factors of importance in the formation of the NAACP: Ida B. Wells's activism around lynching through the media, the impact of white progressives mobilizing on behalf of African American citizenship, further deteriorating racial conditions and the ideological shift away from Booker T. Washington's accommodationist strategy for African American advancement, and the rise of a new cadre of African American radicals, led by W. E. B. Du Bois and focused on a protest politics approach.

The first person to highlight the injustice of lynching on a national scale was Wells; however, her impact is curiously missing from mainstream accounts documenting the early years of the NAACP.[7] This chapter argues for the centrality of Wells's anti-lynching activism in laying the groundwork that spurred the development of the NAACP. Wells's anti-lynching work began in 1892 while she was living in Memphis and editing *Free Speech*, a newspaper where she discussed controversial issues of local and national significance, even when that meant harshly criticizing the African American and white communities. In the same year, racial tensions climaxed over competition between an established white grocery store and the opening, across the street, in the African American section of town, of the African American–owned People's Grocery Company. The success of the People's Grocery Company embittered a number of white residents who viewed its success as a threat to the racial power dynamics in Memphis. At the beginning of March, after a violent exchange broke out between whites and African Americans at the People's Grocery Company, more than 100 African American men in Memphis were dragged from their homes and thrown into jail on suspicion charges. On March 9, 1892, a mob of seventy-five white men disguised with black masks dragged three of Wells's closest friends, who were the owners of the People's Grocery Company, from jail and savagely lynched them in a railroad yard.[8]

The lynchings of her three friends marked a transformative moment in Wells's life. The lynchings created numerous questions for Wells because they

[7] Later in this chapter, I will discuss in greater detail why Wells is missing from NAACP narratives such as Charles Flint Kellogg, *NAACP: A History of the National Association for the Advancement of Colored People*, Baltimore: Johns Hopkins University Press, 1973; Mark Tushnet, *The NAACP's Legal Strategy Against School Segregation, 1925–1950*, Chapel Hill: The University of North Carolina Press, 1987; Manfred Berg, *The Ticket to Freedom: The NAACP and the Struggle for Black Political Integration*, Gainesville: University of Florida Press, 2005.

[8] Ida B. Wells, *Crusade For Justice: The Autobiography of Ida B. Wells*, Chicago: The University of Chicago Press, 1970; Paula Giddings, *Ida: A Sword Among Lions*, New York: HarperCollins, 2008.

were contrary to the accepted belief that lynchings were punishment for rape; her three friends had not been charged with the crime of rape, but they were still lynched. If lynchings were not always contingent on a charge of rape, then what other reasons existed for lynching African Americans? Wells's inquiry led her to conduct independent lynching investigations across the South where she interviewed eyewitnesses and members of the community to gather information. Using the findings from a select number of these investigations, Wells wrote what would be her last article for *Free Speech* on May 21, 1892. Drawing attention to the lynchings of eight African American men in the short time period since the Memphis incident, Wells refuted the notion that rape was the motive for the lynchings, calling it "the old thread-bare lie."

Despite threats on her life in Memphis after the article was printed, Wells was convinced a lot of power lay in the media and moved to New York where she continued writing, this time for T. Thomas Fortune's *New York Age*, an African American weekly newspaper with a substantial white following. For her first article, Wells drew on the full extent of the material collected from her lynching investigations. On June 25, 1892, it became the first published exposé of lynching in America. Wells reported on facts she gathered, giving names, dates, and places of many lynchings that had taken place as alleged punishment for the accused crime of rape. The *New York Age* placed the article on its front page, printed 10,000 copies, and distributed them across the country. Her facts revealed that rape was a cover-up for a consensual but socially forbidden relationship between African American men and white women. Wells's facts made clear lynching was not a response to rape or to a greater level of criminality among African Americans. Lynching, Wells determined, was used as a strategy to keep African Americans "in their place."[9]

Wells's work in exploding the lynching myth is noteworthy in that it went at the very foundation of lynching. During this time, the most common justification for lynching was the racist myth that African American men were prone to raping white women. In this elaborate mythology, rape became the justification of lynching. Because of its constant repetition by state and city politicians in government, pastors in churches, and reporters in the white press, many citizens believed the myth. The fact that charges of rape were not even alleged prior to the majority of lynchings did not weaken the power of the rape myth. Under the false pretense of protecting white womanhood from rape and the clutches of African American male aggression, the propaganda around lynching and mob violence came to be rooted deep in white racial mores. Wells, through her investigations, told another story: that lynching was used to maintain the total (economic, educational, social) subordination of African Americans. The resulting conclusion was not hard to draw: that if lynching

---

[9] Ida B. Wells, *Crusade For Justice: The Autobiography of Ida B. Wells*, Chicago: The University of Chicago Press, 1970.

was not a response to African American criminality and instead was a tool to maintain white power, then it was unjust.[10]

Never before had anyone questioned the veracity of lynching justifications with such authority. This was groundbreaking, since a majority of African Americans and whites accepted the explanation that lynching was a response to rape or excessive violence. The great abolitionist Frederick Douglass visited Wells and applauded her for this revelation, as Douglass himself had been previously misled into believing the myth and assumed lynching was a response to increases in African American criminal activity.[11] Even white northerners had become desensitized to the lynching of African Americans. Writing about the sentiments of whites regarding lynching, Mary White Ovington, a white suffragette, settlement worker, and future founder of the NAACP, observed, "New Yorkers were not interested in anti-lynching. Nearly all believed that, when a Negro was lynched, it was for the crime of rape, and, while mob violence was wrong, it was easily excused."[12] Wells's focus on writing newspaper articles stemmed from her view that "there was no chance for a fair trial in these cases" and that pursuing recourse through the political or legal system was futile.[13] Newspapers offered Wells a platform to share her perspective and an opportunity to change the court of public opinion.

As a result of the publishing of Wells's findings, $500 was raised for Wells to publish her *New York Age* article into a pamphlet. The pamphlet was retitled *Southern Horrors: Lynch Law in All Its Phases*, and published in 1892. Not long afterward, in 1895, Wells published a more ambitious project called *The Red Record*. Similar to her first pamphlet but on a larger scale, Wells provided details of lynchings including the victims' names, dates, locations, and alleged motives. *The Red Record* was an account of the research on lynchings she conducted between 1892 and 1894 across the country. The book also included narratives and lynching photographs. The pamphlets were useful in dispelling the rape myth as they established a clear pattern of using lynchings in the service of white supremacy.[14]

---

[10] Ida B. Wells-Barnett, *On Lynchings: Southern Horrors, A Red Record, Mob Rule in New Orleans*, New York: Arno Press, 1969; Ida B. Wells-Barnett, *Crusade for Justice: The Autobiography of Ida B. Wells*, Chicago: University of Chicago Press, 1970; Donald Grant, *The Anti-Lynching Movement, 1883–1932*. San Francisco: R and E Research Associates, 1975; Walter Francis White, *Rope & Faggot: A Biography of Judge Lynch*, New York: A. A. Knopf, 1929.

[11] Ida B. Wells, *Crusade For Justice: The Autobiography of Ida B. Wells*, Chicago: The University of Chicago Press, 1970, p. 72; Paula Giddings, *Ida: A Sword Among Lions*, New York: HarperCollins, 2008, pp. 238–239.

[12] Mary White Ovington, "Early Years of the NAACP and the Urban League," *Baltimore Afro-American*, December 10, 1932.

[13] Ida B. Wells, *Crusade For Justice: The Autobiography of Ida B. Wells*, Chicago: The University of Chicago Press, 1970, p. 84.

[14] Ida B. Wells-Barnett, *On Lynchings: Southern Horrors, A Red Record, Mob Rule in New Orleans* (reprints of original pamphlets), New York: Arno, 1969; Paula Giddings, *Ida: A Sword Among Lions*, New York: HarperCollins, 2008.

Wells continued writing scathing critiques against lynching, traveled internationally to drum up support in Europe, and helped in organizing African Americans to abolish lynchings. Wells is responsible for a number of extraordinary firsts in the effort to rid America of lynchings. She was the first person to risk her life, time after time, while conducting dangerous lynching investigations. Wells was the first American to travel abroad to seek international support in the fight against lynchings. She also wrote the first article and pamphlet exposing and condemning lynching. Finally and perhaps most importantly, Wells was the first to effectively situate lynching at the crux of American democracy: in order to protect the voting, education, and workplace rights of African Americans, the senseless killings of African Americans had to stop.

The NAACP would later mobilize over the lynching issue but without Wells's early work in exposing the lynching myth and her courageous crusade to abolish lynching, it is difficult to imagine that the NAACP would have formed. Wells created the context that made the formation of the NAACP possible, by helping both whites and African Americans see that lynching was the greatest obstacle to equality.[15] As long as lynching persisted as a check on African American advancement, African Americans would never be treated as equal citizens. Thus, it became a rallying point and white progressives and African Americans alike began to mobilize over the need to end lynching.

Around the same time, many African Americans grew frustrated with Booker T. Washington's prominent Tuskegee Institute's emphasis on silent accommodation in the face of violent racism. Cautioning African Americans against social protest activities, Washington said, "agitation of questions of social equality is the extremest folly, and that progress in the enjoyment of all the privileges that will come to us must be the result of severe and constant struggle rather than of artificial forcing."[16] Advocating a gradualist approach focused on vocational and agricultural training, Washington called on African Americans to "cast down your bucket where you are," arguing that if African Americans worked hard and refrained from challenging the boundaries of the southern white power structure, whites would eventually grant them political and social equality.[17] Many white progressives believed in the power of education as a way for African Americans to overcome the obstacles in their lives and were supporters of Washington's emphasis on education as a way to uplift the African American community.[18]

---

[15] Moorfield Storey to Oswald Garrison Villard, letter, January 17, 1906, Folder 3714. Oswald Garrison Villard Papers (MS Am 1323). Houghton Library, Harvard University.

[16] Booker T. Washington, speech, Atlanta Cotton States and International Exposition Speech, September 18, 1895.

[17] Booker T. Washington, speech, Atlanta Cotton States and International Exposition Speech, September 18, 1895; Booker T. Washington, *Up From Slavery*, New York: Doubleday, Page & Co., 1901, 1st ed.

[18] Cary Wintz ed., *African American Political Thought, 1890–1930: Washington, Du Bois, Garvey, and Randolph*, Armonk, NY: M. E. Sharpe, 1996; Wilson Jeremiah Moses, *Creative Conflict in*

However, they would soon be disappointed. Washington, the most prominent and well-funded African American man in America, was reluctant to speak out against lynching. A significant attack on lynching would require Washington to address the caste system in the South. Washington was afraid to do this; he feared his purse strings would be cut off if he offended many of his wealthy white benefactors. Instead, he played into their stereotypes by performing "darky jokes" in front of white audiences, and reinforced the propaganda surrounding lynching by affirming, "The men who are lynched are invariably vagrants, men without property or standing."[19] In these ways, he fueled the idea that lynching happened only to people who were on the lowest rung of society or the people that likely deserved to be lynched.

The rare instances when Washington made a public statement, he emphasized the harm lynching did to whites – how it reflected upon the moral character of whites in the South and the impact it had on their economic situation.[20] A long time went by before Washington verbalized the terror lynchings inflicted upon African American communities.[21] After a while, many white progressives who initially supported Washington became disaffected when the realization began to set in that African Americans would not earn equal citizenship rights by hard work and sacrifice alone. Oswald Garrison Villard, a prominent white supporter of Washington who later became one of the founders of the NAACP, described his frustrations with the Washington school of thought,

They are silent in the face of all this wrongdoing unless at times and places where it is safe to speak out against the growing lynching habit. They look with ill-concealed uneasiness upon those who would make each single wrongdoing as a fire bell in the night to alarm the conscience of the people. Their duty as they see it is to serve, but not to protect; to sit silent if need be in the presence of sin, with their eyes fixed only upon the numerous and encouraging signs that this republic will in the long run not tolerate injustice against a class or race among its citizens.[22]

African American Thought: Frederick Douglass, Alexander Crummell, Booker T. Washington, W.E.B. Du Bois, and Marcus Garvey, New York: Cambridge University Press, 2004.

[19] Booker T. Washington in the *Indianapolis Freeman,* August 28, 1897. Even if we accept the claim in recent scholarship that Washington did not completely ignore lynching, it is also true that he did not actively contribute to an anti-lynching agenda. See: Robert Norrell, *Up From History: The Life of Booker T. Washington,* Cambridge: Harvard University Press, 2009.

[20] August Meier, *Negro Thought in America, 1880–1915: Radical Ideologies in the Age of Booker T. Washington,* Ann Arbor: The University of Michigan Press, 1963, pp. 108–109; James McPherson, *The Abolitionist Legacy: From Reconstruction to the NAACP,* Princeton, NJ: Princeton University Press, 1975, p. 363.

[21] Finally, in 1912, Washington made a strong statement against lynching declaring that most lynching victims were black and innocent of any wrongdoings, but this was after the NAACP had already formed and elucidated its agenda. See Booker T. Washington, "Is the Negro Having a Fair Chance?," *Century* 75 (November 1912): 46–55.

[22] Oswald Garrison Villard, Address before the Fourth Annual Conference of the National Association for the Advancement of Colored People, 1912, Box 120, Oswald Garrison Villard Papers (MS Am 1323), Houghton Library, Harvard University.

If anything, since 1890 African Americans had lost more civil rights, and those African Americans who were the most schooled faced the most virulent type of hatred from whites.[23] It became clear that lynching tracked African American intellectual and financial success. Washington's formula for African American advancement was not working.

W. E. B. Du Bois, Washington's most vocal critic in the African American community, came out in firm opposition to Washington's program of gradual advancement in 1903 with the publication of *The Souls of Black Folk*.[24] Desiring a direct approach to the litany of social ills, including lynching, that African Americans faced, Du Bois, along with a number of prominent African American leaders, formed the Niagara Movement in 1905 as a counter to the accommodationist policies of Washington.[25] Members of the Niagara Movement advocated that African Americans "should protest emphatically and continually against the abridgment of political and civil rights and against inequality of economic opportunity."[26] Though they faced financial and organizational troubles, they managed to establish thirty branches in different cities across the United States and became the first significant African American protest organization of the twentieth century. The Niagara Movement's programmatic agenda and action-oriented philosophy resonated with a number of white progressives who were discouraged with Washington's uplift ideology.[27] It was not long before many white progressives began withdrawing support from Washington and brainstormed in 1906 about creating a national organization

---

[23] C. Van Woodward, *Origins of the New South, 1877–1913*, Baton Rouge: Louisiana State University Press, 1951; August Meier, *Negro Thought in America, 1880–1915: Radical Ideologies in the Age of Booker T. Washington*, Ann Arbor, The University of Michigan Press, 1963, pp. 161–170; Rayford Logan, *The Betrayal of the Negro: From Rutherford B. Hayes To Woodrow Wilson*, New York: Collier Books, 1969; Kevin Gaines, *Uplifting the Race: Black Leadership, Politics, and Culture in the Twentieth Century*, Chapel Hill: The University of North Carolina Press, 1996, pp. 21–31.

[24] W. E. B. Du Bois, *The Souls of Black Folk*, Chicago: A. C. McClurg & Co., 1903; David Levering Lewis, *W.E.B. Du Bois: Biography of a Race, 1868–1919*, New York : H. Holt, 1993.

[25] For more on the Niagara Movement, see: W. E. B. DuBois, *Dusk of Dawn: An Essay Toward an Autobiography of a Race Concept*, New York, Harcourt, Brace & Co., 1940, p. 224; Gunnar Myrdal, *An American Dilemma: The Negro Problem and Modern Democracy*, New York, London: Harper & Brothers, 1944, pp. 742–744; E. Franklin Fraizer, *The Negro in the United States*, New York: Macmillan Co., 1949, pp. 523–524; Elliott M. Rudwick, "The Niagara Movement," *Journal of Negro History* 42 (1957): 177–200; Raymond Baker, *Following the Color Line: American Negro Citizenship in the Progressive Era*, New York: Harper & Row, 1964; John Hope Franklin, *From Slavery to Freedom : A History of African Americans*, 8th ed, New York : A.A Knopf, 2000, pg 438.

[26] Elliott M. Rudwick, "The Niagara Movement," *Journal of Negro History* 42 (1957): 178.

[27] For example, on numerous occasions, prominent abolitionists such as Oswald Garrison Villard argued that farm ownership and education were of little use if blacks were going to be burned at the stake every week. Also, Mary White Ovington wrote flattering accounts of the Niagara Movement, and Du Bois honored her with an invitation to join the movement. See James McPherson, *The Abolitionist Legacy: From Reconstruction to the NAACP*, Princeton: Princeton University Press, 1975, pp. 380–386.

focused on an aggressive approach to securing the basic citizenship rights guaranteed by the U.S. Constitution.[28]

The efforts of African Americans and progressive whites to create an alternative organization focused on securing equal rights to African Americans would soon cohere in the NAACP. The event that led to the formation of the NAACP was a vicious race riot in Springfield, Illinois, on August 14, 1908. The riot was sparked by a number of claims in the local press of a white woman being violated by George Richardson, an African American man who was in police custody. After Richardson's hearing, a menacing crowd of 4,000 began to form around the jail. Worried about the safety of Richardson, the sheriff sent him to a nearby town. Upon finding out that Richardson had been taken away, whites in Springfield became enraged. The result was the formation of white mobs comprised of many prominent white citizens who set about terrorizing the African American section of town. In the midst of their rampage, mob members cried out, "curse the day that Lincoln freed the nigger" and "niggers must depart from Springfield."[29] Realizing the unruly nature of the mob, town officials tried without success to stop the violence, and the governor was forced to call on the militia to help quell the unrest. It took two days and more than 3,500 militiamen to stop the carnage. In the words of James Crouthamel, who completed a monograph on the riot, "Springfield resembled a city in wartime on the morning after the riot, with squads of soldiers patrolling the streets, and entire battalions concentrated in the Negro area."[30] When the dust cleared, numerous deaths and injuries had been reported, property had been destroyed, and thousands of African Americans had fled town.[31]

The Springfield race riot is noteworthy due to its origin, location, and timing. First, violence erupted after the usual lynching trope was deployed when a white woman falsely named an African American man as her rapist.[32] Second, it occurred outside of the South – in Springfield, Illinois, the home of Abraham "The Great Emancipator" Lincoln. The occurrence of a race riot in Springfield created great alarm among white progressives as it meant that lynchings and

---

[28] James McPherson, *The Abolitionist Legacy: From Reconstruction to the NAACP*, Princeton: Princeton University Press, 1975.

[29] James Crouthamel, "The Springfield Race Riot of 1908," *Journal of Negro History* 45 (1960): 170.

[30] Crouthamel, p. 174. For another account on the riot, see Roberta Senechal de la Roche, *The Sociogenesis of a Race Riot: Springfield, Illinois in 1908*, Urbana: University of Illinois Press, 1990.

[31] For the most detailed treatment of the NAACP's development, see Patricia Sullivan, *Lift Every Voice: The NAACP and the Making of the Civil Rights Movement*, New York: New Press, 2009. See also Charles Flint Kellogg, *NAACP: A History of the National Association for the Advancement of Colored People*, Baltimore: Johns Hopkins University Press, 1973.

[32] The wife of a streetcar conductor accused George Richardson, an African American who had been working in the neighborhood, of attacking her. Richardson was arrested and jailed. Later, before a special grand jury, the woman admitted that she had been severely beaten by a white man and that Richardson had nothing to do with the attack.

mob violence were not solely a southern phenomenon and could occur with similar viciousness in the North. It was a jarring reminder that mob violence was a national rather than a sectional problem, and that something radical would have to be done before race relations deteriorated further. Third, it came at a time when white progressives were aware of the urgent need to set up a national civil rights organization focused on directly addressing the most blatant denials of African American citizenship.

William English Walling, a white progressive from the South, investigated the race riot at Springfield and, disturbed by what he saw, wrote an important article, "The Race War in the North," a charge to white progressives to get involved in the movement against lynching and mob violence. Mary White Ovington and Henry Moskowitz, a prominent Jewish man in the administration of the mayor of New York, responded and met with Walling in a small New York City apartment. In the meeting, which lasted hours, the three expressed their indignation at the state of race relations and vowed to organize a larger gathering of like-minded individuals.[33] After the meeting, they immediately approached Oswald Garrison Villard, the grandson of abolitionist William Lloyd Garrison and president of the *New York Evening Post* newspaper, whereupon they decided to issue a call for a national conference to discuss the political and social rights of African Americans. On Lincoln's birthday, February 12, 1909, Villard issued his now-famous "Lincoln's Birthday Call," which focused on the serious denials of freedom and equality for African Americans since the Emancipation Proclamation and which was signed by fifty-three prominent African American and white writers, activists, and scholars, including Wells and Du Bois.[34] Of particular significance, the call drew attention to the problem of mob violence:

The spread of lawless attacks upon the Negro, North, South and West – even in the Springfield made famous by Lincoln – often accompanied by revolting brutalities, sparing neither sex nor age nor youth, could but shock the author of the sentiment that government by the people, for the people, should not perish from the earth.[35]

The call led to the formation of a conference in 1909, and the small group was called the National Negro Committee. During the conference a number of relevant topics pertaining to African American citizenship rights were raised, including disenfranchisement, education, lynching, and the enforcement of the Fourteenth Amendment.

On the final day of the two-day conference, the committee on nominations for the Committee of 40 (those who were to become the main leaders

---

[33] Mary White Ovington, "How the National Association for the Advancement of Colored People Began," pamphlet, 1914, Box 120. Oswald Garrison Villard Papers (MS Am 1323). Houghton Library, Harvard University.

[34] "The Call" was published in the *New York Evening Post* on February 12, 1909, on the 100th anniversary of President Lincoln's birth.

[35] *New York Evening Post*, February 12, 1909.

of the formal organization) congregated in a contentious meeting that lasted until midnight. Acutely aware of Washington's power and chest of financial resources, a few members on the committee were concerned about how they were going to receive funding if the NAACP did not have his endorsement. At the end of the long debate, the anti-Washington contingent of whites won, but at a tremendous cost: two of the most active but radical leaders in the African American community, Ida B. Wells and Monroe Trotter (outspoken African American activist and Washington critic) were left off of the final Committee of 40 list. Ovington rightly observed that the committee "took a middle course and suited nobody."[36] In a compromise foreshadowing the complicated racial dynamics of twentieth-century civil rights struggles, the burgeoning NAACP had to make a choice between embracing the more radical movement veterans who were doing valuable work or walking a middle line in hopes of reaching increased numbers of moderate white supporters with financial resources. Rationalizing this decision in her memoir, Ovington tried to explain the committee's decision to exclude Wells and Trotter: "They were powerful personalities who had gone their own ways, fitted for courageous work, but perhaps not fitted to accept the restraint of an organization."[37] Although Wells was later listed on the Committee of 40 after many complaints from her supporters at the conference, the snub by senior NAACP leadership led to Wells withdrawing from the NAACP.[38] The formation of the NAACP allowed it to offer America a new vision of a race organization – one that did not include its most conservative and radical elements.

Later, in May 1910, a permanent body was established, which called itself the National Association for the Advancement of Colored People. Recognizing the need to include more African Americans (the board of directors was all white), the organization asked Du Bois to assume a leadership position as director of publicity and research. Du Bois accepted the offer as he realized the similarities in organizational platforms between the NAACP and the Niagara Movement. Subsequently, he encouraged members to join the NAACP, and the Niagara Movement was dissolved. Thus began the formation of a biracial

---

[36] Mary White Ovington, *The Walls Came Tumbling Down*, New York: Harcourt Brace, 1947, p. 106.

[37] Mary White Ovington, *The Walls Came Tumbling Down*, New York: Harcourt Brace, 1947, p. 106.

[38] For more on this, see Ida B. Wells, *Crusade For Justice: The Autobiography of Ida B. Wells*, Chicago: The University of Chicago Press, 1970, pp. 321–333; Charles Flint Kellogg, *NAACP: A History of the National Association for the Advancement of Colored People*, Baltimore: Johns Hopkins University Press, 1973; Thomas C. Holt, "The Lonely Warrior: Ida B. Wells Barnett and the Struggle for Black Leadership," in *Black Leaders of the Twentieth Century*, edited by John Hope Franklin and August Meier, Urbana: University of Illinois Press, 1982, pp. 38–61; David Levering Lewis, *W.E.B. Du Bois: Biography of a Race, 1868–1919*, New York: H. Holt, 1993, pp. 386–407; Paula Giddings, *Ida: A Sword Among Lions*, New York: HarperCollins, 2008.

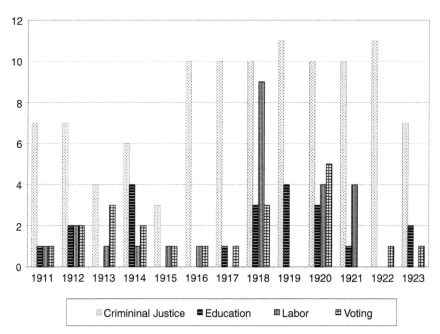

FIGURE 2.1 NAACP monthly board minutes, mentions of the important issue areas.
Note: This figure is an indication of the breadth of the early NAACP's agenda during
the time period that this book covers. I read and content coded all the minutes from
the NAACP meetings from 1911 to 1923, eleven per year for twelve years. The purpose
was to compare the frequency with which the organization addressed issues of lynching
and mob violence in comparison to three other areas that are more commonly associated with the NAACP in the literature: labor, education, and voting. The coding scheme
that I developed used the following key words for each issue area: "labor unions" or
"unions" for labor; "schools" or "education" for education, "ballot" or "voting rights"
or "disenfranchisement" for voting, and "mob violence" or "lynching" or "accused of
murder" for criminal justice. Because I read through and did not simply do a key-word
search, I was able to dismiss those occurrences of code words such as "education" that
were not really about the issue and referred to something else. This figure ignores the
frequency with which a topic was discussed in a given month. In other words, this figure
does not explain the magnitude with which the NAACP discussed an issue item each
month, even though, quite often, it was brought up more than once.
Source: NAACP Board of Director Minutes 1911–1923, NAACP Papers, Reel 1,
Manuscript Division, Library of Congress, Washington DC.

struggle for African American equality with the fight against lynching and mob
violence as one of the most prominent concerns.[39]

---

[39] For accounts of the development of the NAACP see the following: Charles Flint Kellogg, *NAACP
     A History of the National Association for the Advancement of Colored People*, Baltimore: Johns
     Hopkins University Press, 1967; Langston Hughes, *Fight for Freedom*, New York: W. W. Norton,

This should be no surprise. Lynching and mob violence were at the top of the NAACP's issue agenda because racial violence was believed to be the greatest obstacle that African Americans faced to gaining equality in America. In the original NAACP platform in 1909 it was stated, "We regard with grave concern the attempt manifest South and North to deny black men the right to work and to enforce this demand with violence and bloodshed."[40] Seven years later, racial violence remained high on the list of NAACP's concerns. As explained by Secretary Roy Nash in 1916 in response to criticism from Ovington that the NAACP's program of advancement was not radical enough, "All he [the American Negro] wanted was a chance to live without a rope around his neck."[41] As the NAACP saw it, before the organization could appropriately address other problematic areas of civil rights such as voting, labor, and housing, it was necessary to focus on ending lynching and mob violence so that African Americans could live to enjoy the benefits of their struggle. NAACP board minutes are particularly elucidative (see Figure 2.1), showing that for every year from 1911 to 1923, the NAACP focused most of its attention on lynching and mob violence in comparison with other areas of racial injustice.

The NAACP Develops a Formal Strategy Against Lynching

The most important thing which can be done immediately toward stopping lynching is to gather all the facts of lynching and give them the widest publicity.
                                                            – W. E. B. Dubois, 1916

The NAACP had identified ending racist violence as its most important issue area but it was not yet clear how the organization was going to go about meeting this goal. In the era that preceded the heyday of civil rights activism – before the marches and the sit-ins and without repertoires of successful civil rights movement tactics to draw from – how did early groups map their strategies? The most prominent approach – education, hard work, and patience as advocated by Booker T. Washington – had not produced a substantive change in the occurrence of racial violence in the United States. The NAACP was left with the daunting task of formulating a strategy for civil rights before there were actual civil rights in society.

Fortunately for the NAACP, there was protest work the organization admired – even if someone the NAACP was at odds with was carrying it out. Ida

1962; B. Joyce Ross, *J.E. Spingarn and the Rise of NAACP, 1911–1929*, New York: Atheneum, 1972; Minnie Finch, *The NAACP: Its Fight for Justice*, London: The Scarecrow Press, 1981; Patricia Sullivan, *Lift Every Voice: The NAACP and the Making of the Civil Rights Movement*, New York: New Press, 2009.

[40] Platform of the National Negro Committee, 1909. NAACP Papers, Manuscript Division, Library of Congress, Washington, DC.

[41] As quoted in Charles Flint Kellogg, *NAACP: A History of the National Association for the Advancement of Colored People*, Baltimore: Johns Hopkins University Press, 1973, p. 134.

B. Wells's personal crusade against lynching was noteworthy for demonstrating the importance of public opinion to creating a change in the national con- science of America. Building and expanding upon the foundation that Wells laid, the NAACP endeavored to use its organizational resources to fill a void in media portrayals of African American criminality and to bring the concerns of African American civil society into mainstream discourse. As social move- ment studies have made clear, movements often matter to the broader culture because they can shift values and beliefs and ultimately encourage people to think radically differently.[42] An analysis of the NAACP's early strategy reveals that the organization was very much engaged in this type of social movement action. The problem was not simply that lynchings and mob violence were occurring; these acts existed in a racially caustic environment that supported and justified the carrying out of racist violence. The NAACP wanted to change the way in which issues about racial violence were framed in public media and language in the hope that lynchings would cease. The rest of this chapter details how the NAACP used different forms of media, first its own publications and then mainstream newspapers, to raise national awareness about lynching and mob violence.

In 1915, the NAACP began the first of many public awareness campaigns to fight negative perceptions of African Americans when the film *Birth of a Nation* was released. A film that pioneered new elements of filmmaking – the facial close-up, the tracking shot, the iris effect, parallel action – the sociopo- litical elements of the film were not lost on the audience. Based on Thomas Dixon's novel *The Clansmen, Birth of a Nation* portrayed a nostalgic view of a slaveholding South before the Civil War.[43] African American freedom during Reconstruction, in this rendition, was a vile mistake. In its execution, the film characterized African Americans as rapists, idiots, and deviants. In stark con- trast, the white-cloaked members of the Ku Klux Klan (KKK) were cast as the saviors of the South and the protectors of good government, order, and white women's virtue. It is no surprise, then, that the visceral reaction created by the

---

[42] William Gamson and Andre Modigliani, "Media Discourse and Public Opinion of Nuclear Power: A Constructionists Approach," *American Journal of Sociology* 95 (1989): 1–37; Leo d'Anjou, *Social Movements and Cultural Change: The First Abolition Campaign Revisited*, New York: Aldine De Gruyter, 1996; Leo d'Anjou and John Van Male, "Between Old and New: Social Movements and Cultural Change," *Mobilization* 3 (1998): 207–226; Thomas Rochon, *Culture Moves: Ideas, Activism, and Changing Values*, Princeton: Princeton University Press, 1998. For a great review of the literature on the cultural consequences of social movements, see Jennifer Earl, "The Cultural Consequences of Social Movements," in *The Blackwell Companion to Social Movements*, edited by David Snow, Sarah Soule, and Hanspeter Kresi, Oxford: Blackwell Publishing, 2004, pp. 508–530.

[43] John Hope Franklin, "Propaganda as History," *The Massachusetts Review* 20, no. 3 (1979): 417–434; Michael Rogin, "'The Sword Became a Flashing Vision': D.W. Griffith's *The Birth of a Nation*," *Representations* 9 (1985): 150–195; Melvyn Stokes, *The Birth of a Nation: A History of "The Most Controversial Motion Picture of All Time,"* New York: Oxford University Press, 2007.

movie helped to ignite the rebirth of the KKK after a lull in activity. In response to the movie's incendiary content, the NAACP held public demonstrations across the country and distributed thousands of pieces of literature denouncing the film. The NAACP's campaign to suppress the film did not prevent the release of *Birth of Nation* to huge crowds, but it helped to create a sense of the possibilities for using media in the service of racial justice.[44]

One year after the film's release, with racist violence on the rise, the NAACP launched an anti-lynching campaign. Though the NAACP had always made lynching a key focus of its organizational activities since the beginning, the ad hoc manner in which it fought against lynchings and mob violence hampered the organization's efforts. Feeling that a coordinated attack was needed in 1916, the NAACP formalized an anti-lynching strategy. A committee of five board members assembled on April 10, 1916, to prepare a report. They spoke about the hostility of working in the South and the need to call "the attention of the press and of the Federal Government to the breakdown of democracy in the South."[45] The NAACP eventually agreed the anti-lynching campaign should follow three central goals in ascending order of importance: "(1) Gathering and compiling the facts in regard to lynching; (2) investigating specific cases as they occur; (3) organizing the existing southern opinion of practical business and political leaders who are opposed to lynching."[46] After the committee report, a formal anti-lynching campaign was established along with a fundraising drive to finance activities.

The NAACP's anti-lynching campaign was officially operational. At the December 1916 NAACP board meeting, Du Bois reported, "All [on the anti-lynching committee] were agreed that the most important thing which can be done immediately toward stopping lynching is to gather all the facts of lynching and give them the widest publicity."[47] The NAACP quickly developed a sophisticated understanding of the way different forms of media reached different populations of people. In order to educate white Americans about lynchings, the NAACP was deliberate about when and what forms of media it used. To give the facts of lynching the "widest publicity," the NAACP started with citizens who could be easily mobilized and enlarged its orbit to reach those who

[44] For more on the NAACP's campaign to suppress and then censor *The Birth of a Nation*, see Charles Flint Kellogg, *NAACP: A History of the National Association for the Advancement of Colored People* Vol. 1, 1909–1920, Baltimore: Johns Hopkins University Press, 1967, pp. 142–145; Melvyn Stokes, *The Birth of a Nation: A History of "The Most Controversial Motion Picture of All Time,"* New York: Oxford University Press, 2007, pp. 134–170; Patricia Sullivan, *Lift Every Voice: The NAACP and the Making of the Civil Rights Movement*, New York: New Press, 2009, pp. 48–59.

[45] BOD Minutes, April 10, 1916, NAACP Papers, Manuscript Division, Library of Congress, Washington, DC.

[46] BOD Minutes, April 9, 1916, NAACP Papers, Manuscript Division, Library of Congress, Washington, DC.

[47] BOD Minutes, December 10, 1916, NAACP Papers, Manuscript Division, Library of Congress, Washington, DC.

were viewed as being on the fence or curious; later, the organization reached out further to individuals who were hostile to learning about lynching.

At the beginning, the NAACP utilized its own newspaper, *The Crisis*. Printed at the NAACP's headquarters, the newspaper informed individuals about lynching on a monthly basis and made clear that it was a problem that citizens needed to work actively to end. *The Crisis* did not require reliance on mainstream media and offered the NAACP significant control over its message. Still, *The Crisis* was distributed mainly to people that subscribed to it or who voluntarily sought it out to read, which did not address the huge numbers of white Americans the NAACP wanted to influence that would never pick up an NAACP newspaper. Pamphlets, the NAACP's next line of defense in its opinion-shaping campaign, filled in this gap: in-depth reports of specific lynching investigations were distributed or mailed out to individuals the NAACP hoped to influence. While useful at educating people to the horrors of lynching, pamphlets were not printed with any level of regularity. After the NAACP built up its capacity to report on lynchings through these indigenous media outlets, they placed renewed emphasis on mainstream media. The NAACP understood that in order to educate whites and other groups, the organization had to get the facts of lynching into what people generally regarded as credible sources of information: white-controlled newspapers and magazines. By articulating the terror of lynching and broadcasting it to a wider audience through these different channels, the NAACP hoped that familiarity with and careless disregard for lynching could be transformed into critique and protest.[48]

In-House Publication: *The Crisis*

After all, publicity is the main thing. The world does not know, it does not realize evil or its significance in nine cases out of ten. This is particularly true of the situation of American Negroes. We count them as our greatest assets, the various methods by which we make the truth known. First of all comes The Crisis Magazine.
       – NAACP Annual Report for the Year 1916

The Crisis, the official magazine of the NAACP, was a powerful in-house publicity tool used to inform the American public about the state of African Americans and NAACP policy.[49] Du Bois, NAACP director of publicity and research, strongly felt protest organizations should publicize their work through their own newspaper and pushed the board in this direction from the outset. The first issue, titled *The Crisis: A Record of the Darker Races*, was published on November 10, 1910. From the beginning, *The Crisis* had a wide readership comprised of mostly African Americans and a few whites and included editorials

---

[48] August Meier, *Negro Thought in America, 1880–1915: Radical Ideologies in the Age of Booker T. Washington*, Ann Arbor, The University of Michigan Press, 1963, p. 161.

[49] Executive Session, May 14, 1910, in BOD Minutes, NAACP Papers, Manuscript Division, Library of Congress, Washington, DC.

by Du Bois, articles about the NAACP's initiatives, poems, and reports on investigations of racial injustice. Reflecting the NAACP's social reform goals, *The Crisis* presented material debunking false racial stereotypes and protested injustices against African Americans. But it did more than this: Du Bois used *The Crisis* as a platform of agitation and with incisive candor launched attacks on the U.S. government for denying democracy to African Americans and for not doing anything about the evil of lynching. Few were free from the wrath of Du Bois's pen – he even criticized other African American newspapers for sloppy grammar and for focusing mostly on weddings and murders instead of taking up some of the more categorically complicated issues such as lynching investigations and campaigns for equal rights.[50]

The Crisis was the successor to a tradition of advocacy journalism, which focused on using the written word to expose, challenge, and educate in hopes of advancing equality for African Americans. The precursors to *The Crisis* include the *Freedman's Journal,* the first newspaper published by Africans in the United Sates; Frederick Douglass's *North Star*, William Lloyd Garrison's *Liberator*; Ida B. Wells's *Free Speech*, and the *New York Age*, edited by T. Thomas Fortune. Considered by many to be a "militant newspaper," *The Crisis*'s expanding influence was made evident by the state authorities in Mississippi and Arkansas who attempted to ban the publication from being distributed.[51]

Since Du Bois was at the helm of *The Crisis,* he set the agenda and dedicated the majority of its content in the first decade of publication to exposing lynching to the world. *The Crisis* insisted that lynching was the outgrowth of white supremacy, not African American savagery. In describing the lynching of an African American man, Du Bois sought to explain the hypocrisy associated with lynching justifications in the white press:

The point is he was black. Blackness must be punished. Blackness is the crime of crimes .... It is therefore necessary, as every white scoundrel in the nation knows, to let slip no opportunity of punishing this crime of crimes. Of course, if possible, the pretext should be great and overwhelming – some awful stunning crime, made even more horrible by the reporters imagination. Failing this, mere murder, arson barn burning or impudence may do.[52]

[50] David Levering Lewis, *W.E.B. Du Bois: Biography of a Race, 1868–1919*, New York: Henry Holt, 1993, p. 416.

[51] Mississippi passed legislation forbidding the sale of publications "tending to disturb relations between the races," as a result of which a *Crisis* agent was arrested in April 1920, badly beaten, fined, and sentenced to six months in prison for selling the magazine (reported in Charles Flint Kellogg, *NAACP: A History of the National Association for the Advancement of Colored People*, Baltimore: Johns Hopkins University Press, 1973, p. 290). Also in 1919, after the Phillips County race massacre, the Arkansas governor told the postmaster general not to distribute any more issues of *The Crisis*.

[52] David Levering Lewis, *W.E.B. Du Bois: Biography of a Race, 1868–1919*, New York: H. Holt, 1993, pp. 426–427.

The task of *The Crisis*, as Du Bois saw it, was to create a counternarrative of lynching that depended on the very real danger of unrestrained white violence instead of imaginary claims of African American criminality.

The value of *The Crisis* in exposing lynchings was not confined to the written word; Du Bois problematized lynching for white Americans through the use of photos. Photographs of lynchings provided a visual representation of what the NAACP was writing about in *The Crisis*. Du Bois skillfully used photos to create a different frame from which to interpret lynchings: whereas lynching photos had been used to celebrate the carrying out of justice, *The Crisis* used photographs to expose that myth and convey the sheer injustice of lynching. The juxtaposition of text and horrific photographs made the logic of lynching harder to navigate in the white mind; it was one thing to read stories of African American innocence and another to see the consequences of white vigilante violence meted out on a mutilated African American body.

The first time *The Crisis* linked the reporting of a lynching with multiple photographs was after the shocking lynching in May 1916 of Jesse Washington, a mentally disabled boy in Waco, Texas.[53] An investigation was completed by the NAACP; the report detailed how Washington was dragged by a mob from a Waco courtroom after receiving the death sentence for the murder of a white woman and taken to a public square where he was viciously stabbed and beaten before a chain was thrown over his neck and he was pulled over a blazing bonfire and burned alive. A crowd of 15,000, including the mayor of Waco, the chief of police, and other city officials, cheered as the body burned.[54]

Du Bois was appalled at the cruelty, and so in July 1916, *The Crisis* went where no other journalism publication had gone before and unapologetically featured pictures of the charred corpse of nineteen-year-old Washington hanging by a chain from a tree (Illustrations 2.1 and 2.2). The July issue included an eight-page spread complete with numbing pictures and lengthy transcripts of lynch-party participants. The horror in these photos was not just in what had been done to the body of Washington – the horror was also about the thousands of white spectators who celebrated in the murder of Washington. It didn't matter that Washington's mangled body and the faces of many of the spectators were unrecognizable: Washington's body symbolized the vulnerability of African American life and in the oppressive crowd, Du Bois saw the complicity of white America in the lynching of African American citizenship. Members on the board cautioned Du Bois about publishing such disturbing photographs, but Du Bois argued that these were the daily realities African Americans faced and that they should not be censored.[55] If it took shocking the

---

[53] BOD Minutes, June 12, 1916, NAACP Papers, Manuscript Division, Library of Congress, Washington, DC.

[54] Elizabeth Freeman, The Waco Lynching, report, 1916, Anti-Lynching File, 15 pages. NAACP Papers, Manuscript Division, Library of Congress, Washington, DC.

[55] David Levering Lewis, *W.E.B. Du Bois: Biography of a Race, 1868–1919*, New York: H. Holt, 1993, p. 514.

ILLUSTRATION 2.1 The Torture of Jesse Washington, printed in *The Crisis*. "Large crowd looking at the burned body of Jesse Washington, 18 year-old African American, lynched in Waco, Texas, May 15, 1916."
Source: Photographed by Fred Gildersleeve. Courtesy of the Library of Congress, Prints and Photographs Division, LC-USZ62–35348, LOT 13093, no. 38.

sensibilities of Americans with gruesome photographs, so be it; Du Bois was not in the business of making white people feel comfortable – he wanted to unsettle in hopes of engendering change.

Many more lynching exposés would grace the pages of *The Crisis*.[56] While often controversial, Du Bois's stubborn refusal to assuage the realities of lynching in *The Crisis* helped to raise considerable support for the fight to end lynching and pushed the NAACP to the forefront of that struggle. As stated by Du Bois, the intent of *The Crisis* was to set forth "those facts and arguments which show the danger of race prejudice."[57]

The Crisis was soon established as America's leading publication focused on the state of African Americans. Signifying the importance of *The Crisis* in

[56] Others include "Massacre At East St. Louis," *The Crisis*, September 1917; "The Burning at Dyersburg," *The Crisis*, February 1918; "The Burning of Jim McIlherron," *The Crisis*, May 1918.
[57] David Levering Lewis, *W.E.B. Du Bois: Biography of a Race, 1868–1919*, New York: H. Holt, 1993, p. 411.

ILLUSTRATION 2.2 Mob Surrounding Lynching of Jesse Washington, printed in *The Crisis*. "Large crowd watching the lynching of an African American, possibly, Jesse Washington, in Waco, Texas."
Source: Photographer unknown. Courtesy of the Library of Congress, Prints and Photographs Division, LC-USZ62–36635, LOT 13093, no. 29.

the public sphere is the growth in distribution from 1,000 copies a month in 1910 to a peak of 100,000 copies a month in 1919 (see Figure 2.2).[58] This made it more popular than long-standing journals such as *The Nation* and *The New Republic*.[59] Even more surprising, unlike these journals, *The Crisis* could not use ordinary channels for distribution and was instead distributed chiefly through its own agents, affectionately referred to by Du Bois as "missionaries in a crusade," in mostly big urban cities.[60] Despite this logistical hurdle, *The Crisis* quickly became popular among upper-class African Americans living in northern cities. Distribution of *The Crisis* to African Americans in the South took place after James Weldon Johnson came on board to the NAACP in 1917,

[58] In June, 1919, circulation went to 104,000. BOD Minutes, NAACP Papers, July 11, 1919. Average monthly circulation during 1919 was 94,908. See Twelfth Annual Report for the Year 1921, p. 81 for *The Crisis* circulation from 1911 to 1921. NAACP Papers, Manuscript Division, Library of Congress, Washington, DC.
[59] David Levering Lewis, *W.E.B. Du Bois: The Fight For Equality and the American Century, 1919–1963*, New York: Henry Holt, 2000, p. 2. Lewis acknowledged: "Du Bois was the founding editor of one of the most remarkable journals of opinion and propaganda in America. Its monthly circulation of 100,000 and better exceeded that of Herbert Croly's four-year-old *New Republic* and Oswald Villard's *Nation*, and was four times larger than Max Eastman's *Liberator*, the successor to the banned *Masses*." See also John Tebbel and Mary Ellen Zuckerman, *The Magazine in America: 1741–1990*, New York, Oxford University Press, 1991, pp. 203–206.
[60] Editorial, *The Crisis*, November 1912, p. 28.

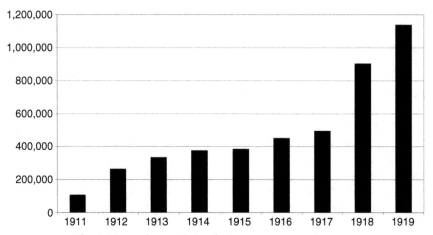

FIGURE 2.2 *The Crisis* total annual circulation, 1911–1919.
Source: Twelfth Annual Report for the Year 1921, p. 81, NAACP Papers, Manuscript Division, Library of Congress, Washington, DC.

and a field agent, F. J. Calloway, led a four-month circulation drive based on commission.[61]

Pamphlet Publications

The use of pamphlets in the NAACP's anti-lynching campaign grew out of *The Crisis*. Despite initial rumblings about the selection of photos in the Waco Horror, the NAACP's leadership determined it was of great value. The NAACP made the Waco Horror a stand-alone report, called it a pamphlet, and sent it out to a wide audience who did not already subscribe to *The Crisis*. In an effort to advance its anti-lynching campaign, the NAACP mailed the pamphlet to 700 white newspapers. In addition, the pamphlet was distributed together with an appeal for contributions to a list of 500 wealthy men in New York, 670 members of the New York City Club, 600 members of the Indian Rights NAACP, 900 members of the Intercollegiate Socialist Society, 1,800 New York churches, and all members of Congress.[62] As a result of the short pamphlet detailing the Waco lynching, many people across the nation expressed indignation and outrage. The NAACP's success in using the pamphlet was realized at

---

[61] Report of the Director of Publications and Research for The Crisis, 1919, NAACP Papers, Box F-1, Manuscript Division, Library of Congress, Washington DC; Charles Flint Kellogg, *NAACP: A History of the National Association for the Advancement of Colored People*, Baltimore: Johns Hopkins University Press, 1973, p. 153.

[62] Roy Nash, "Waco Horror Stirs to Action," letter, 1916, Anti-Lynching File; BOD Minutes, July 10, 1916; BOD Minutes, November 13, 1916, NAACP Papers, Manuscript Division, Library of Congress, Washington, DC.

the end of the year when NAACP Board Chairman Joel Spingarn announced the organization had succeeded in raising $11,869 for the anti-lynching fund, the greatest amount for any single-issue area in the NAACP's history up to that point.[63] They were able to do this off the response from the *The Waco Horror* pamphlet.

Aware of the potential of pamphlets to rally public opinion, the NAACP significantly increased the publication of pamphlets from one in 1916 to twenty in 1919.[64] The NAACP viewed pamphlets as valuable educational resources since they offered the organization the opportunity to expand its reach outside of *The Crisis* readership. Pamphlets filled in an important information void between *The Crisis*, which inundated its readers with lynching reports on a monthly basis and the mainstream newspaper outlets, which swept lynchings under the rug. Through pamphlets, the NAACP could do something to stop the erasure of African American lynching from the public sphere.

Pamphlets were self-published reports that addressed specific areas of the NAACP's concern. For example, the headline that jumped out to readers on the cover of an April 1919 pamphlet was: *Twelve Months of Lynching in America: Is this Democracy?*, and beneath was a photo of a frenzied lynch mob. The seven-page report went on to document atrocious lynchings that had taken place in Georgia, Mississippi, Tennessee, Texas, Florida, and Kentucky. Another eight-page pamphlet, published in September 1919, attempted to rally public support for the federal government to get involved in addressing lynchings with the title *Why Congress Should Investigate Race Riots and Lynching*. The pamphlet, which was distributed to members of Congress as well as the public, listed statistics of race riots and lynching victims in the North and South and argued that "states have proved themselves unable or unwilling to stop lynching" and thus "lynching and mob violence have become a national problem."[65]

Pamphlets were also used to raise support abroad. The pamphlet *An Appeal to the Conscience of the Civilized World* focused on exposing the injustice of lynching to an international audience. The twelve-page pamphlet was sent to 100 leading newspapers in England, Ireland, Scotland, Holland, Belgium, France, Switzerland, Italy, Austria, Germany, Denmark, Sweden, Norway, Spain, Cuba, Argentina, and Canada.[66] The NAACP reported in May 1920

[63] Patricia Bernstein, *The First Waco Horror: The Lynching of Jesse Washington and the Rise of the NAACP*, College Station: Texas A&M Press, 2005, p. 169.

[64] Tenth Annual Report for the Year 1919. NAACP Papers, Manuscript Division, Library of Congress, Washington, DC. Some titles of lynching-related pamphlets include *An American Lynching, A Ten Year Fight Against Lynching, Massacring Whites in Arkansas, Burnings at a Stake, A Lynching Uncovered, Laws Against Lynching, The Mobbing of John R. Shillady,* and *Three Thousand Will Burn Negro.*

[65] "Why Congress Should Investigate Race Riots and Lynching," pamphlet, September 1919. Part 7: Anti-Lynching, NAACP Papers, Manuscript Division, Library of Congress, Washington, DC.

[66] BOD Minutes, March 8, 1920, NAACP Papers, Manuscript Division, Library of Congress, Washington, DC.

that the foreign appeal "has received considerable comment in the press" and that a letter from a representative in London had come "assuring us that [the representative] will give the pamphlet the widest publicity possible."[67]

The most valuable pamphlet publication on lynching ever completed was *Thirty Years of Lynching in the United States, 1892–1918*. To address the population of white Americans that still believed lynchings were punishment for the rape of white women, the NAACP decided to undertake the first statistical study of lynching in America. To obtain the necessary data, two researchers were sent to the Library of Congress in Washington, DC, and instructed to read through newspapers back over a period of thirty years and extract data regarding every lynching that had been published. They reported on the name, sex, and age of the victim and the place, date, and manner of each lynching.[68] The library data was supplemented by information on lynchings that could be verified by the NAACP but that had not been reported in the press. These data were analyzed by Franklin Morton and published in a 105-page pamphlet showing that over the thirty-year period, of the 3,224 Americans who had been lynched, 2,522 were African American and 702 were white.[69] Of the African Americans who had been lynched, less than 19 percent had been charged with rape; the study revealed African Americans had often been lynched for much lesser offenses such as "talking back to whites," "killing a cow," and for "protecting a wife and child from the beating of belligerent white men."[70] The publication made unequivocally clear that rape accusations were not the main reason African Americans were being lynched and helped to solidify the NAACP's credibility.

The pamphlet went to libraries in the United States and throughout the world and received the attention of numerous media outlets.[71] The *Chicago Tribune* relayed to its readers, "In the last thirty years 3,224 persons have been put to death by mobs according to a report made public today by the National Association for the Advancement of Colored People."[72] The pamphlet also helped the leading newspaper in the South, *The Atlanta Constitution*, bring home to its readers the magnitude of lynchings when it declared boldly in a subtitle, "Georgia Leads the States With 386 – 2,834 of the Total Number

---

[67] BOD Minutes, May 5, 1920, NAACP Papers, Manuscript Division, Library of Congress, Washington, DC.

[68] James Weldon Johnson, *Along This Way: The Autobiography of James Weldon Johnson*, New York: The Viking Press, 1933, p. 330.

[69] Mary White Ovington, *The Walls Came Tumbling Down*, New York: Harcourt Brace, 1947, p. 150; *Thirty Years of Lynching in the United States, 1889–1918*, New York: National Association for the Advancement of Colored People, April 1919.

[70] *Thirty Years of Lynching in the United States, 1889–1918*, New York: National Association for the Advancement of Colored People, April 1919, p. 16.

[71] Mary White Ovington, *The Walls Came Tumbling Down*, New York: Harcourt Brace, 1947, p. 152.

[72] "Many Lynchings Taking Place in the United States," *Chicago Daily Tribune*, May 3, 1919.

Lynched in the South."[73] According to Johnson, "This publication was of a value beyond estimation in the Association's fight against lynching."[74] The NAACP used the study over and over again in appealing to the general public and politicians.

Newspapers

Despite the NAACP's inroads through pamphlets and *The Crisis*, the organization certainly viewed mainstream newspapers as the cornerstone to a successful media strategy. The hardest-to-reach citizens, those who viewed NAACP publications as biased, could conceivably be reached through their local newspaper. In a period before televisions were commercially available, newspapers were deeply influential in shaping public opinion. As the NAACP saw it, the slanderous reporting of lynchings in white newspapers as the consequence of African American crime and the absence of reporting of white crimes against African Americans contributed to the public acceptability of lynchings and mob violence. Since newspapers were considered an authoritative public record of events (official account, reporting of facts, eyewitness testimony) the NAACP understood that if the organization was going to achieve the change it wanted to see in the consciousness of America, it needed to shift the way mainstream newspapers reported on the lynching of African Americans. Writing about the NAACP's work with the press, Ovington reveals, "The newspapers usually showed the Negro as a criminal. It made, they thought, interesting reading. We, then, would show the criminality of the white; we would publicize lynching, interpret the story."[75] If the NAACP could show that lynchings were not a response to an innate propensity of African Americans to commit crimes through mainstream newspapers and instead were a result of white savagery, then the belief structure supporting lynching would begin to crumble.

In the first year of its anti-lynching campaign, the NAACP laid the groundwork for what they hoped would be a national newspaper presence. In 1916, the NAACP developed five lists of 289 newspapers where they sent every story that had any conceivable chance of being published: fifty leading colored papers, sixty-six friendly white papers, ninety-two northern, forty-four southern, and seventy-seven foreign newspapers.[76] While useful in showing that the NAACP was acutely concerned about getting printed in mainstream newspapers, the association lacked a calculated method for how to achieve this goal. When John Shillady, a hardworking social worker, came onboard as

---

[73] "3,224 Persons Lynched by Mobs in Last 30 Years," *The Atlanta Constitution*, May 3, 1919.
[74] James Weldon Johnson, *Along This Way: The Autobiography of James Weldon Johnson*, New York: The Viking Press, 1933, p. 331.
[75] Mary White Ovington, *The Walls Came Tumbling Down*, New York: Harcourt Brace, 1947, p. 112.
[76] Annual Report for the Year 1916, NAACP Papers, Manuscript Division, Library of Congress, Washington, DC.

NAACP secretary in 1918, he took a lead role in expanding and systematizing the NAACP's newspaper reach. He set up a regular press service and pressed the board of directors to hire someone to focus specifically on a targeted newspaper strategy.[77]

A significant boost in the NAACP's ability to use the media was the addition of Herbert Seligmann, a reporter for the *New York Evening Post*. Since 1911, Oswald Garrison Villard had attempted to acquire an individual with newspaper experience to directly handle all of the NAACP's publicity efforts. Villard's previous attempts were thwarted by financial constraints, but in April 1919, Seligmann was contracted to take charge of the publicity for the National Conference on Lynching and he stayed on to become the first director of publicity for the NAACP. He quickly published a number of articles centered on drawing attention to racist violence, including "Race War?" and "Democracy and Jim-Crowism" in *The New Republic*; "Chicago in Grip of Rising Fear" in the *New York Call*; "Protecting Southern Womanhood" and "The Press Abets the Mob" in *The Nation*; and "Everybody's Say-So" in *The Chicago Evening Post*.[78] He also issued a pamphlet comprising four articles previously published by staff members, wrote thirteen press stories, and sent letters to selected newspapers in 1919.[79] By the end of the year, the publicity department reported distributing 427,000 pieces of literature, an increase of nearly 300,000 over the previous year. In addition, 134 press releases were sent out, and special articles were written by Seligmann, White, and Ovington.[80]

The lynching of Berry Washington, a respectful 72-year-old African American man living in Milan, Georgia, is illustrative of the NAACP's ability to place racist violence on the agenda of mainstream media. On May 25, 1919, at one o'clock in the morning, two drunk white men stumbled into the African American section of town and attempted to break into the home of a widow living with two young girls. The girls screamed out of fright and attempted to run away with the white men chasing after them. Hearing the noise, Washington ran out with his shotgun in hand to ascertain what the commotion was all about. Without the slightest provocation, one of the white men fired at him, and Washington shot back in self-defense, killing one of the white

---

[77] Charles Flint Kellogg, *NAACP: A History of the National Association for the Advancement of Colored People*, Baltimore: Johns Hopkins University Press, 1973, p. 148.

[78] Tenth Annual Report for the Year 1919, NAACP Papers, Manuscript Division, Library of Congress, Washington, DC, p. 61. See also Herbert Seligmann, "Race War?," *The New Republic*, August 13, 1919, pp. 48–50; "Democracy and Jim Crowism," *The New Republic*, September 3, 1919, pp. 151–152, "Protecting Southern Womanhood," *The Nation* 108, no. 2815, June 14, 1919: pp. 938–939, "The Press Abets the Mob," *The Nation* 109, no. 2831, October 4, 1919: pp. 460–461.

[79] Charles Flint Kellogg, *NAACP: A History of the National Association for the Advancement of Colored People*, Baltimore: Johns Hopkins University Press, 1973.

[80] BOD Minutes, October 13, 1919, NAACP Papers, Manuscript Division, Library of Congress, Washington, DC; *The Crisis* 19, March 1920, p. 244.

men. A short while later, Washington woke up the sheriff and turned himself in, only to be taken out of jail at noon the next day by a mob of between 75 and 100 angry white men. The mob dragged him back to the place where he had fired his gun, hanged him to a post, shot his body to pieces, and left it hanging for hours while the African American residents were forced to come out of their homes to view the mutilated body.[81]

The lynching was not reported in the newspapers, and the authorities in Milan tried to cover it up. However, the NAACP got wind of it through a lengthy sworn statement from a clergy member, desperate for someone to look into the matter.[82] NAACP secretary Shillady sent out a letter to a number of newspapers with the statement from the clergy member.[83] In July, the wheels started to turn when the editor of the *Richmond Virginian* forwarded the NAACP's letter to Clark Howell, editor of *The Atlanta Constitution*, who sent it to a prominent white citizen of Milan for verification. *The Atlanta Constitution's* high-placed contact corroborated the NAACP's version of events, declaring it a "disgraceful occurrence" and explained that local officials refused to act. As soon as Howell had this report, he published it along with the NAACP's letter and statement from the clergy member and wrote a strong editorial in *The Atlanta Constitution* in which he declared the lynching of Washington a "monstrous affair."[84] The community was shamed, the Democrat governor of Georgia, Hugh Dorsey, promptly offered up $1,000, and another prominent citizen offered up $500 to convict the lynchers the day after the article was published.[85] The attempted cover-up by local authorities and the exposé initiated by the NAACP made national headlines and was reported in many newspapers including *The Washington Post, New York Globe, Baltimore Daily Herald, Pittsburg Post, St. Louis Morning Star* and *The New York Times*.[86] The

---

[81] *A Lynching Uncovered*, pamphlet, Anti-Lynching File, 1919, NAACP Papers, Manuscript Division, Library of Congress, Washington, DC.

[82] Rev. Judson Dinkins, letter, in Anti-Lynching File, May 26, 1919, NAACP Papers, Manuscript Division, Library of Congress, Washington, DC.

[83] John Shillady, letter, Anti-Lynching File, July 17, 1919, NAACP Papers, Manuscript Division, Library of Congress, Washington, DC.

[84] "Moonshine Whisky and Lynch Law Raise Tumult in Telfair County," *The Atlanta Constitution*, July 25, 1919; "No Wonder?," *The Atlanta Constitution*, July 25, 1919.

[85] "Rewards Offered in Lynching Case," *The Atlanta Constitution*, July 27, 1919; Tenth Annual Report for the Year 1919, NAACP Papers, Manuscript Division, Library of Congress, Washington, DC, p. 27; *A Lynching Uncovered*, pamphlet, Anti-Lynching File, 1919, NAACP Papers, Manuscript Division, Library of Congress, Washington, DC.

[86] "Negro Lynched in Courtyard," *The Washington Post*, July 27, 1919; "Lynched for Guarding Girls," *New York Globe*, July 21, 1919; "Aged Negro Lynched On May 26th – Authorities Conceal News Under Claim of Investigation to Find Guilty Parties – No Arrests Have Been Made," *Baltimore Daily Herald*, July 25, 1919; "The South Awakening," *Pittsburgh Post*, July 26, 1919; Untitled, *St. Louis Morning Star*, July 25, 1919; "Lynching Kept Secret," *The New York Times*, July 25, 1919. Interesting to note, except for the *Atlanta Constitution Journal*, no other newspapers mentioned the NAACP by name in describing how the lynching in Milan was uncovered.

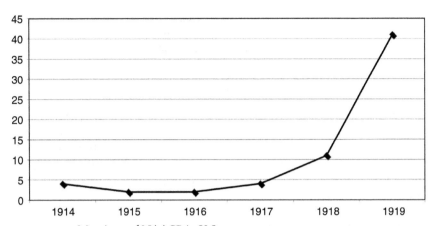

FIGURE 2.3 Mentions of NAACP in U.S. newspapers.

Source: Search combines three mainstream newspapers (*The New York Times, The Atlanta Constitution,* and *The Washington Post*) with the results from the America's Historical Newspaper index (a database of nearly 2,000 titles from fifty states from important repositories of early American newspapers such as the Library of Congress and the Wisconsin Historical Society and many others). For both searches I searched for articles containing the following search terms: National Association for the Advancement of Colored People AND lynching OR riot OR mob OR violence for the years 1914–1919.

NAACP's investigation and immediate public fallout as a result of the press coverage underscored the NAACP's belief that if the organization could get its story out in mainstream newspapers, the public acceptance surrounding lynching would wane.

It is difficult to ascertain the full magnitude of the NAACP's reach in mainstream media because there is no known record of the exact list of newspapers to which the NAACP sent press releases and tried to influence. The other complication for completing a retrospective assessment of the NAACP's impact in mainstream media is the fact that the organization often asked not to be explicitly named in print so as not to provoke anger or retaliation against its members. During this time period, many people, especially in the South, viewed the NAACP as "troublemakers," and the NAACP did not want to aggravate the situation further. Nevertheless, despite these obstacles, it still is possible to get a sense of the impact of its mobilization efforts through mainstream newspapers.[87] Figure 2.3 examines mentions of the NAACP in articles in mainstream newspapers and smaller local newspapers. The figure shows correspondence

---

[87] In press releases, they often highlighted obscured lynchings or other racial injustices that escaped the attention of the white press. White publications would then report these cases as if they had uncovered them.

between the main surge in NAACP media activity after the establishment of its anti-lynching campaign in 1916 and a higher proportion of articles published about the NAACP's activities during 1919 when Seligman came on board.

Conclusion: Institutionalized State Racism

The battery of NAACP activities focused on transforming public opinion about lynching provided a necessary shock to a society that was at best ambivalent over the lynching of African Americans. Aided by financial resources, contacts, and well-placed white board members, the NAACP battled stereotypes surrounding lynchings and mob violence. The infusion of an alternative perspective into the public domain provided the nation with another way to interpret the violent spectacle. Inroads were made as evidenced by the expressed outrage and growing support for the organization's activities by white Americans.

As was detailed at the beginning of this chapter, the NAACP's publicity strategy was greatly influenced by Ida B. Wells. Indeed, one cannot help but wonder how much more successful the NAACP would have been if it had not sidelined Wells in the early years of the organization's development. Consumed with the need to raise funds to sustain the organization, the NAACP believed Wells was more of a threat and a liability than a resource and that she would ultimately undermine the organization. Writing about Wells's omission from the Committee of 40, Ovington observed, "she was a great fighter, but we knew that she had to play a lone hand. And if you have too many players of lone hands in your organization, you soon have no game."[88] As a result, the NAACP was without the counsel of the most courageous crusader against lynching in the United States. If Wells had been actively involved from the outset, it is likely the NAACP's opinion-shaping strategy through indigenous African American media sources and through the white press would have been even more far-reaching. By the time the NAACP developed, Wells had already traveled internationally and lectured to huge crowds in Europe about the evils of lynching in the United States. Drumming up international support was of, course, something the NAACP had yet to do. I am not suggesting that if Wells had been included that everything would have changed and lynching would have been eliminated – only that the NAACP's sphere of influence could have been wider.

An overall evaluation of the struggle to end lynching and mob violence in the United States – with or without Wells's valiant contributions – reveals the somber conclusion that the written word and pictures were powerful, but they ultimately were not enough. The history of the NAACP's public opinion campaign demonstrates the importance of using media in the service of civil rights, but it also underscores the durability of racism in American society and politics in the

---

[88] Mary White Ovington, "Early Years of the NAACP and the Urban League," *Baltimore Afro-American*, November 26, 1932.

early twentieth century. The widely held assumption that lynchings and mob violence stemmed from racist beliefs that whites held about African Americans and that these heinous acts would end if the NAACP could just reach whites' hearts and minds was shattered when lynchings of African Americans escalated to record levels in 1918 and 1919. The seventy-five recorded lynchings of African Americans in 1919 was the highest number of lynchings of the previous ten years. The NAACP noted with disappointment at the end of 1919, "An increase of twenty-four percent in the number of lynchings for 1919 as compared with 1918, and 1918 itself an increase over 1917, is distinctly discouraging."[89] Though the numbers were down from the turn of the century, they were climbing upward again, a fact that alarmed the NAACP.

Even more disturbing, the national office of the NAACP noticed that the lynchings were becoming more gruesome. In his autobiography, Johnson provides detail of the barbarous manner in which African Americans were put to death in 1919:

Inch by inch the Negro was fairly cooked to death. Every few minutes fresh leaves were tossed on the funeral pyre until the blaze had passed the Negro's waist. As the flames were eating away his abdomen, a member of the mob stepped forward and saturated the body with gasoline. It was then only a few minutes until the Negro had been reduced to ashes.[90]

Aggravating the situation even further, 1919 marked the bloodiest summer in recent memory when racial tensions flared and a record twenty-six race riots broke out across the United States. The most violent riots occurred in major cities such as Charleston; Longview, Texas; Washington, DC; Chicago; Knoxville; Omaha; and Phillips County, Arkansas.[91] Despite the NAACP's efforts in the public sphere, racial violence was on the rise.

The NAACP achieved to many what had seemed impossible in the first quarter of the twentieth century: shift the narrative of lynchings in local, state, and national media. Yet, at the same time of this purported achievement, the most gruesome and highest numbers of African American lynchings were being reported. The juxtaposition of a successful media campaign and an escalation in the number of lynchings forced the NAACP to reassess its strategy. The benign view that racist violence stemmed from irrational individual prejudice was inherently flawed by the undeniable presence of the state as a complicit player in the violence. Many whites acted on their racial prejudice because southern states made it safe to do so by minimizing and often times eliminating the repercussions for such violent acts as lynching. The NAACP's anti-lynching

---

[89] Tenth Annual Report for the Year 1919, NAACP Papers, Manuscript Division, Library of Congress, Washington, DC, p. 17.

[90] James Weldon Johnson, *Along This Way: The Autobiography of James Weldon Johnson*, New York: Viking Press, 1933, p. 361.

[91] Arthur Waskow, *From Race Riot to Sit-in: 1919 and the 1960s*, Garden City, NY: Anchor Books, 1967.

committee acknowledged in 1919, "Not only do local authorities fail to protect mob victims but after a lynching has occurred indictments are rarely found and if found, either no trial is held or no convictions result."[92] Furthermore, local and state political institutions across the South encouraged an environment of tolerance around lynching and mob violence, which was evidenced by the many government and law enforcement officials that participated in mob violence.

It became clear to the NAACP that it was no longer simply a problem of "the soul of America": the real problem was the amount of power that local and state governments possessed. Declaring that there is a "new spirit" during 1919 and that "the Negro everywhere is determined to press his right to the citizenship guaranteed him by the federal constitution" as well as "to strive by every legal and constitutional method for complete Negro citizenship in accordance with established law," the NAACP sounded the trumpet that moving forward, it would place renewed energy on political and legal institutions in hopes that the change it sought through its media campaign could be achieved in combination with another approach.[93] Indeed, it was the realization that its media campaign could not outright end lynching that encouraged the NAACP to focus more of its efforts on enlarging the governing capacity of the federal government.

---

[92] NAACP Anti-Lynching Committee, Meeting Notes, November 14, 1919, NAACP Papers, Manuscript Division, Library of Congress, Washington, DC.
[93] Tenth Annual Report for the Year 1919, NAACP Papers, Manuscript Division, Library of Congress, Washington, DC.

3

The Unsteady March into the Oval Office

There have been many lynchings and every one of them has been a blow at the heart of ordered law and humane justice. No man who loves America, no man who really cares for her fame and honor and character, or who is truly loyal to her institutions, can justify mob action while the courts of justice are open and the governments of the States and the Nation are ready and able to do their duty.
— President Woodrow Wilson, July 26, 1918

Congress ought to wipe the stain of barbaric lynching from the banners of a free and orderly, representative democracy.
— President Warren G. Harding, April 12, 1921

At an early stage in the NAACP's movement against racial violence, the organization targeted the executive branch as a possible institution in the federal government whereby a civil rights agenda could be entrenched. Of course, the president, the highest political office in the United States, has often appeared off-limits to marginalized groups, as the obstacles to gain the ear of the president are often insurmountable, and the likelihood of success is lower than with other branches in government. However, in two successive presidential administrations, the National Association for the Advancement of Colored People (NAACP) garnered unprecedented access to the Oval Office and secured presidential denouncements of lynching and mob violence. President Woodrow Wilson conceded to NAACP demands during his second term, and President Warren G. Harding complied with NAACP requests for a strong statement against lynching as soon as he assumed office. The statements by Wilson and Harding admonishing lynchings are particularly remarkable because both came from men who initially expressed an unwillingness to publicly address the issue. How did the NAACP push the issues of lynching and mob violence onto the presidential agenda? Furthermore, how did the idea of lynching as antithetical to a healthy democracy become recognized as persuasive and powerful in the

Oval Office? And finally, why did the NAACP consider a presidential statement as a necessary step in the march toward racial equality in the first quarter of the twentieth century? To answer these questions, this chapter unveils how the NAACP transformed the realm of what was possible in the presidential administrations of Wilson and Harding.

In presidential studies that seek to measure a change in attitude on a particular issue area, rhetorical shifts are often the key dependent variable. Since the status quo during this period was racist rhetoric, the effectiveness of the NAACP's strategy can be gauged by examining whether Wilson's or Harding's rhetoric shifted on the acceptability of racist violence. In this context, the statements condemning lynching made by each president are particularly noteworthy because they evidence how a group of nonelite actors were able to influence the president to change positions on an issue, presumed by most to be beyond reproach.

The NAACP's advocacy of Wilson and Harding, while interesting singularly and considered together, demonstrate a broader strategy of the organization's use of the executive office in its campaign to end racial violence. Though these statements did not reflect any particular shift in federal civil rights legislation, they illustrate how the NAACP was reshaping the political landscape and that it had altered the behavior of the nation's chief executive. Reflecting on the broader significance of Wilson's statement to the African American freedom struggle, a delegation from the National Race Congress of the United States of America expressed in a letter, "It gave encouragement to the heart of every true American, and is the harbinger of hope to all colored men in the United States."[1] Robert Russa Moton, president of the Tuskegee Institute, thanked Wilson for his "wise, strong, frank, patriotic statement on mob violence."[2] Harding's address to Congress was met with a similar level of jubilation in the African American community. James Weldon Johnson immediately wrote, "These utterances from you as President of the United States will give heart to millions of colored American citizens who were rapidly losing hope in American democracy."[3] The NAACP publicity department, which monitored the content of the African American press, found that many newspapers were hailing Harding's statement and recommendations on the lynching issue as "the strongest ever made by a President to Congress."[4] Insofar as the

---

[1] The National Race Commission to Woodrow Wilson, enclosure, October 1, 1918. Reprinted in *The Papers of Woodrow Wilson*, edited by Arthur Link, Princeton: Princeton University Press, 1985, pp. 191–192.

[2] Robert Russa Moton to Woodrow Wilson, letter, July 27, 1918. Reprinted in *The Papers of Woodrow Wilson*, edited by Arthur Link, Princeton: Princeton University Press, 1985, pp. 113–114.

[3] James Weldon Johnson to Warren G. Harding, letter, April 13, 1921, Special Correspondence File, NAACP Papers, Manuscript Division, Library of Congress, Washington, DC.

[4] "Since the delivery of your message to Congress we have been receiving from our branches all over the United States expressions of the great satisfaction with which your utterances on the race question have been received by the colored people of the country. They have been stirred as

NAACP is concerned, it is clear the presidential statements were viewed as a "stupendous" achievement for the organization and served to reinvigorate its fight against lynching and mob violence.[5]

However, if one examines the existing presidential scholarship from the end of Reconstruction to the New Deal, it appears as if U.S. presidents made no significant concessions to African Americans. In particular, when interpreting the race relations component in the administrations of Wilson and Harding, scholars have offered up a one-dimensional view that describes each president as vehemently against (Wilson) or completely uninterested (Harding) in the goal of racial equality. Assessing the impact of the Harding administration on the black freedom struggle, Robert Sherman ruefully concludes: "Negroes learned that they could by no means count upon the Republican leaders to support their battle for fuller citizenship."[6] The scholarship examining Wilson's race relations is the most resolute and appears to agree that his administration moved the federal government to an unprecedented level of racial segregation and was disastrous to the struggle for equal rights in America.[7] David Levering Lewis makes clear Wilson was no friend of civil rights when he asserted,

In every man's life, there's the possibility of making a considerable difference. By attitude, by word spoken, by something done or not done. You would have to say that in the area of race relations, Woodrow Wilson was deficient on all those points. He neither said what should have been said, he neither did what should have been done, nor did he understand what needed doing.[8]

seldom before by your straightforward words. The same sentiments are reflected in the Negro press. Our publicity department scans the colored newspapers very closely and we find that many of them are hailing your recommendations on this question as the most practical, the most concrete and at the same time the strongest ever made by a President to Congress. I myself have met and talked with a large number of leading colored men in various cities and they have expressed the same sentiments." James Weldon Johnson to Warren G. Harding, letter, April 20, 1921, Special Correspondence File, NAACP Papers, Manuscript Division, Library of Congress, Washington, DC.

[5] NAACP founder Mary White Ovington wrote to NAACP executive secretary John Shillady, "The one thing we must all be thinking is the president's stupendous denunciation of lynching. That is surely your monument and Mr. [James Weldon] Johnson's. It's such a splendid thing that I feel as a general must feel who sees his side win a great victory." July 27, 1918, Special Correspondence File, Reel 20, NAACP Papers, Manuscript Division, Library of Congress, Washington, DC.

[6] Robert Sherman, "The Harding Administration and the Negro: An Opportunity Lost," *The Journal of Negro History* 49, no. 3 (1964): 158. Desmond King also argues that Harding did little to support the NAACP's anti-lynching campaign: *Making Americans: Immigration, Race, and the Origins of the Diverse Democracy*, Cambridge: Harvard University Press, 2000.

[7] Philip Klinkner and Rogers Smith, *The Unsteady March: The Rise and Decline of Racial Equality in America*, Chicago: The University of Chicago Press, 1999. See also Nancy Weiss, "The Negro and the New Freedom: Fighting Wilsonian Segregation," *Political Science Quarterly*, 84, no. 1 (1969): pp. 62–79; Kenneth O'Reilly, *Nixon's Piano: Presidents and Racial Politics from Washington to Clinton*, New York: The Free Press, 1995; Nicholas Patler, *Jim Crow and the Wilson Administration*, Boulder: The University of Colorado Press, 2004.

[8] David Levering Lewis, film transcript, PBS documentary: *Woodrow Wilson, Episode One: A Passionate Man*, directed by Carl Byker and Mitch Wilson, 2001.

Philip Klinker and Rogers Smith leave little room to question if Wilson can be imagined as anything but damaging to civil rights, "In regard to blacks, Wilson was probably the most racist president of this century."[9] But these traditional characterizations of Wilson and Harding obscure just as much as they illuminate.

This chapter challenges previous presidential studies that place the beginnings of presidential concern for civil rights with President Franklin Delano Roosevelt.[10] Scholars of the American presidency have tended to locate the origins of presidential civil rights rhetoric in the New Deal era, not in the first quarter of the twentieth century. The American presidents before Roosevelt are assumed to be hostile to the struggle for racial justice. Moreover, when describing civil rights concessions, the presidential literature has rarely accounted for how marginalized groups can successfully influence the president. Important changes in the presidential agenda regarding civil rights are interpreted as the result of the goodwill of individual presidents. This theory owes to a considerable amount of scholarship that has established the importance of presidential leadership on expansions in African American civil rights.[11] These scholars situate the origins of the civil rights movement with actions originating from the office of the president such as courtpacking, governmental appointments, implementation of new policies benefiting African Americans, and the creation of new agencies not with the activities of social justice organizations. However, the ground that was exploited in the Roosevelt, and the subsequent John F. Kennedy and Lyndon B. Johnson, administrations built on earlier efforts. The tactics necessary to secure inroads in the fight for African American citizenship during these presidential administrations were sown during the first quarter of

---

[9] Philip Klinker and Rogers Smith, *The Unsteady March: The Rise and Decline of Racial Equality in America*, Chicago: The University of Chicago Press, 1999.

[10] Garth Pauley writes, "The modern civil rights movement had its genesis during the presidency of Franklin Roosevelt and declined during Richard Nixon's presidency: never was the expectation that a president should speak out on civil rights so urgent as it was during the era between the Roosevelt and Nixon administrations," in *The Modern Presidency and Civil Rights: Rhetoric on Race from Roosevelt to Nixon*, College Station: Texas A&M University Press, 2001, p. 6. See also Gunnar Myrdal, *An American Dilemma: The Negro Problem and Modern Democracy*, New York: Harper & Brothers, 1944; Harvard Sitkoff, *A New Deal for Blacks: The Emergence of Civil Rights as a National Issue*, New York: Oxford University Press, 1978; Nancy Weiss, *Farewell to the Party of Lincoln: Black Politics in the Age of FDR*, Princeton: Princeton University Press, 1983; Kevin McMahon, *Reconsidering Roosevelt on Race: How the Presidency Paved the Road to Brown*, Chicago: University of Chicago Press, 2004.

[11] Harvard Sitkoff, *A New Deal for Blacks: 1945–1992*, New York: Hill and Wang, 1993; Kenneth O'Reilly, *Nixon's Piano: Presidents and Racial Politics from Washington to Clinton*, New York: The Free Press, 1995; Philip Klinkner and Rogers Smith, *The Unsteady March: The Rise and Decline of Racial Equality in America*, Chicago: The University of Chicago Press, 1999; Garth Pauley, *The Modern Presidency and Civil Rights: Rhetoric on Race from Roosevelt to Nixon*, College Station: Texas A&M University Press, 2001; Kevin McMahon, *Reconsidering Roosevelt on Race: How the Presidency Paved the Road to Brown*, Chicago: University of Chicago Press, 2004.

the twentieth century. Despite the hostile racial conditions during this period, the NAACP was able to make progress and create a foundation of knowledge from which future struggles could draw. In outlining this connection between celebrated "civil rights" presidents and the NAACP's struggle in the Oval Office during the administrations of Wilson and Harding, I hope to make clear that there is much more continuity and much less of a decisive break in the struggle for civil rights in the executive branch.

The current state of the literature fits with the critique I make in the first chapter. In tying the emergence of civil rights in the executive office to the actions of individual presidents, scholars have provided a stunted view of the development of civil rights in the Oval Office. To properly understand how U.S. presidents came to adopt a more expansive understanding of racial equality in the Roosevelt administration and in subsequent presidential administrations, one must go further back in the causal chain to an earlier era and examine what changed in the political climate. Continuing with the main thrust of the book, this chapter asks if we might be able to tell a different story about institutional change and civil rights progress by focusing on the actions of marginalized citizen actors instead of on the supposed benevolence of individual presidents. In pursuit of this goal, the rest of this chapter details the NAACP's program of protest that persuaded President Wilson and President Harding to make these statements and offer their symbolic support to end lynching.

Whites Only: Woodrow Wilson's New Freedom

Born in Virginia and raised in Georgia and South Carolina, Wilson chose a career as a scholar, and in 1902 he became president of Princeton University. In 1910 Wilson assumed the office of governor of New Jersey where he fought machine politics and quickly established a reputation as a progressive reformer. His work in New Jersey attracted a tremendous amount of positive attention, and Wilson was nominated for president at the 1912 Democratic Convention. He campaigned on a program called the New Freedom, a progressive platform aimed at reforming the banking system, increasing economic competition, and promoting individual freedom and opportunity. In the general election of 1912, Wilson defeated Theodore Roosevelt and William Howard Taft by a substantial margin.[12] Domestically, Wilson's presidency enlarged the role of the federal government in managing the economy. And in foreign affairs, he established a powerful presence of the United States in the world. Wilson's biographers have painted him as a man of extraordinary vision, idealism, and expertise, despite a few mishaps that

---

[12] Wilson received 41.8 percent of the popular vote, Roosevelt secured 27.4 percent, and Taft received 23.2 percent.

are easily explained away.[13] On the whole, Wilson is considered one of the great presidents of American politics.[14]

However, if Wilson's presidency is looked upon as one of the greatest, African Americans and their supporters certainly hold a different opinion. On the scorecard of African American civil rights, Wilson failed miserably, especially during his first term.[15] The blow dealt by Wilson's presidency to the African American freedom struggle was exacerbated because he rescinded on a promise to increase racial equality while in office. During the campaign of 1912, Wilson appealed to African Americans for support. In a letter to Alexander Walters, head of the National Colored Democratic League, Wilson wrote, "should I become President of the United States they [African Americans] may count on me for absolute fair dealing and for everything by which I could assist in advancing the interests of their race in the United States."[16] The letter was widely printed in African American newspapers and magazines. Wilson went out of his way to court leaders of African American public opinion and secured endorsements from NAACP vice president Oswald Garrison Villard, NAACP director of publicity and research W. E. B. Du Bois, and National Equal Rights League founder Monroe Trotter, all of whom worked for his election. To help quell concerns about Wilson's southern upbringing, Du Bois penned in *The Crisis,*

---

[13] Kendrick Clements, *Woodrow Wilson, World Statesman*, Boston: Twayne, 1987; Kendrick Clements, *The Presidency of Woodrow Wilson*, Lawrence: University of Kansas Press, 1992; August Heckscher, *Woodrow Wilson*, New York: Scribner's, 1991; Arthur Walworth, *Woodrow Wilson*, Baltimore: Penguin Books, 1978; Ray Stannard Baker, *Woodrow Wilson: Life and Letters*, Vol. 4, Garden City, NY: Doubleday, 1931.

[14] Robert Murray and Tim Blessing, *Greatness in the White House: Rating the Presidents, Washington Through Carter*, University Park: Pennsylvania State University Press, 1988; John Milton Cooper Jr., *Pivotal Decades: The United States, 1900–1920*, New York: W. W. Norton, 1990. Wilson was ranked ninth in a survey in which a cross-section of sixty-five presidential historians ranked the forty-two former occupants of the White House on ten attributes of leadership. See C-SPAN, *Historians Presidential Leadership Survey*, February 15, 2009, http://www.c-span.org/PresidentialSurvey/presidential-leadership-survey.aspx.

[15] Wilson biographer Arthur Link writes, "The dearth in administration circles of any impelling passion for social justice was nowhere better illustrated than in the government's policy toward Negroes during Wilson's magistracy." In *Woodrow Wilson and the Progressive Era, 1910–1917*, New York: Harper and Brothers, 1954, p. 63.

[16] As quoted in Kathleen Long Wolgemuth, "Woodrow Wilson's Appointment Policy and the Negro," *The Journal of Southern History* 24, no. 4 (1958): 457; Nancy Weiss, "The Negro and the New Freedom: Fighting Wilsonian Segregation," *Political Science Quarterly* 84, no. 1 (1969), p. 63. Wilson met with the president of the Washington, DC NAACP branch, J. Milton Waldron. Waldron's memo from the meeting stated that Wilson wanted the support of African Americans and that there was nothing to fear from a Democratic Congress, as he assured Waldron that as president, he would veto hostile legislation and would not exclude blacks from office holding on account of color. As described in Charles Flint Kellogg, *NAACP: A History of the National Association for the Advancement of Colored People*, Baltimore: Johns Hopkins University Press, 1973, p. 157; *The Crisis*, September 1912, pp. 216–217.

We sincerely believe that even in the face of promises disconcertingly vague, and in the face of the solid caste-ridden South, it is better to elect Woodrow Wilson President of the United States and prove once for all if the Democratic party dares to be Democratic when it comes to black men.[17]

The Crisis also published a two-page advertisement from the National Colored Democratic League, encouraging readers to vote for the Democratic Party because it is "the one party which has the power to restore to the Negro the right of suffrage."[18] NAACP president Moorfield Storey added his opinion that "Governor Wilson has shown rare courage in dealing with the corrupt men, even in the Democratic party, and has achieved in New Jersey the most satisfactory results during his term as Governor."[19] Though they were nervous about a southerner occupying the White House, African Americans were swayed by the arguments of their leaders, and Wilson became the Democratic presidential candidate to receive the most African American votes to that date in history.[20]

As soon as he was inaugurated, Villard went to meet Wilson to present a plan for a National Race Commission with the stated purpose of engaging "[a] non-partisan, scientific study of the status of the negro in the life of the nation, with particular reference to his economic situation."[21] Villard and Du Bois spent a great deal of time on the plan, which included a list of supportive organizations and recommendations of a bipartisan committee of fifteen people from the North and the South to serve on the race commission. Villard believed that if the race commission was instituted, "It would be a great step forward in the history of the Negro race in America," and he walked away from the meeting elated at Wilson's reception and reported that it was his best meeting with Wilson. However, formalization talks were put on hold while Villard traveled to Europe for two months and were scheduled to continue when he returned stateside. The talks never resumed. Wilson refused to meet with Villard about the commission, explaining, "The situation is extremely delicate" and that "it would be a blunder on my part to consent to name the commission you speak

[17] *The Crisis*, November 1912.

[18] *The Crisis*, October 1912, pp. 306–307.

[19] Box 4, Letter to Colored Voters, October 1912, Moorfield Storey Papers, Manuscript Division, Library of Congress, Washington DC.

[20] August Heckscher, *Woodrow Wilson: A Biography*, New York: Collier Books, Macmillan, 1991, p. 290; Aurthur Link, "The Negro as a Factor in the Campaign of 1912," *Journal of Negro History* 32 (1947): 98; August Meier, "The Negro and the Democratic Party, 1875–1915," *Phylon: The Atlanta University Review* 17 (1963): 190; Nicholas Patler, *Jim Crow and the Wilson Administration: Protesting Federal Segregation in the Early Twentieth Century*, Boulder: University Press of Colorado, 2004, p. 20; Kathleen Long Wolgemuth, "Woodrow Wilson's Appointment Policy and the Negro," *The Journal of Southern History* 24, no. 4 (1958): 457, footnote 1.

[21] *A Proposal for a National Race Commission*, pamphlet, Box 120, Oswald Garrison Villard Papers (MS Am 1323), Houghton Library, Harvard University.

of."[22] He argued that senators from various parts of the country had his hands tied. Villard was dismayed at Wilson's apparent change of heart on the race commission as there were no specifics attached; it was simply a commission with a vague mandate to study and report on racial conditions in the country. When invited to lunch by Wilson months afterward to discuss another matter, Villard nearly declined out of frustration, writing Storey, "Of course, I shall go down, though I would rather take the course that I would not see him except with a committee."[23] Wilson's reversal on Villard's race commission marked the beginning of a long line of disappointments that eventually led to the unraveling of the friendship between the two men.

Indeed, Wilson's withdrawal of support on the race commission paled in comparison to the way racist southern norms were gaining prominence in his administration. As his close advisers, Wilson chose outspoken white supremacists such as senators James Vardaman (D-Mississippi) and Hoke Smith (D-Georgia), both notorious for exploiting African American convict labor for state benefit.[24] The leading biographer of Wilson noted, "Southerners were riding high in Washington for the first time since the Civil War, demanding segregation in the government departments and public services and dismissal or down-grading Negro civil servants."[25] It wasn't long before southerners began to implement a system of Jim Crow segregation in national governmental office. It started on April 11, 1913 when Postmaster General Albert Burleson recommended segregating the federal services during a cabinet meeting.[26] Not long afterwards, the Bureau of the Census, the Post Office Department, and the Bureau of Printing and Engraving attempted to quietly segregate employees in offices, shops, toilets, and restaurants.[27] Villard obtained a copy of the Treasury Department's letter mandating "this toilet room is exclusively for the use of white employees" and relegating African American employees to

[22] Wilson to Villard, letter, August 21, 1913. Reprinted in *The Papers of Woodrow Wilson* Vol. 28, edited by Arthur Link, Princeton: Princeton University Press, p. 202.

[23] Villard to Storey, letter, October 8, 1913, Box 120, Oswald Garrison Villard Papers (MS Am 1323), Houghton Library, Harvard University.

[24] Nancy Weiss, "The Negro and the New Freedom: Fighting Wilsonian Segregation," *Political Science Quarterly* 84, no. 1 (1969): 65; Charles Flint Kellogg, *NAACP: A History of the National Association for the Advancement of Colored People*, Baltimore: Johns Hopkins University Press, 1973, p. 163. Vardaman, while governor of Mississippi, began Parchman Farm, the largest and most inhumane state-run convict labor prison. Smith, while governor of Georgia, abolished the convict lease to use convicts for state benefit and greatly expanded the chain gang in Georgia.

[25] Arthur Link, *Woodrow Wilson and the Progressive Era, 1910–1917*, New York: Harper and Brothers, 1954, p. 64.

[26] E. David Cronon, ed., *The Cabinet Diaries of Josephus Daniels, 1913–1921*, Lincoln: University of Nebraska Press, 1963, pp. 32–33.

[27] Arthur Link, *Woodrow Wilson and the Progressive Era, 1910–1917*, New York: Harper and Brothers, 1954; Nancy Weiss, "The Negro and the New Freedom: Fighting Wilsonian Segregation," *Political Science Quarterly* 84, no. 1 (1969): 61–79; Charles Flint Kellogg, *NAACP: A History of the National Association for the Advancement of Colored People*, Baltimore: Johns Hopkins University Press, 1973.

use the substandard toilets on the third floor. When asked about this policy of restroom segregation, Secretary of the Treasury William McAdoo, who ordered the segregated restrooms, feigned innocence, writing Villard, "There is no 'segregation issue' in the Treasury Department. It has always been a mischievous exaggeration."[28] Villard knew this couldn't be further from the truth.

In the South, the changes were bolder: officials in the Post Office and Treasury were given permission to discharge or demote African Americans as they pleased. Later, in May 1914, the Civil Service Commission required photographs to accompany applications. African Americans became concentrated in menial jobs for which they were overqualified. Jobs with greater responsibilities and prestige were no longer open to qualified African Americans. Segregation had been around before Wilson, but it was limited and unofficial, and African Americans were assessed equally to whites.[29] The Wilson administration succeeded in rolling back progress through segregation policies, most telling in the losses in high-ranking government jobs; of the thirty-one African Americans holding important government jobs in 1913, only eight were retained in 1916.[30] Assessing the situation, Villard observed, "the intense feeling of bitterness and outrage among the colored people grows daily."[31] This was not maintenance of a norm of racial inequality; this was retrogression.

Racial segregation in government was vigorously protested. Villard put his friendship with Wilson on the line and wrote a letter calling attention to the evils of segregation and the many African Americans who supported Wilson, and implored Wilson to turn the situation around. Wilson attributed Villard's letter to a misunderstanding:

It is as far as possible from being a movement against the negroes. I sincerely believe it to be in their interest. And what distresses me about your letter is to find that you look at it in so different a light. I am sorry that those who interest themselves most in the welfare of the negro should misjudge this action on the part of the departments, for they are seriously misjudging it.

Claiming public-safety concerns, Wilson argued segregation would protect African Americans from discrimination.[32]

[28] Treasury Department Memo, July 16, 1913, Box 120, Oswald Garrison Villard Papers (MS Am 1323), Houghton Library, Harvard University; William G. McAdoo to Oswald Garrison Villard, letter, October 27, 1913, Oswald Garrison Villard Papers (MS Am 1323), Houghton Library, Harvard University.

[29] Desmond King, *Separate and Unequal: Black Americans and the US Federal Government*, Oxford: Oxford University Press, 1995.

[30] Kathleen Long Wolgemuth, "Woodrow Wilson's Appointment Policy and the Negro," *The Journal of Southern History* 24, no. 4 (1958): 467.

[31] Villard to Representative A. Mitchell Palmer, letter, November 20, 1913, Box 120, Oswald Garrison Villard Papers (MS Am 1323), Houghton Library, Harvard University.

[32] Wilson to Villard, letter, July 23, 1913. Reprinted in *The Papers of Woodrow Wilson* Vol. 28, edited by Arthur Link, Princeton: Princeton University Press, p. 65.

However, government segregation was never about protecting African American interests; it was always about solidifying white supremacy. Wilson's position on the proper place for African Americans was confirmed when Thomas Dixon, author of *The Clansman*, wrote Wilson complaining about the nomination of Adams Edward Patterson, an African American, to the position of register of the Treasury. Wilson, six days after writing Villard asserting segregation as a means of public safety, wrote Dixon a letter arguing segregation as a way of protecting the sanctity of whiteness:

I do not think you know what is going on down there. We are handling the force of colored people who are now in the departments in just the way in which they ought to be handled. We are trying – and by degrees succeeding – a plan of concentration which will put them all together and will not in any one bureau mix the two races.[33]

The racism of Wilson's first administration was obvious to everyone. In August, the senior leadership of the NAACP wrote a formal letter of protest to Wilson, calling the justification that African Americans would be safer in segregated facilities "fallacious" and "humiliating." Appropriating Wilson's campaign slogan for the NAACP's purposes, the letter reasoned: "They [African Americans] desire a 'New Freedom,' too, Mr. President, yet they include in that term nothing else than the rights guaranteed to them under the Constitution."[34] Later, Trotter led a delegation of African American leaders to the White House to discuss segregation and the impact on African Americans. Wilson still maintained that segregation was to protect African Americans and threw the delegation out of the White House when they disagreed.

In addition to Wilson's countenance of segregation in the civil service, he contributed to the acceptance of Thomas Dixon's racist film *Birth of a Nation* as a brilliant work of historical accuracy. On February 18, 1915, in the East Room of the White House, Wilson allowed Dixon to conduct a private screening for his family and members of his cabinet and their families.[35] Throughout the film, which lauded the role of the Ku Klux Klan in restoring white supremacy to southern state governments after Reconstruction, Dixon had placed screen shots of quotes from Wilson's writing to add credibility to the film. After watching the film, Wilson is said to have confessed, "It is like writing history with lighting. And my only regret is that it is all so terribly true."[36]

---

[33] Thomas Dixon to Woodrow Wilson, letter, July 27, 1913; Wilson to Dixon, letter, July 29, 1913. Reprinted in *The Papers of Woodrow Wilson* Vol. 28, edited by Arthur Link, Princeton: Princeton University Press, pp. 88–89, 94.

[34] Moorfield Storey, W. E. B. Du Bois, and Oswald Garrison Villard to Woodrow Wilson, letter, August 15, 1913, NAACP Papers, Manuscript Division, Library of Congress, Washington, DC.

[35] Representative Thomas Thacher to Joseph Tumulty, letter, April 17, 1915; Wilson to Tumulty, letter, April 1915; Tumulty to Thacher, letter, April 28, 1915. Reel 332, Woodrow Wilson Papers, Manuscript Division, Library of Congress, Washington, DC.

[36] John Hope Franklin, "Propaganda as History," *The Massachusetts Review* 20, no. 3 (1979):; Lloyd E. Ambrosius, "Woodrow Wilson and *The Birth of a Nation*: American Democracy and International Relations," *Diplomacy and Statecraft* 18, no. 4 (2007): 689–718; Michael Rogin,

After the film was released to sold-out audiences, Dixon sent Wilson a dozen newspaper clippings of reviews that praised *The Birth of a Nation*. In the letter, Dixon singles out Villard who, unlike Wilson, did not enjoy the film. In a revealing contrast to Wilson's adoration of the film was Dixon's contempt for Villard:

The *New York Evening Post* is the only one I have not sent you – it's a rag, I never allow in my home or touch without a pair of tongs. Oswald Villard, a noted negro lover owns it – you may have heard of him! I understand from the gossip in our office that he gave me a column of voluble abuse.[37]

The differences in responses to the film between Villard and Wilson help to illustrate the wide gulf of difference that existed at the time between the Wilson administration and the supporters of the NAACP. Wilson is said to have enjoyed *The Birth of a Nation* so much that Dixon was able to use his endorsement in organizing a larger screening that included Supreme Court justices, the secretary of the Navy, U.S. senators, and approximately fifty members of the House of Representatives.[38] As a result, when the NAACP and other organizations protested and tried to suppress distribution of the film, Dixon was able to argue that it had been screened and received favorably in front of the president and members of Congress.

His presidency would soon come to represent one of the greatest disappointments to African Americans since the dismantling of Reconstruction. Six months after Wilson took office, Du Bois could no longer mask his disappointment and penned an open letter in *The Crisis* where he stated, "It is no exaggeration to say that every enemy of the Negro race is greatly encouraged; that every man who dreams of making the Negro race a group of menials and pariahs is alert and hopeful."[39] In advising Storey for his *Yale Law Review* piece about Wilson's administration, a scorned Villard wrote, "I hope you will be unsparing in your criticism of Mr. Wilson, particularly because of his betrayal of our highest American ideals."[40] During his first term, Wilson's administration expressed obvious indifference to the plight of African Americans and eroded the progress that had been made before he assumed the presidency.

"'The Sword Became a Flashing Vision': D.W. Griffith's *The Birth of a Nation*," *Representations* 9 (1985): 150–195.

[37] Dixon to Wilson, letter, March 5, 1915, Reel 332, Woodrow Wilson Papers, Manuscript Division, Library of Congress, Washington, DC.

[38] Melvyn Stokes, The Birth of a Nation: *A History of "The Most Controversial Motion Picture of All Time"*, New York: Oxford University Press, 2007.

[39] W. E. B. Du Bois, *The Crisis*, September 1913; W. E. B. Du Bois, "My Impressions of Woodrow Wilson," *The Journal of Negro History* 58, no. 4 (1973): pp. 453–459.

[40] Villard to Storey, letter, February 5, 1916, Folder 3714, Oswald Garrison Villard Papers (MS Am 1323), Houghton Library, Harvard University.

NAACP Makes Inroads During Wilson's Second Term

Despite the tremendous barriers erected to African American civil rights during Wilson's first term, the NAACP refused to give up: it believed the road to racial equality went directly through the executive branch. After the establishment of a formal campaign against lynching in April 1916, the NAACP renewed its commitment to fight lynching in the federal government. The NAACP realized that in order for its program of political protest to succeed, the organization would have to continue to work to change Wilson's attitude on racial issues. The NAACP's majority white board members (with the exception of Du Bois) retained a sense of liberal idealism and were convinced that they could change Wilson's mind about racial violence during his second term by educating him and applying pressure through its leadership. In a few years the NAACP had succeeded in its quest and Wilson, the staunch southern conservative, met with a delegation concerned about lynching, followed the NAACP's request for clemency of African American soldiers, and made a public address against lynching. However, the road was not an easy one for the NAACP; only through an unyielding onslaught of protest was it able to obtain support from Wilson.

Pressure started before Wilson was elected for a second term. In the wake of the presidential election of 1916, Villard sent Wilson a note expressing disappointment in Wilson's handling of race issues. In addition, Villard reminded him of the upcoming election and accused him of being uninterested in African American votes.[41] Wilson was dismissive in his response, writing:

I am sorry to think from the general tone of your letter that you feel I am really not interested in the colored people and in the colored vote. If you do, you are very much mistaken, though perhaps you and I do not hold exactly the same views about the best way in which to promote the welfare of the colored people.[42]

Wilson's letter did little to persuade a weary Villard or anyone else in the NAACP's leadership. It did convince them, however, that it was now time to shift course. Moving forward, the NAACP chose to back away from the futile struggle against the segregation of African American civil service workers and turned its attention toward lynching and mob violence in hopes that it would receive more favorable results from Wilson.

Once Wilson was reelected, the NAACP began to press the lynching issue more forcefully as the NAACP viewed executive support crucial to a successful anti-lynching campaign strategy. Before Wilson was inaugurated for his second term, a letter on behalf of the NAACP, signed by six of the ranking members, was sent to Wilson requesting that he say something in his inaugural address "against the barbaric system of lynching which prevails in various parts of

---

[41] Villard to Wilson, letter, October 26, 1915, Folder 4236, Oswald Garrison Villard Papers (MS Am 1323), Houghton Library, Harvard University.

[42] Wilson to Villard, letter, October 28, 1915, Folder 4236, Oswald Garrison Villard Papers (MS Am 1323), Houghton Library, Harvard University.

this country." Most interesting about the letter was the couching of claims for increased federal government power in terms of the inability of state governments to properly punish those responsible for lynching. As the NAACP made clear, lynching and mob violence were not simply problems of a few wayward southern states but that "disgrace falls upon the nation as a whole" and thus the national government must get involved. The NAACP letter ended with a call to Wilson to "help the cause of civilization and good government" by making a statement against lynching.[43] Unsurprisingly, nothing immediately happened. This was a disingenuous appeal as the NAACP did not believe Wilson, the president who had increased the obstacles toward racial equality, would take the opportunity of his inaugural address to denounce lynching. This letter is best interpreted as a calculated move: the NAACP sent the letter as a signal to Wilson that lynching would be the organization's top agenda concern during his second term in accordance with its anti-lynching campaign.

A few months after Wilson assumed his second term as president, the massacre of African Americans in East St. Louis, Illinois occurred and strengthened the NAACP's resolve to pressure Wilson to address lynching and mob violence. In July 1917, racial and labor tensions arising from African American migration exploded in a massacre of African Americans living in East St. Louis. The trouble resulted over the labor competition between long-time white residents and the influx of recently migrated African Americans from the South. After the laying off of thousands of white workers and the hiring of recently migrated African Americans, white labor leaders used racist propaganda, and the anger over lost jobs was directed against African Americans. This anger manifested itself in many violent clashes between African Americans and whites during the month of May. On May 10, 1917 a committee from one of the largest labor unions met with the Mayor and pleaded with him to "inform Negroes in the South that there were no jobs in East St. Louis;" the committee threatened a holocaust that would make previous race riots look tame if conditions were not improved.[44] Tensions between the two groups climaxed during July 1917, and whites waged a brutal race war against African Americans. Men, women, and children as young as one year old were viciously stoned, shot to death, and lynched. Most disturbing was the premeditated nature of the massacre. As noted by Elliott Rudwick, who has written the most detailed account on the riot, there was a strategy for killing African Americans: whites would light African American homes on fire and wait outside for them to come running out. Thus, it was either burn alive inside or run out and face a firing squad of angry whites. African Americans who were found on the street were beaten and

---

[43] Villard, Storey, Du Bois, Spingarn, Archibald Grimke, and John Hurst to Wilson, letter, February 13, 1917, Reel 285, Woodrow Wilson Papers, Manuscript Division, Library of Congress, Washington, DC.

[44] Elliott Rudwick, *Race Riot at East St. Louis*, Urbana: University of Illinois Press, 1964; Martha Gruening and W. E. B. Du Bois, "The Massacre of East St. Louis," *The Crisis*, September 1917.

then lynched by a clothesline or a rope. When the violence ceased, hundreds of African Americans were dead and their corpses were strewn along the road.

The NAACP was enraged by the events that unfolded in East St. Louis and felt it could reach Wilson through this incident. Undoubtedly, part of what made the NAACP seize this as the issue it was going to bring to Wilson was the public visibility of this violent spectacle. It was one thing to ignore individual lynchings and another to turn a blind eye to the mowing down of hundreds of African Americans and the burning up of the African American section of town. The need for outside attention became all the more obvious when reports began to surface revealing that the East St. Louis Police and the Illinois National Guard, both law enforcement agencies in charge of handling the violence during the riot, stood idly by and even participated in the violence against African Americans. The incident highlighted the inability of states to prevent or even halt racial violence.[45]

Though many in the nation expressed outrage about the violence, Wilson ignored the incident. The *Cleveland Gazette* reported on July 21, 1917 that a delegation from Baltimore went to the White House and attempted to meet with President Wilson but was denied and given the excuse that Wilson was trying to conserve his time.[46] Other attempts of reaching Wilson such as petitions and open letters in many newspapers fell on deaf ears. If the president of the United States could not be convinced that racial violence was a national problem, there was little hope of convincing the other two branches of government. Wilson's callous indifference to the East St. Louis violence angered many throughout the nation.

After the riot, the NAACP felt a dramatic public demonstration would be helpful in raising awareness about mob violence. In Harlem, NAACP secretary James Weldon Johnson organized the largest mass demonstration of African Americans in the twentieth century to that date in the "Silent Protest Parade."[47] On July 28, 1917, more than 10,000 African Americans marched in respectful silence down Fifth Avenue in New York City against mob violence and racist oppression to the sound of muffled drums.[48] Dressed in all white, close to 800 African American children held hands in the front, thousands

---

[45] Martha Gruening and W. E. B. Du Bois, "The Massacre of East St. Louis," *The Crisis*, September 1917, pp. 225–226; Elliott Rudwick, *Race Riot at East St. Louis*, Urbana: University of Illinois Press, 1964.

[46] Elliott Rudwick, *Race Riot at East St. Louis*, Urbana: University of Illinois Press, 1964, p. 134.

[47] Though it was the largest, it was not the first. The first demonstration of African Americans occurred two years prior in response to the film *The Birth of a Nation*, when thousands came out in protest in Philadelphia and Boston. See August Meier and Elliott Rudwick, *Along the Color Line: Explorations in the Black Experience*, Urbana: University of Illinois Press, 1976; James Weldon Johnson, *Along This Way: The Autobiography of James Weldon Johnson*, New York: The Viking Press, 1933.

[48] *The New York Times*, July 29, 1917; BOD Minutes, August 1917, NAACP Papers, Manuscript Division, Library of Congress, Washington, DC.

of women, also in white, followed them, and the men in dark suits took up the rear. Police estimated that an additional 10,000 African Americans lined along Fifth Avenue to show their solidarity.[49] Protesters held signs reading: Mr. President: Please Make America Safe for Democracy; Mother, Do Lynchers Go to Heaven?; Give Me a Chance to Live; Race Prejudice is the Offspring of Ignorance and the Mother of Lynching; If You Hate Me on Account of my Color, Blame Yourselves and God, and next to the man who carried the American flag was a bold indictment against the nation on a streamer: Your Hands Are Full of Blood.[50] In addition, circulars were distributed by African American boy scouts that explained the NAACP's drive against lynching, discrimination, brutality, and other forms of racism.

It was one thing to read about the struggles African Americans faced, and it was another to see thousands come together in organized mass protest against those struggles. Demonstrations helped magnify the humanity of African Americans in a very powerful way. In reflecting on the larger significance of the parade, Johnson wrote:

The power of the parade consisted in its being not a mere argument in words, but a demonstration to the sight. More than twelve thousand of us marching along the greatest street in the world, marching solemnly to no other music than the beat of muffled drums, bearing aloft our banners on which were inscribed not only what we have suffered in this country, but what we have accomplished for this country, this was a sight as has never before been seen.[51]

According to reports, the parade drew respect from city officials and many white onlookers. *The New York Times* observed the protesters marched "as a people of one race, united by ties of blood and color, and working for a common cause."[52] The mayor of New York John Purroy Mitchel diverted traffic and established a protective police presence for the protesters on their route.

The executive branch was the NAACP's first point of direct protest in the federal government and was the institution the organization perceived significant change would flow from if enough pressure was brought to bear. In this light, it makes sense that the NAACP did not attempt to litigate or pursue legislation as a way to prevent further injustices similar to East St. Louis; the NAACP engaged in protest focused specifically on reaching President Wilson. The NAACP continued to apply pressure through a twenty-member delegation representing the Silent Protest Parade. The delegation journeyed to the White House to present the president with a resolution containing a statement of their grievances and a petition on August 1, 1917. Wilson's secretary Joseph Tumulty acted as a buffer, and they were forced to leave the petition with him.

[49] *Thousands March in Silent Protest, The Chicago Defender*, August 4, 1917.
[50] Mottoes Used in the Negro Silent Protest Parade, Memo, NAACP Papers, Box C-334, Manuscript Division, Library of Congress, Washington, DC.
[51] James Weldon Johnson, *The New York Age*, August 3, 1917.
[52] *Negroes in Protest March in Fifth Ave, The New York Times*, July 29, 1917.

In their resolution, the delegation called attention to the "spirit of lawlessness" that allows lynching and mob violence to continue and stated:

We come asking that the President use his great powers to have granted to us some redress of the grievances set forth in our petition, and we come further praying that the President may find it in his heart to speak some public word that will give hope and courage to our people, thus using his great personal and moral influence in our behalf.[53]

The petition also included information about the number of lynching victims and the prevalence of mob violence. Most interesting, the NAACP's petition displays an expansive understanding of the potential power of the President in the fight against mob violence. Tumulty gave the petition to Wilson shortly after the delegation left.

The mounting pressure was more than Wilson's administration could ignore. Though Wilson refused to meet with the delegation, a considerable effort was taking place behind the scenes. Hours after the Silent Protest delegation left, Tumulty, hoping to keep Wilson from directly addressing the East St. Louis violence, attempted to call in a favor. Tumulty wrote the Governor of Illinois explaining, "the request for some statement on our part with reference to the East St. Louis affair will not down" and requesting that he make a statement denouncing the violence. If this was not done, Tumulty worried, "I am afraid the pressure will grow greater and greater."[54] Tumulty reasoned that a statement from the governor would deflect attention from Wilson and help to quiet African Americans.

However, Wilson already felt his hand forced and for the first time in any private or official correspondence, expressed interest in wanting to do something about the violence at East St. Louis. In a letter to Tumulty on the same day as the Silent Protest Parade delegation visited, Wilson asked:

I wish very much that you would think this [Silent Protest petition] over and tell me just what form and occasion you think such a statement ought to take. I want to make it if it can be made naturally and with the likelihood that it will be effective.[55]

Not long afterward, President Wilson kept good on his word to follow up and on August 16, 1917, Wilson personally met with a smaller delegation representing the Silent Protest Parade. The delegation sat down with Wilson in the Oval Office and told him about the race riot in East St. Louis and about

[53] Joseph Patrick Tumulty to Governor Frank Orren Lowden, letter with enclosures, August 1, 1917. Reprinted in *The Papers of Woodrow Wilson* Vol. 43, edited by Arthur Link, Princeton: Princeton University Press, pp. 342–343.

[54] Joseph Patrick Tumulty to Governor Frank Orren Lowden, letter, August 1, 1917. Reprinted in *The Papers of Woodrow Wilson* Vol. 43, edited by Arthur Link, Princeton: Princeton University Press, pp. 342–343.

[55] President Woodrow Wilson to Joseph Patrick Tumulty, letter, August 1, 1917. Reprinted in *The Papers of Woodrow Wilson* Vol. 43, edited by Arthur Link, Princeton: Princeton University Press, pp. 342–343.

violence in other parts of the country. Wilson expressed shock and promised that the federal government would do everything it could do to prevent future occurrences of mob violence.[56] Though these assurances did not mount to any immediate action on Wilson's behalf, the meeting represented a rare accommodation from Wilson in addressing African American concerns.

Another incident of racial violence intensified the NAACP's pressure on Wilson. On August 23, 1917, a detachment of the African American army battalion called the Twenty-Fourth Infantry (one of the Buffalo Soldier regiments) was charged with the shooting up of the city of Houston in which seventeen white people were killed. The bloody violence in Houston was the climax to racial anxieties surrounding African American soldiers who were stationed at a base near Houston and white Houstonians embittered by their presence.[57] Upon finding out about the Houston incident, the NAACP quickly sent down an investigator to gather facts. Further NAACP investigation revealed:

> The friction was due chiefly to the fact that the local authorities had objected to the policing of the men while in the city by the usual methods of establishing a provost guard, and had insisted on that duty being placed at the hands of the local police; that the police had been insulting and brutal in enforcing their powers.[58]

Though the NAACP attempted to intervene, sixty-three members of the regiment were court-martialed, and thirteen were quickly hung on the early morning of December 11, 1917. Leniency was granted only to those that agreed to testify against their fellow soldiers. In subsequent court-martials, sixteen more were sentenced to be hanged and fifty-one to life imprisonment.

The NAACP rallied behind this issue, as they believed it was a blatant example of the racial terrorism they were working so hard to overcome. The conclusion was easy to draw that if African American soldiers could become the victims of racist violence, then ordinary African Americans certainly would not be protected. As far as the NAACP was concerned, the Houston incident fell squarely in line with their fight against lynching and mob violence. On a macro level, the Houston riot provided the NAACP with additional evidence in making the case that the federal government had to do something to stop the spread of lawlessness and racial violence in the states.

A committee of four, headed by Johnson, went to the White House on February 19, 1918, to seek executive clemency for the men sentenced to death. They brought a petition of 12,000 signatures, both African American and

---

[56] "Wilson Pledge to Negroes," *The Washington Post*, August 17, 1917, p. 2; Alfred B. Cosey to President Wilson, letter, August 9, 1917. Reprinted in *The Papers of Woodrow Wilson* Vol. 43, edited by Arthur Link, Princeton: Princeton University Press, p. 412.

[57] For more on the Houston Riot of 1917, see Edgar Schuler, "The Houston Race Riot, 1917," *Journal of Negro History* 29 (1944): pp. 300–338; Robert Haynes, *A Night of Violence: The Houston Riot of 1917*, Baton Rouge: Louisiana State University Press, 1976.

[58] James Weldon Johnson, *Along This Way: The Autobiography of James Weldon Johnson*, New York: The Viking Press, 1933.

white, in support of their request. They were received warmly by President Wilson and they asked specifically for:

Executive clemency to the five Negro soldiers of the Twenty-Fourth Infantry now under sentence of death by court martial. And understanding that the cases of the men of the same regiment who were sentenced to life imprisonment by the first court martial are to be reviewed.[59]

They also used the time with Wilson to talk about the continuance of mob violence and lynchings and ended their plea with a request that Wilson make a public statement against this lawlessness. After the presentation by Johnson, Wilson continued to talk at length with the delegation about the spread of racial violence, and though he initially declined to make a public announcement, after continued prodding, Wilson promised the group that he would "seek an opportunity" to say something.[60] This represented the first time Wilson gave his word to make a statement about racial violence.

The petition of 12,000 signers left a mark on Wilson, and he immediately took action on the NAACP's requests. He wrote his secretary of war, Newton Diehl Baker, the same day of the visit, telling him, "This document, which was left with me today, accompanied by a gigantic petition, that is, gigantic in the bulk of its signatures, has I must say moved me very much." In this letter, he told Baker he wanted to reconsider the cases of both the men who had been condemned to death and the men who had been condemned to life sentences.[61] Directly following the NAACP delegation, Wilson prohibited the execution of any more American soldiers before the sentences of the court-martial had been reviewed by the War Department. Also, of the sixteen men who were condemned to death, he reviewed the cases and commuted the sentences of ten to life imprisonment and affirmed the death sentences of six.[62] Wilson's actions in regards to the Twenty-Fourth Infantry directly followed the NAACP's requests and provide evidence that the NAACP's efforts in raising the issue of racial violence to Wilson were resonating.

The NAACP continued to push for a presidential statement against lynchings, and soon pressure was coming from all over the nation. Shillady sent telegrams and letters to forty-four of the most active NAACP branches, urging them to instruct their members to write or telegraph Wilson, asking that he condemn lynching in his Address to the Nation in July.[63] Organizing their

---

[59] James Weldon Johnson, *Along This Way: The Autobiography of James Weldon Johnson*, New York: The Viking Press, 1933, p. 323.

[60] James Weldon Johnson, *Along This Way: The Autobiography of James Weldon Johnson*, New York: The Viking Press, 1933, p. 324.

[61] President Wilson to Newton Diehl Baker, letter, February 19, 1918. Reprinted in *The Papers of Woodrow Wilson* Vol. 43, edited by Arthur Link, Princeton: Princeton University Press, p. 385.

[62] James Weldon Johnson, *Along This Way: The Autobiography of James Weldon Johnson*, New York: The Viking Press, 1933.

[63] BOD Minutes, July 8, 1918, Box 3, Moorfield Storey Papers, Manuscript Division, Library of Congress, Washington DC.

local branches in this letter-writing campaign was useful as many NAACP members had influential contacts. Emblematic of the strength of their base, in West Virginia, Mordecai Johnson, head of the Charleston branch of the NAACP and later president of Howard University, succeeded in persuading the governor and two judges of the West Virginia Supreme Court and other influential white citizens to send telegrams.[64] While these letters were flooding Wilson's office, racial violence broke out in Washington, and Shillady sent Wilson a telegram calling his attention "to the shame put upon the country by the mobs, including United States soldiers, sailors and marines, which have assaulted innocent and unoffending negroes in the National Capital."[65] The telegram, which was printed in the *Washington Post* and *The New York Times*, called on Wilson to make a statement condemning mob violence.

The very next day, a special newspaper dispatch reported that Wilson was considering making a statement about mob violence. The NAACP was elated and felt more emboldened than ever before. Shillady quickly compiled a memo in support of a presidential statement against lynching. Shillady's memo outlined eleven reasons why such a statement was necessary.[66] The next day, President Wilson complied directly with the NAACP's request and made a strong statement denouncing lynching in his Address to the Nation, pledging the support of the entire nation to rid the country of this evil.[67] In his speech, he declared:

I take the liberty of addressing you upon a subject which so vitally affects the honor of the Nation and the very character and integrity of our institutions that I trust you will think me justified in speaking very plainly about it. I allude to the mob spirit which has recently here and there very frequently shown its head amongst us, not in any single region, but in many and widely separated parts of the country. There have been many lynchings and every one of them has been a blow at the heart of ordered law and humane justice. No man who loves America, no man who really cares for her fame and honor and character, or who is truly loyal to her institutions, can justify mob action while the courts of justice are open and the governments of the States and the Nation are ready and able to do their duty.... I therefore very earnestly and solemnly beg that the governors of all the States, the law officers of every community, and, above all, the men and women of every community in the United States, all who revered America and wish to keep her name without stain or reproach, will cooperate – not passively merely,

---

[64] Charles Flint Kellogg, *NAACP: A History of the National Association for the Advancement of Colored People*, Baltimore: Johns Hopkins University Press, 1973.

[65] John Shillady, "Negroes Call on Wilson to Act on Mob Violence; Fear Outbreaks Elsewhere," July 23, 1919, *The Washington Post*.

[66] John R. Shillady to President Wilson, letter, July 25, 1918. Reprinted in *The Papers of Woodrow Wilson* Vol. 49, edited by Arthur Link, Princeton: Princeton University Press, pp. 88–89.

[67] President Woodrow Wilson, *A Statement to the American People*, July 26, 1918. Reprinted in *The Papers of Woodrow Wilson* Vol. 49, edited by Arthur Link, Princeton: Princeton University Press, pp. 97–99.

but actively and watchfully – to make an end of this disgraceful evil. It cannot live where the community does not countenance it.[68]

For African Americans trying to fight against lynching and for equality of citizenship in the first quarter of the twentieth century, Wilson's statement was an important sign that the federal government had not completely forgotten about them.

Certainly, President Wilson was no advocate for African Americans rights, but the tenor of his approach toward mob violence and lynching softened during his second term. This did not occur in a vacuum: the NAACP was responsible for this shift as the organization felt Wilson's support was critical to its campaign. In Wilson's personal correspondence after the meeting with NAACP representatives from the Silent Protest Parade and the Twenty-Fourth Infantry, he exhibited a desire to take affirmative action as a direct result of the NAACP appeal, going so far as to say he was "moved very much"[69] by one of the petitions from the NAACP. Most telling of the NAACP's influence was Wilson's statement against lynching; it was made on the exact date and in the forum the NAACP had requested.

Harding's Return to Normalcy and the NAACP's Return to the Presidency

Warren G. Harding took office as the twenty-ninth president of the United States and served from 1921 until a heart attack took his life less than three years later. Harding was a Republican from Marion, Ohio, where he became a newspaper publisher and quickly climbed the ladder of state politics serving as state senator and lieutenant governor. He was later elected and served as a U.S. senator from 1915 to 1921. Harding's political philosophy was closer to the conservative than the progressive side of the Republican Party, but he was viewed as a peacemaker and called upon to heal the rift in the party during the Republican National Convention of 1916.[70] He decided to run for president with Calvin Coolidge as his running mate against James Cox and his running

---

[68] President Woodrow Wilson, *A Statement to the American People*, July 26, 1918. Reprinted in *The Papers of Woodrow Wilson* Vol. 49, edited by Arthur Link, Princeton: Princeton University Press, pp. 97–99.

[69] President Wilson to Newton Diehl Baker, letter, February 19, 1918. Reprinted in *The Papers of Woodrow Wilson* Vol. 46, edited by Arthur Link, Princeton: Princeton University Press, p. 385.

[70] There was a rift between the conservative and progressive wings of the Republican Party that emerged during the 1912 convention, which is considered one of the most contentious conventions in history. During this convention, William Howard Taft won the Republican nomination in large part because he controlled the party machinery and was able to block progressive Theodore Roosevelt. When this happened, the progressives split off, and the progressive Bull Moose Party was born, with Roosevelt as the presidential candidate. In the convention of 1916, both factions came together, and Harding gave a speech aimed at bringing the Republican Party together.

mate Franklin Delano Roosevelt in the 1920 election. During this campaign, he promised a "return to normalcy" after World War I and inaugurated a new style of "front porch politics" that captivated the nation. He would go on to win by the largest margin in a presidential election, but evidence of government corruption surfaced posthumously, marring his legacy. Most notable was the "Tea Pot Dome" scandal, which, until Watergate was the most infamous scandal involving a presidential administration.[71]

However, perhaps most remarkable about Harding is what is missing from accounts of his presidency.[72] While Harding is frequently remembered as one of America's worst presidents, he responded to the NAACP in a way that had never been done before by someone in the Oval Office. A considerable amount of archival evidence demonstrates that Harding directly attended to NAACP grievances and made surprising concessions. This was partially due to political expediency, but was mostly the result of pressure brought by the NAACP and the actions of a president who seemed genuinely interested in the plight of African Americans. In hopes of shining light on this forgotten area, the next section of this chapter will detail the NAACP's lobbying efforts in persuading Harding to address the issues of lynching and mob violence.

In 1920, the political presence of African Americans was growing. Many southern African Americans came North during the first phase of the Great Migration for work, and, with the passage of the Nineteenth Amendment, African American women could vote.[73] Understanding the importance of new African American voters and encouraged by the inroads made with Wilson, the NAACP started to make its presence felt early in the 1920 presidential election when it attempted to place the issues of lynching and race on the agenda of the presidential candidates through a questionnaire that Du Bois created and sent out. The first question was: "Will you favor the enactment of laws making

---

[71] Secretary of the Interior Albert Fall, a former senator from New Mexico and a friend of Harding's, was responsible for the valuable oil lands known as "Teapot Dome" and Elk Hills that were meant for the long-term use of the U.S. Navy. However, in secret dealings, he leased out oil rights to friends Harry Sinclair to drill for oil at Teapot Dome, Wyoming, and Edward Doheny for reserves at Elk Hills, California. Fall received approximately $400,000 in cash and gifts from Doheny and Sinclair. He was later convicted of taking bribes and sent to jail – the first cabinet member ever sent to prison as a result of misconduct while in office.

[72] Writing about Harding's presidency in 2004, John Dean canvases the available material and determines, "The conclusion that Harding was our worst president endures because the actual record of his presidency has, in fact, been largely overlooked." *Warren G. Harding*, New York: Henry Holt, 2004, p. 1. For more on Harding, see Samuel Adams, *Incredible Era: The Life and Times of Warren Gamaliel Harding*, Boston: Houghton Mifflin Company, 1939; Andrew Sinclair, *The Available Man: The Life Behind the Masks of Warren Gamaliel Harding*, New York: Macmillan, 1965; Robert Murray, *The Harding Era: Warren G. Harding and His Administration*, Minneapolis: University of Minnesota Press, 1969; Randolph Downes, *The Rise of Warren Gamaliel Harding, 1865–1920*, Ohio University Press, 1970; John Dean, *Warren G. Harding*, New York: Henry Holt, 2004.

[73] Joe Trotter, *The Great Migration in Historical Perspective: New Dimensions of Race, Class, and Gender*, Bloomington: Indiana University Press, 1991.

lynching a federal offense?"[74] Presidential hopeful Harding responded that he was interested in the work of the NAACP but that:

I do not find it consistent with my views to take up the categorical questions which you address to me, because I am a very firm believer in the doctrine that conventions are called upon to enunciate platforms and policies for our Party, and the candidate selected must be expected to stand on the platform thus made.

In this letter, Harding made clear he was not going to take any independent stand away from the Republican Party on the issue of lynching or any of the other issues concerning race. Using the Republican Party as a shield from NAACP demands, Harding ended, "I can well believe that the Republican National convention will make every becoming declaration on behalf of the negro citizenship, which the conscience of the Party and the conditions of this country combine to suggest."[75]

Shortly afterward, aware they would have to address the growing vocal discontent of African Americans, Republican Party leaders sought to pacify African Americans by making a few amends and lukewarm promises of racial equality. For example, at the 1920 Republican National Convention, NAACP Secretary James Weldon Johnson and four more African Americans were appointed to sit on a platform advisory committee. The small African American committee met with Republican Party chairman Will Hays, Senator James Watson (R-Indiana) who served as chairman of the resolutions committee, and Harding's campaign manager for a mere twenty minutes.[76] The African American committee requested a plank assuring the right to vote for African Americans in the South, a civil rights act abolishing segregation, and a general commitment that the United States should be made safe for democracy at home before it pursued democracy on foreign soil. Seeking to quiet demands from African American activists while not disrupting the party's base, a meager accommodation was made to place one sentence in the Republican Party platform that read, "We urge Congress to consider the most effective means to end lynching in this country which continues to be a terrible blot on our American civilization."[77] African Americans were disappointed, and Johnson called his service on the advisory committee an

---

[74] BOD Minutes, February 9, 1920, NAACP Papers, Manuscript Division, Library of Congress, Washington, DC.

[75] Harding to Shillady, letter, February 20, 1920, Series 1: C, Box 64, NAACP Papers, Manuscript Division, Library of Congress, Washington, DC.

[76] James Weldon Johnson, *Along This Way: The Autobiography of James Weldon Johnson*, New York: The Viking Press, 1933, p. 357; Richard Sherman, "The Harding Administration and the Negro: An Opportunity Lost," *The Journal of Negro History* 49, no. 3 (1964): 151–168; Robert Zangrando, *The NAACP Crusade Against Lynching, 1909–1950*, Philadelphia: Temple University Press, 1980, p. 56.

[77] Donald McCoy, "Election of 1920," *History of American Presidential Elections, 1789–1968* Vol. 3, edited by Arthur Schlesinger Jr. and Fred Israel, New York: Chelsea House, 1971, p. 2413.

"empty honor."[78] In his acceptance speech one month later on July 22 at the Republican National Convention, Harding continued this bare-bones equality rhetoric: "I believe the Negro citizens of America should be guaranteed the enjoyment of all their rights, that they have earned their full measure of citizenship bestowed."[79] Through this speech and the lynching plank in the Republican Party platform, the Republicans hoped they had dodged specifics and subsequently launched a publicity campaign with the clear objective "to keep things moderate and general and to curb the militants who wanted more specifics."[80]

While Harding steered clear of specifics, the small accommodations he made toward African Americans elicited a savage white backlash. After it became known that Harding was reaching out to African Americans with vague promises of racial equality during his campaign, lily-white Democrats in the North and border states mounted two substantial attacks aroused by the dubious research of historian William Estabrook Chancellor. The first was the charge that Harding had "mixed blood and was of Negro ancestry" and the second was the claim that Harding was trying to undermine white supremacy.[81] The former proved more damaging, so much so that the Republican National Committee was prepared with genealogical data proving Harding's whiteness. But whatever reservations whites had with Harding's racial background, it paled in comparison to their growing dislike of the Wilson administration. In 1920, the wartime economic boom had come crashing down and strikes in meatpacking and steel were taking place in major cities. Americans were war-weary, and Irish Catholic and German communities were especially outraged at Wilson's support of the League of Nations. Harding capitalized on the growing anti-Wilson sentiment and ran his campaign as if he were running against Wilson, not Cox. Harding argued he would be the change the country needed, and Americans agreed – delivering to him a landslide victory of 60.3 percent compared to Cox's 34.1 percent.[82]

Harding's small accommodations, however, did not placate the NAACP, and the organization began to marshal its expertise as a pressure group to convince Harding to address issues on its agenda. So the question becomes, after he was elected and had nothing to gain from African American voters, how did the NAACP convince Harding to make the most specific and firm concession to

---

[78] James Weldon Johnson, *Along This Way: The Autobiography of James Weldon Johnson*, New York: The Viking Press, 1933, p. 357.

[79] Donald McCoy, "Election of 1920," *History of American Presidential Elections, 1789–1968* Vol. 3, edited by Arthur Schlesinger Jr. and Fred Israel, New York: Chelsea House, 1971.

[80] Randolph Downes, "Negro Rights and White Backlash in the Campaign of 1920," *Ohio History Journal* 75 (1966): 89.

[81] Randolph Downes, "Negro Rights and White Backlash in the Campaign of 1920," *Ohio History Journal* 75 (1966): 85–107.

[82] Harding won all the states except Kentucky and ten states of the former Confederacy. Tennessee went to Harding, marking the first time since the end of Reconstruction that a Confederate state voted for a Republican presidential candidate.

African American demands to date in the form of a strong public statement denouncing lynching? This is especially noteworthy, as Harding had repeatedly declined to make such a statement during his campaign. The rest of this section will draw a direct link between Harding's lynching statement and the NAACP's education strategy. The focus on educating Harding may seem peculiar to some, but records of meetings between Harding and Johnson reveal that the NAACP was certain that, unlike with Wilson, Harding's reluctance to speak out against lynching was directly connected to his ignorance of the issue. Conveyed bluntly by Johnson, "Mr. Harding will need to be educated on the race question."[83] After a January 1921 meeting with Harding, Johnson admitted, "More serious still, from our point of view, is the fact that he knows absolutely nothing about the race question. All that he seems to know about Negroes is what he has gathered from the rather sorry specimens in and about Marion, Ohio."[84]

Harding's lack of familiarity about the extreme levels of racism and violence that many African Americans were forced to endure brings up a critical point in this presidency analysis: the NAACP's starting positions in the struggle to convince Wilson and Harding to make a public statement against lynching were different. With Wilson, the NAACP had to fight against entrenched racism in his administration and a president who was well aware of Jim Crow violence but chose to look the other way. It was a decidedly larger mountain to climb. Harding did not appear to have the kind of strong deep-seated biases against African Americans that Wilson harbored. With Harding, the NAACP faced the task of bringing the facts of lynching to him, presenting them as a problem of American democracy, and suggesting a solution. This seemingly simple focus on agenda setting is important because controversial issues do not arrive on the presidential speaking agenda by themselves. Issues existing on the periphery have to be placed there. So, although the NAACP's advocacy of Harding did not mirror the intensity that was exhibited in the effort to pressure Wilson into making a public statement, it did not have to because of the different circumstances surrounding each president. It should not be interpreted, however, that the NAACP did not matter in Harding's decision to speak out against lynching. On the contrary, I contend that the NAACP's ability to agenda set and raise Harding's awareness about the dangers of racial violence were critical in understanding Harding's eventual anti-lynching statement.

The movement to educate Harding started soon after Harding secured the Republican nomination; Johnson and Harry E. Davis, the Cleveland member of the NAACP Board of Directors, met with Harding at his home in Marion,

---

[83] James Weldon Johnson, Report of the Field Secretary on Interview with Senator Warren G. Harding, August 9, 1920, Series 1: C, Box 66, NAACP Papers, Manuscript Division, Library of Congress, Washington, DC.

[84] James Weldon Johnson, Report of the Secretary's Visit to Senator Harding, January 15, 1921, Series 1: C, Box 66, NAACP Papers, Manuscript Division, Library of Congress, Washington, DC.

Ohio, on August 9, 1920, in hopes of "having him make several pre-election statements regarding his attitude and that of the Republican Party on the Negro."[85] During the meeting, Johnson and Davis took turns in disclosing "a great many things about the race question which had never before been brought to his [Harding's] attention, especially the present state of mind of the Negro race in America."[86] Johnson and Davis presented Harding with seven points regarding the current state of African Americans: the right to vote, abolition of government segregation, enactment of anti-lynching legislation, investigation of the conditions in Haiti, federal aid to education, greater apportionment of African American officers and privates in the armed services, and investigation by the Interstate Commerce Commission of Jim Crow car conditions. They explained to Harding why each point was important to African Americans and urged him to make statements about all of the seven points. Harding affirmed his earlier statement and explained that as a matter of principle, he agreed with them on all points with the exception of federal aid to education but was unwilling to make them into a campaign issue as he felt it would hurt the Republican Party in the general election.

Not only was Harding unaware of the dangerous issues that African Americans had to contend with on a daily basis, but also, over the course of the meeting, it became clear that Harding had little knowledge of the NAACP. So time was spent informing Harding of the mission of the NAACP and explaining "it was an organization composed not merely of executives on a letterhead but that it was a thoroughly organized and effective machine with branches and members all over the United States."[87] After describing the focus and goals of the NAACP, Johnson wrote that Harding "was especially impressed" and that there was reason to believe that "if that impression is followed up and strengthened, Mr. Harding, in case of his election, will turn to this organization for information and advice on Negro policies rather than to petty politicians."[88] This favored position of the NAACP in Harding's organizational hierarchy was confirmed in January 1921, when Harding told Johnson that "he had been obliged to refuse hundreds of persons who wished to talk with him but that he granted the Secretary (Johnson) an interview feeling that he spoke for an organization

[85] James Weldon Johnson, Report of the Field Secretary on Interview with Senator Warren G. Harding, August 9, 1920, Series 1: C, Box 66, NAACP Papers, Manuscript Division, Library of Congress, Washington, DC.

[86] James Weldon Johnson, Report of the Field Secretary on Interview with Senator Warren G. Harding, August 9, 1920, Series 1: C, Box 66, NAACP Papers, Manuscript Division, Library of Congress, Washington, DC.

[87] James Weldon Johnson, Report of the Field Secretary on Interview with Senator Warren G. Harding, August 9, 1920, Series 1: C, Box 66, NAACP Papers, Manuscript Division, Library of Congress, Washington, DC.

[88] James Weldon Johnson, Report of the Field Secretary on Interview with Senator Warren G. Harding, August 9, 1920, Series 1: C, Box 66, NAACP Papers, Manuscript Division, Library of Congress, Washington, DC.

which represented the Negro race."[89] Johnson was Harding's first meeting with an African American representative following the election.

Once Harding secured the nomination, Johnson visited president-elect Harding in January 1921 at his home in Marion, Ohio. The meeting was a continuation of their August 1920 conference. In this meeting, the NAACP removed federal aid to education from its list of demands and pressed the other six points – two of which would make their way into Harding's public statement in March 1921. Johnson spoke at length about the NAACP's anti-lynching fight and the organization's desire to appoint a national interracial commission for the purpose of making a study of racial conditions in the United States. Still reluctant to make a public statement denouncing lynching, Harding stalled when asked to by Johnson and cautioned him that he did not consider the conversation an interview and switched topics. Johnson reported that Harding was most interested in the interracial commission and had remarked that it was "a novel ideal worth considering." Overall, the meeting went well, and Harding invited Johnson to come to Washington after he was inaugurated to speak more about racial conditions in the United States.[90]

After his meeting in Marion, Johnson was on the lookout for additional opportunities to educate Harding and to strengthen the NAACP's case for federal intervention. Fortunately for Johnson, he soon received word that Harding was vacationing in Florida and sent a letter requesting Harding meet with a small delegation of African Americans while in Florida to learn more about conditions of African Americans in the South.[91] Harding responded to Johnson's letter that he was "anxious, of course, to get the viewpoint of leading colored citizens of the South."[92] Subsequently, on February 22, 1921, Harding met with a group that included Bishop John Hurst of the African Methodist

[89] James Weldon Johnson, Report of the Secretary's Visit to Senator Harding, January 15, 1921, Series 1: C, Box 66, NAACP Papers, Manuscript Division, Library of Congress, Washington, DC. Harding's perspective that the NAACP was an authoritative voice on African Americans was apparent in his dismissive treatment of other prominent African American organizations. After sending many letters, the president of the Tuskegee Institute Robert Moton was able to visit Harding as he vacationed in Florida in February 1921. Moton brought along other influential African Americans such as Will Alexander of the Commission on Interracial Cooperation; and John Eagan, president of the American Cast Iron Pipe Company. An account of the meeting by the participants reveals that Harding had never heard of Moton, Booker T. Washington, or the Tuskegee Institute. Even worse, as the meeting went on, it became apparent that Harding was uninformed about the purpose of the meeting as he assumed the members of the delegation were job-seeking African American politicians. See Robert Sherman, *The Republican Party and Black America: From McKinley to Hoover 1896–1933*, Charlottesville: University Press of Virginia, 1973, pp. 146–147.

[90] James Weldon Johnson, Report of the Secretary's Visit to Senator Harding, January 15, 1921, Series 1: C, Box 66, NAACP Papers, Manuscript Division, Library of Congress, Washington, DC.

[91] James Weldon Johnson to Warren G. Harding, letter, February 11, 1921, Warren G. Harding Papers, Manuscript Division, Library of Congress, Washington, DC.

[92] Warren G. Harding to James W. Johnson, letter, February 14, 1921, Series 1: C, Box 64, NAACP Papers, Manuscript Division, Library of Congress, Washington, DC.

Episcopal Church, Captain James W. Floyd of Jacksonville, and several other business and professional men in St. Augustine, Florida. Desiring to exploit every opportunity to educate Harding, the NAACP was able to chip away at his wall of ignorance by shining a spotlight on the precarious state of African American citizenship – especially in the Jim Crow South.

Once Harding took office on March 4, 1921, the NAACP wasted no time in trying to win him over. One month into Harding's presidency, Johnson met with him at the White House to discuss in greater detail steps that could be taken by the federal government "to relieve oppressive conditions affecting colored people and causing friction between the races."[93] In the meeting, Johnson presented Harding with a memo stating the top issues the NAACP wanted Harding to address; the first demand was the following:

The National Association for the Advancement of Colored People earnestly request the President to include in his message to Congress convening April 11 a recommendation that it take action to end lynching, the most terrible blot on American civilization.[94]

This meeting marked the most aggressive the NAACP would be in asking for a presidential statement concerning lynching, going so far as directing Harding to where it would like to see such a statement. In addition, the NAACP asked for "the appointment of a National Inter-Racial Commission to make a thorough and sincere study of race conditions and race relations in the United States with particular reference to the causes of friction."[95] The NAACP viewed the appointing of such a committee as key to addressing issues of racial inequality and of permanently ridding the nation of lynching and mob violence.

Harding did not completely dismiss the NAACP's recommendations, but he did not heartily embrace them either. He seemed to be on the fence and still in the process of making up his mind about where he stood on these matters. Hoping to sway Harding, Johnson followed up their meeting with a letter, again calling attention to the NAACP's request that he include a recommendation to end lynching in his address to Congress. Johnson included a number of southern newspaper clippings as evidence "that even Southern sentiment was now expressing a conviction that the Federal Government would and ought to take a hand in this matter."[96] The newspaper clippings made clear that lynchings were not abating; some of the headlines read: "May Lynch 3 to 6 Negroes This Evening," "Kill Negro by Inches," "Negro Burned At Stake," "Avengers

---

93 Christian to Johnson, letter, March 30, 1921, Series 1: C, Box 64, NAACP Papers, Manuscript Division, Library of Congress, Washington, DC; *Cause of the Negro Presented to President Harding*, April 5, 1921, Series 1: C, Box 66, NAACP Papers, Manuscript Division, Library of Congress, Washington, DC.

94 James Weldon Johnson, *Memorandum to the Honorable Warren G. Harding*, April 4, 1921, Warren G. Harding Papers, Manuscript Division, Library of Congress, Washington, DC.

95 James Weldon Johnson, *Memorandum to the Honorable Warren G. Harding*, April 4, 1921, Warren G. Harding Papers, Manuscript Division, Library of Congress, Washington, DC.

96 James W. Johnson to President Harding, letter and newspaper enclosures, April 6, 1921, Warren G. Harding Papers, Manuscript Division, Library of Congress, Washington, DC.

Set 6 O'Clock As Lynching Hour," and "Feed Dry Leaves to Slow Fire Which Cooks Lowry: Tries to End Life by Swallowing Hot Coals as Flames Eat Flesh from Legs."[97]

Six days later, on April 12, 1921, in his first public speech after being inaugurated, Harding addressed a joint session of Congress and challenged:

Congress ought to wipe the stain of barbaric lynching from the banners of a free and orderly, representative democracy. We face the fact that millions of people of African descent are numbered among our population, and that in a number of States they constitute a very large proportion of the total population. It is unnecessary to recount the difficulties incident to this condition nor to emphasize the fact that it is a condition which can not be removed.[98]

But he did not stop there. In a direct reference to Harding's correspondence with the NAACP, he stated while talking about ameliorating the situation of African Americans:

One proposal is the creation of a commission embracing representatives of both races to study and report on the entire subject. The proposal has real merit. I am convinced that in mutual tolerance, understanding, charity, recognition of the interdependence of the races, and the maintenance of the rights of citizenship lies the road to righteous adjustment.[99]

The establishment of a commission was brought up as a possible solution that would help to address the task of wiping lynching from the nation. The NAACP's campaign for Harding to make a bold statement about ending lynching in his address to Congress was fulfilled in the manner in which the NAACP requested. It is especially important to note the timing: Harding's statement to Congress (Illustration 3.1) came one day after Representative Leonidas Dyer (R-Missouri) introduced the NAACP-supported anti-lynching bill into the House of Representatives.

Harding's support for the anti-lynching campaign can be traced directly to the NAACP's work. The following day, Johnson sent a telegram to Harding in which he thanked the president for his message to Congress and his endorsement of the NAACP's proposal of a commission to study race relations in the United States. Johnson, who wrote about it most eloquently, describes the importance of President Harding's statement:

We are confident that the adjustment of race relations in the United States can be arrived at through understanding, through the recognition of the interdependence of the races

---

[97] James W. Johnson to President Harding, letter and newspaper enclosures, April 6, 1921, Warren G. Harding Papers, Manuscript Division, Library of Congress, Washington, DC.

[98] President Warren G. Harding, *Address to Joint Session of Congress*, April 12, 1921, Warren G. Harding Papers, Manuscript Division, Library of Congress, Washington, DC. For section on lynching and race commission, see pp. 39–41.

[99] President Warren G. Harding, *Address to Joint Session of Congress*, April 12, 1921, Warren G. Harding Papers, Manuscript Division, Library of Congress, Washington, DC. For section on lynching and race commission, see pp. 39–41.

ILLUSTRATION 3.1 President Warren G. Harding addressing the joint session of Congress on April 12, 1921. "Harding delivering first address to Congress, 1921." *Source*: Photographer unknown. Courtesy of the Library of Congress, Prints and Photographs Division, National Photo Company Collection, LC-USZ62–35268, LOT 12282.

and the maintenance of the equal rights of citizenship. Your action is a long step toward that adjustment.[100]

Providing further support to the NAACP's influence at the executive level, Harding wrote Johnson a letter that was read at the NAACP's Twelfth Annual Conference in which Harding disclosed,

I hope the Association may enjoy a larger and constantly enlarging usefulness, and that in the near future, it may be possible to set up some instrumentalities with which your cooperation will be very much desired. I will be glad to be informed of the transactions of the convention and to receive any suggestions from it that may be helpful in developing a constructive policy.[101]

This letter from Harding in which he discusses a cooperative relationship between the president and the NAACP provides indication that the NAACP's

[100] James Weldon Johnson to President Warren G. Harding, letter, April 13, 1921, Series 1: C, Box 66, NAACP Papers, Manuscript Division, Library of Congress, Washington, DC.
[101] President Warren G. Harding to James Weldon Johnson, letter, June 18, 1921, Series 1: C, Box 66, NAACP Papers, Manuscript Division, Library of Congress, Washington, DC.

advocacy was achieving an admirable degree of success. More importantly, Harding's anti-lynching statement and this letter both evidence significant rhetorical shifts in Harding's understanding of the executive branch's responsibility to helping to quell racial violence.

Even Du Bois, who had been skeptical about Harding, rejoiced about Harding's anti-lynching statement in *The Crisis*, "This is the strongest pronouncement on the race problem ever made by a President in a message to Congress."[102] It is worth emphasizing that over the course of a year, President Harding went from declining to make a statement on race to making the boldest presidential denouncement on lynching to that point. This is not happenstance. The NAACP's constant pressuring around Harding helps to explain this statement to Congress.

Harding was not through responding to the NAACP's requests. Not long after Harding addressed Congress, one of the most devastating displays of racial violence in American history broke out in Tulsa, Oklahoma, after a young African American man was arrested for the alleged sexual assault of a young white woman. In response, from May 31, 1921, to June 1, 1921, angry whites crossed the railroad tracks and attacked Greenwood District (also known as "Negro Wall Street"), where the wealthiest African American community in the United States lived, and burned it to the ground. But the horrific violence did not stop there – whites looted and carried out deadly drive-by shootings of surrounding African American neighborhoods. An estimated 10,000 African Americans were left homeless and a reported 100–300 African Americans were murdered.[103]

Walter White conducted an investigation for the NAACP of the underlying reasons for the racial bloodshed and revealed that one of the accusations whites made was that African Americans were being too "radical." Often the one to delve deeper into the race psyche of whites, White pressed a bit more regarding the meaning of this radicalism and found

it means that Negroes were uncompromisingly denouncing "Jim Crow" [rail] cars, lynching, peonage; in short, they were asking that the federal constitutional guarantees of "life, liberty, and the pursuit of happiness" be given regardless of color.[104]

An outraged NAACP telegrammed Harding, stating, "An utterance from you at this time on the violence and reign of terror at Tulsa, Oklahoma, would have an inestimable effect not only upon that situation but upon the whole country."[105] Interestingly, the NAACP's request was also printed two days later

---

[102] *The Crisis*, June 1921, p. 68.
[103] Scott Ellsworth, *Death in a Promised Land: The Tulsa Race Riot of 1921*, Baton Rouge: Louisiana State Press, 1982; Tim Madigan, *The Burning: Massacre, Destruction, and the Tulsa Race Riot of 1921*, New York: St. Martin's Press, 2001; Alfred Brophy, *Reconstructing the Dreamland: The Tulsa Riot of 1921: Race Reparations, and Reconciliation*, New York: Oxford University Press, 2002.
[104] Walter White, "The Eruption of Tulsa," *The Nation*, June 29, 1921, pp. 909–910.
[105] James Weldon Johnson to President Harding, telegram, June 2, 1921, microfilm edition, Reel 193, File 266, Warren G. Harding Papers, Ohio Historical Society.

in *The New York Times* under a headline and a short article that took sides with the white establishment in Tulsa, asking rhetorically if the violence was a "Plot by Negro Society?"[106] Despite a skeptical mainstream press and a white business community in Tulsa that was in the process of covering up the tragedy, President Harding used the opportunity of an impromptu speech to African American graduates at Lincoln University, a historically black college, on June 6, 1921, to address the violence at Tulsa. After commending the university for preparing its students for citizenship, Harding turned his attention to the Tulsa riots, calling them an "unhappy and distressing spectacle" and expressing his hope that "in the soberness, the fairness and the justice of this country, we shall never have another spectacle like it."[107] Harding's private secretary George Christian confirmed that it was done at the behest of the NAACP, writing Johnson: "Following the receipt of your telegram of June 2, the President, as you will have noticed, made a public expression of his regret and horror at the recent Tulsa tragedy, which reflected his sentiments."[108] The NAACP thanked Harding for his words and reported that it had given them "wide publicity" through its press.[109] Harding's willingness to wade into the controversial waters of the Tulsa massacre and Christian's subsequent letter provide surprising insight to the influence the NAACP was able to carve out for itself in the executive branch.

After Harding acquiesced to the NAACP's appeals for a statement against lynching and the Tulsa riots, the organization continued to press Harding to make additional amends. In particular, the NAACP implored him to make good on his suggestion to Congress and formally establish a race commission and later, when the anti-lynching bill was stalled in Congress, the NAACP requested another public statement from him. Villard sent Harding his plan for a race commission, which he had proposed to President Wilson, and the NAACP sent many follow-up letters recommending prominent whites and African Americans to serve on the commission.[110] Feeling that his 1921 address to Congress to stop lynching was a sufficient statement on how he felt about the issue and that the race commission would be overstepping his bounds, Harding declined to do either task in the remaining time that he was in office. Though Harding did not attend to everything the NAACP asked for during his tenure in office, the correspondence between both sides is remarkable for its friendly tone and the

---

[106] "Military Control is Ended at Tulsa. Plot by Negro Society?" *The New York Times*, June 4, 1921, p. 1.

[107] "Harding Exhorts Negroes to Study," *The New York Times*, June 7, 1921, p. 3.

[108] George Christian to James Weldon Johnson, letter, June 7, 1921, microfilm edition, Reel 193, File 266, Warren G. Harding Papers, Ohio Historical Society.

[109] James Weldon Johnson to George Christian, letter, June 16, 1921, microfilm edition, File 93, Warren G. Harding Papers, Ohio Historical Society.

[110] Oswald Garrison Villard to George Christian, letter and proposal for a national race commission, December 22, 1921, microfilm edition, Reel 193, File 266, Warren G. Harding Papers, Ohio Historical Society.

apparent way the NAACP had the ear of Harding.[111] For example, in responding
to Johnson's request that Harding address the constitutionality concerns that
were holding up the Dyer Anti-Lynching Bill in Congress, Christian responded
supportively that while Harding did not want to meddle in the business in
Congress, "He feels that the purpose which the Dyer Bill is intended to further
is so important that the legislation ought not to be held up by reason of some
uncertainties as to what the court might finally decide about it."[112] Johnson
appeared to agree with Christian's assessment of Harding's attitude, writing,
"Personally, I have no misgivings regarding the President's attitude on the Dyer
Anti-Lynching Bill because I have talked with him personally about the matter."[113] It seemed that even when they disagreed, there was the appearance of a
great deal of respect between Harding and the NAACP.

Unfulfilled Wartime Dreams

Of course a number of questions remain about the role of exogenous factors.
It could be that the NAACP's activism occurred at an opportune time and the
real explanation for the changes in Wilson's and Harding's attitudes toward
African Americans has nothing to do with the NAACP. Another possible explanation is that the First World War largely fueled the changes in the social and
political context and forced these presidents to act. This explanation owes to a
considerable amount of scholarship that has demonstrated the importance of
World War II and the resulting Cold War on expansions in African American
civil rights. As discussed in Chapter 1, scholars argue that in the immediate
post–World War II era, U.S. government officials realized that their ability to
promote democracy among people abroad was seriously hampered by continuing racial injustices at home (a claim that African American activists were key

[111] Johnson to Harding, letter, June 1, 1921, Series 1: C, Box 66, NAACP Papers, Manuscript
Division, Library of Congress, Washington, DC; Johnson to Harding, letter, November
28, 1921, Series 1: C, Box 66, NAACP Papers, Manuscript Division, Library of Congress,
Washington, DC; Christian to Johnson, letter, December 1, 1921, Series 1: C, Box 64, NAACP
Papers, Manuscript Division, Library of Congress, Washington, DC; Johnson to Christian, let-
ter, December 2, 1921, Series 1: C, Box 66, NAACP Papers, Manuscript Division, Library of
Congress, Washington, DC; Johnson to Harding, letter, May 9, 1922, Series 1: C, Box 66,
NAACP Papers, Manuscript Division, Library of Congress, Washington, DC; Report of the
Secretary's Trip to Washington, memo, June 15–16, 1922, Series 1: C, Box 66, NAACP Papers,
Manuscript Division, Library of Congress, Washington, DC; Christian to Johnson, letter, June
23, 1922, Series 1: C, Box 66, NAACP Papers, Manuscript Division, Library of Congress,
Washington, DC; Johnson to Harding, telegram, November 16, 1922, Series 1: C, Box 66,
NAACP Papers, Manuscript Division, Library of Congress, Washington, DC; Christian to
Johnson, letter, December 5, 1922, Series 1: C, Box 64, NAACP Papers, Manuscript Division,
Library of Congress, Washington, DC.
[112] George Christian to James Weldon Johnson, letter, September 8, 1922, microfilm edition, Reel
193, File 266, Warren G. Harding Papers, Ohio Historical Society.
[113] James Weldon Johnson to George Christian, letter, September 9, 1922, microfilm edition, Reel
193, File 266, Warren G. Harding Papers, Ohio Historical Society.

in bringing to the fore); in this context, efforts to promote civil rights within the United States were consistent with the central mission of fighting world communism. In other words, the need to fend off international criticism gave the federal government an incentive to promote social change at home.[114]

The work of these scholars necessitates a consideration of the wartime theory of racial change. Indeed, it is plausible that a similar chain reaction between World War I, international pressure, and a change in American attitudes toward lynching occurred. This wartime explanation focuses on the inherent contradiction of America's war "to make the world safe for democracy" and the treatment of African Americans. Under this account, we would expect to find evidence from abroad admonishing the United States' treatment of African Americans during World War I. We would also expect to see the U.S. government responding directly to this criticism. In the public sphere, we would expect international propaganda to be the main motivator for the change in public attitudes about lynching.

However, upon further investigation, it does not appear World War I can explain the changes in Wilson's or Harding's agenda. The most obvious discrepancy has to do with the absence of international pressure on the U.S. government. Unlike during World War II, pressure abroad was targeted specifically at African American soldiers in Europe. German propaganda attempted to weaken the morale of African American soldiers by pointing out how the country they were defending treated them back on their home turf.[115] There is very little evidence of attempts to use the lynching of African Americans as leverage to undermine the American government's aim to make the world safe for democracy. A report from the Department of Defense, detailing the contributions of African Americans to U.S. security, affirmed that despite German propaganda during World War I, "The black American, although disturbed by the messages being received from the enemy, gave his loyalty to the United

---

[114] See Timothy Tyson, *Radio Free Dixie: Robert F. Williams and the Roots of Black Power*, Chapel Hill, London: University of North Carolina Press, 1999; Philip Klinkner and Rogers Smith, *The Unsteady March: The Rise and Decline of Racial Equality in America*, Chicago: The University of Chicago Press, 1999; Mary Dudziak, *Cold War Civil Rights: Race and the Image of American Democracy*, Princeton: Princeton University Press, 2000; Daniel Kryder, *Divided Arsenal : Race and the American State During World War II*, New York: Cambridge University Press, 2000; John Skrentny, *The Minority Rights Revolution*, Cambridge, MA: Belknap Press of Harvard University Press, 2002; Christopher Parker, *Fighting for Democracy: Black Veterans and the Struggle Against White Supremacy in the Postwar South*, Princeton: Princeton University Press, 2009.

[115] On September 12, 1918, Germans scattered a circular to persuade African Americans to lay down their weapons. In the circular they asked: "Do you enjoy the same rights as the white people do in America, the land of Freedom and Democracy, or are you rather not treated over there as second-class citizens? ... Is lynching and the most horrible crimes connected there with a lawful proceeding in a democratic country?" For more on this, see John Hope Franklin, *From Slavery to Freedom: A History of African Americans*, 8th ed., New York: A. A. Knopf, 2000, p. 369.

States, and there were not many who thought differently."[116] A significant reason to explain the lack of worldwide condemnation on the United States as a whole has to do with the press structure during World War I as opposed to World War II. Mary Dudziak argues that the United States received increasing condemnation from other countries because of racism, but before World War I there was very little in the newspapers about lynching, and if there was, it usually justified the "crime."[117] Thus, while the Germans attempted to keep records on lynchings, many of the inconsistencies in the way the U.S. government approached lynching and the war goal of "making the world safe for democracy" were hidden to the international world.

In addition, unlike World War II, which civil rights groups seized on and used as leverage in making equality demands, African Americans, for the most part, were largely supportive of the war effort during the First World War.[118] They exhibited optimism and belief that fighting in the First World War would force white Americans to recognize them as equal citizens.[119] For example, when a separate camp for training African American officers was established, NAACP Chairman Joel Spingarn provided his backing and confidently stated, "The camp is intended to fight segregation, not to encourage it. Colored men in a camp by themselves would get a fair chance for promotion."[120] Du Bois also lent his voice in support of the war effort in an editorial in *The Crisis*: "Let us, while the war lasts, forget our special grievances

[116] *Black Americans in Defense of Our Nation*, Office of the Deputy Assistant Secretary of Defense for Civilian Personnel Policy/Equal Opportunity, Dept. of Defense, Washington, DC, 1991.

[117] Mary Dudziak, *Cold War Civil Rights: Race and the Image of American Democracy*, Princeton: Princeton University Press, 2000.

[118] Arthur Barbeau and Florette Henri, *The Unknown Soldiers: Black American Troops in World War I*, Philadelphia: Temple University Press, 1974; Mark Ellis, *Race, War, and Surveillance African Americans and the United States Government During World War I*, Bloomington: Indiana University Press, 2001; Chad Williams, *Torchbearers of Democracy: African American Soldiers in the World War I Era*, Chapel Hill: University of North Carolina Press, 2010.

[119] August Meier and Elliott Rudwick, *From Plantation to Ghetto: An Interpretive History of American Negroes*, New York, 1966, pp. 193–194; Robert Mullen, *Blacks in America's Wars: The Shift in Attitudes from the Revolutionary War to Vietnam*, New York: Pathfinder, 1973, pp. 45–46; David Kennedy, *Over Here: The First World War and American Society*, New York: 1980, p, 279; Carole Marks, *Farewell – We're Gone and Good: The Great Black Migration*, Bloomington: Indiana University Press, 1989, p. 303; John Hope Franklin, *From Slavery to Freedom: A History of African Americans*, 8th ed., New York: A. A. Knopf, 2000.

[120] Charles Flint Kellogg, *NAACP: A History of the National Association for the Advancement of Colored People*, Baltimore: Johns Hopkins University Press, 1973, pp. 250–256; John Hope Franklin, *From Slavery to Freedom: A History of African Americans*, 8th ed., New York : A. A. Knopf, 2000, p. 362. Monroe Trotter and some of the black press, such as the *Chicago Defender* and the *Baltimore Afro-American*, the *New York Age*, and the *Cleveland Gazette*, opposed the camp. However, numerous others supported the segregated camp including the *Washington Bee*, the *Norfolk Journal and Guide*, and prominent African American colleges such as Hampton and Fisk. For more, see William Jordan, "The Damnable Dilemma": African-American Accommodation and Protest during World War I, *The Journal of American History* 81, no. 4 (1995): 1572.

and close ranks shoulder to shoulder with our white fellow citizens and allied nations fighting for democracy."[121] This is not to say that all African Americans supported the war effort. There was a considerable amount of contestation within the African American community about what their place should be (if any) in World War I. Leaders such as Monroe Trotter, Harry Smith, and Archibald Grimke blasted Du Bois's editorial in *The Crisis*.[122] A. Philip Randolph opposed the war and told African Americans not to enlist while they were still mistreated at home. He believed that Wilson's call on the nation to support the Allied war effort in order to "make the world safe for democracy" referred implicitly to "white democracy four thousand miles away" and pointed out that African Americans were still "denied economic, political, educational, and civil democracy."[123] Even with the valuable perspective of these wartime critics, it appears that a considerable number of African Americans felt that showing their patriotism by supporting the war would help the fight for African American civil rights.

Another proposal to explain the changes in the social context revolves around the notion that African American enlistment in World War I led to a softening of racial attitudes as a result of the increased interaction of African American and white soldiers. However, the idea that fighting alongside whites humanized African Americans in the white mind is problematic because of the racial segregation of soldiers in the military.[124] The 369th Infantry Regiment (formerly the Fifteenth New York National Guard Regiment) was the first all–African American regiment to serve in the trenches in Europe during World War I. It was assigned to the French and was nicknamed the Harlem Hellfighters because the 369th did not give up any ground during the war, no one was captured, and the men stayed in the trenches for 191 days – longer than any other American unit. The 369th became one of the most decorated regiments

---

[121] W. E. B. Du Bois, "Close Ranks," *The Crisis*, July 1918, NAACP Archives. The "Close Ranks" editorial has created a lot of controversy. For arguments that the editorial represented Du Bois's genuine belief that the war would help to bring about racial progress, see Francis Broderick, *W.E.B. Du Bois: Negro Leader in a Time of Crisis*, Stanford: Stanford University Press, 1959, pp. 108–109; Manning Marable, *W.E.B. Du Bois: Black Radical Democrat*, Boston: Twayne, 1986; David Howard-Pitney, *The Afro-American Jeremiad: Appeals for Justice in America*, Philadelphia: Temple University Press, 1990, pp. 102–103. For argument that "Close Ranks" was a calculated move of accommodation, see William Jordan, "'The Damnable Dilemma': African-American Accommodation and Protest during World War I," *The Journal of American History* 81, no. 4 (1995): 1562–1583. For arguments refuting that it depicted Du Bois's views, see: Mark Ellis, "'Closing Ranks' and 'Seeking Honors': W.E.B. Du Bois in World War I, *The Journal of American History* 79, no. 1 (1992): 96–124; David Levering Lewis, *W.E.B. Du Bois: Biography of a Race, 1868–1919*, New York: H. Holt, 1993, pp. 551–560.

[122] David Levering Lewis, *W.E.B. Du Bois: Biography of a Race, 1868–1919*, New York: H. Holt, 1993, p. 556.

[123] A. Philip Randolph, *The Messenger*, July 1918.

[124] African Americans were completely excluded from the Marines and permitted to serve in the Navy in only a menial capacity.

in France. African American Private Henry Johnson was the first French or American to receive the Croix de Guerre – the highest military honor awarded by the French government. And by the time of war's end, 171 members of the 369th were awarded the Legion of Honor.[125]

Despite the valor of the Harlem Hellfighters, combat regiments of African American soldiers were not the norm, and they certainly did not fight along-side whites. Studies of African American soldiers during World War I reveal an army that was deeply segregated. White officers often insulted them, and the War Department received many complaints that African Americans were "grossly maltreated" and were constantly being called "coons," "niggers," and "darkies."[126] The majority of African American enlistments were trained apart from whites and were placed in all-black army battalions so there was little interaction between white and black soldiers. However, most African American soldiers in the army found themselves in labor or stevedore battalions, under-taking a considerable amount of the grunt work and bringing food supplies to officers in combat.[127] Though many African Americans clamored to be in combat battalions where they could be issued a weapon and fight on the front lines, it was clear to many that the army planned to use African Americans not for their skill and intelligence but for their labor. Therefore, in the army, as elsewhere in American society during the early part of the twentieth cen-tury, African Americans were viewed as second-class citizens. Instead of help-ing to deconstruct this caste system, their time spent in the army during the First World War helped to solidify the notion that African Americans did not deserve to be treated as equal citizens.[128]

Perhaps it wasn't fighting alongside whites that humanized African Americans – a final proposal for how the First World War could have directly influenced Wilson's and Harding's conciliatory approach to the NAACP centers around the idea that African Americans' patriotic service to defend this nation engendered a debt of gratitude among whites and led to a softening of racial attitudes once they returned home. Unfortunately, many in the nation were not thankful to African Americans for their service. Violence in 1919 – the

---

[125] Stephen Harris, *Harlem's Hell Fighters: the African-American 369th Infantry in World War I*, Washington, DC: Brassey's, Inc., 2003; Richard Slotkin, *Lost Battalions: The Great War and the Crisis of American Nationality*, New York: Henry Holt, 2005.

[126] John Hope Franklin, *From Slavery to Freedom: A History of African Americans*, 8th ed., New York: A. A. Knopf, 2000; Raymond Wolters, *Du Bois and His Rivals*, Columbia: University of Missouri Press, 2002, pp. 116, 130; Mary White Ovington, *The Walls Came Tumbling Down*, New York: Harcourt Brace, 1947, p. 136.

[127] Out of the 380,000 African Americans who served during wartime, approximately 200,000 were sent to Europe, and roughly 42,000 saw combat.

[128] Emmett Scott, *Scott's Official History of the American Negro in the World War*, Chicago: Homewood Press, 1919; Robert Mullen, *Blacks in America's Wars; The Shift in Attitudes from the Revolutionary War to Vietnam*, New York: Monad Press, 1973; Arthur Barbeau and Florette Henri, *The Unknown Soldiers: Black American Troops in World War I*, Philadelphia: Temple University Press, 1974.

first year after the armistice – spurned in part by the rebirth of the Ku Klux Klan, dramatically increased against African Americans. The sight of African American soldiers in uniform was a sign of a changing social order – one that southern whites were not ready to accept and would actively resist. At least ten of 1919's lynching victims were of African American veterans.[129] As it turned out, the sacrifice of life abroad was no guarantee that African Americans would be treated as equal citizens at home.

Conclusion: Republican Presidential Retreat

The NAACP's advocacy of the executive branch exhibits an organization that viewed the office of the president as a likely place to initiate change in the federal government in the first quarter of the twentieth century. Though the NAACP did not achieve nearly all that it wanted, this chapter has detailed how the NAACP, faced with considerable obstacles, was able to exert a surprising amount of influence on the actions of the president. The NAACP convinced Presidents Wilson and Harding to do what was seen as impossible at the time: make a statement denouncing lynching. The NAACP's savvy lobbying of President Wilson to address racial violence in Houston and to speak out against lynching was particularly interesting considering Wilson's adamant opposition to African American civil rights. The pressure the NAACP brought to bear on Harding also produced notable gains, as he was quickly won over and stepped out of his zone of comfort to make a statement to Congress.

Of course, the relationship the NAACP forged with Harding was a fragile political alliance that was on the ropes before he passed and ultimately fractured after his death. Since Reconstruction, two factions in the Republican Party – the "black and tans" and the "lily-whites" were waging a war about the future of the Republican Party. The lily-white faction was made up of mostly southern white Republicans "who upheld the idea of white supremacy and the social system of segregation in the South."[130] Lily-whites argued that the party would be better off if it were all white and no longer tried to court African American votes. The black-and-tan faction, in contrast, supported full participation in politics and political equality for African Americans. Black and tans were comprised mostly of African Americans though some state organizations had a number of white members. For many years, the rivalry was played out on the state and national political scene as each group employed different tactics in an attempt to gain recognition by the national Republican Party. The coalition of voters during Harding's election gave notice that the lily-white faction had won: all the border states with the exception of Kentucky (which they lost

---

[129] Arthur Barbeau and Florette Henri, *The Unknown Soldiers: Black American Troops in World War I*, Philadelphia: Temple University Press, 1974, p. 177.

[130] Hanes Walton, *Black Republicans: The Politics of the Black and Tans*, Metuchen, NJ: Scarecrow Press, 1975.

by a fraction of 1 percent of the total vote) went Republican, and the party picked up significant gains in all southern states: Harding was able to secure more than 30 percent of the vote in Alabama, Arkansas, Florida, Louisiana, and Virginia; in North Carolina, he got over 40 percent.[131] Republican Party hopes of a two-party South were kindled.

What this meant in terms of race and electoral politics is that it was not in the best interests of Republicans to reach out to African American voters – they did not need their votes to win elections anymore. As evidenced by the actions of Harding's predecessors, the Republican Party moved further and further away from addressing issues important to the African American community. In the succeeding years, Calvin Coolidge spoke out against lynching, but he made no further attempts to do anything else for African Americans.[132] In particular, parting ways with Harding, Coolidge refused to endorse the anti-lynching bill in Congress. Herbert Hoover was adamant about not making any concessions to African Americans: he was an enthusiastic segregationist in civil service departments, outright ignored repeated requests to make a public statement against lynching, and declined to meet with NAACP representatives in the White House. Relations with Hoover deteriorated so much that Walter White labeled Hoover "the man in the lily-White House," and charged that the president "bluntly refused to receive Negro citizens who wished to lay before him the facts of their steadily worsening plight."[133] Unlike Coolidge and Hoover, Harding often met with African American leaders and directly corresponded with them through letters.

In the first few years of its anti-lynching campaign, the NAACP focused on changing public opinion and on the president of the United States to bring some relief. In large part, we have observed, this was because the president was viewed as a barometer of national public opinion. In a period without a proven strategy to secure racial equality, the NAACP assumed that if it could convince the president of the United States to speak out against lynching, a new norm would be created among a majority of white Americans and the subsequent change in the national conscience of American would result in the end of the horrible spectacle of lynching. Everything did not go according to plan. Of course, this strategy was directly connected to the NAACP's naive campaign against public opinion chronicled in Chapter 2 that was based on the idea that the problem of racial violence was in the "hearts and minds" of Americans. But the conscience of America proved very stubborn, and the struggle was

[131] Robert Sherman, *The Republican Part and Black America: From McKinley to Hoover 1896–1933*, Charlottesville: University Press of Virginia, 1973, p. 142; Richard Scher, *Politics in the New South: Republicanism, Race and Leadership in the Twentieth Century*, New York: Paragon House, 1992, p. 108.

[132] John Blair, "A Time for Parting: The Negro During the Coolidge Years," *Journal of American Studies* 3, no. 2 (1969): 177–200.

[133] Walter White, *A Man Called White, The Autobiography of Walter White*, New York: Viking Press, p. 104.

made more difficult by the reluctant acknowledgement that state and federal institutions protected the perpetrators of lynchings. NAACP leaders realized that in order to create substantive changes, it would be necessary to focus on another branch of government. Indeed, it was around the time of Harding's statement that the NAACP looked to the political landscape and began to petition Congress for an anti-lynching law.

4

Anti-Lynching Legislation and the Sinking
of the Republican Ship in Congress

The passage of the Dyer Anti-Lynching Bill in the House of Representatives this afternoon by a vote of 230 to 119 is one of the most significant steps ever taken in the history of America. For the Negro it means that continual agitation has at least been answered and the appeal of the colored man to Congress for relief from mob violence has at last been granted. The reign of terrorism and anarchy must end is the message to lynchers that Congress has sent.

– James Weldon Johnson[1]

The manner of the defeat of the Dyer Anti-Lynching Bill emphasizes the fact that the machinery of the United States Senate is antiquated to the point that millions of people may suffer injustice and death on account of it.

– W. E. B. Du Bois[2]

On January 26, 1922, the House of Representatives gave African Americans a reason to celebrate in national politics. On this day, hundreds of excited African Americans filled the House of Representatives gallery to watch the floor debate of H.R. 13, a bill mandating the federal government take an active role in preventing lynchings. This was the first piece of legislation African Americans felt they had a hand in crafting, and they were not going to miss out. They watched in rapt attention and cheered as white Republicans articulated the threat lynching posed to African Americans and how it violated their constitutional rights. They booed loudly as white southern Democrats attributed lynchings to rape and argued that lynchings were a matter of states' rights and the federal government should not be involved. When the vote was counted, supporters of African Americans won, and the House of Representatives passed its first-ever

---

[1] "Secretary of Advancement Association Declares Passage of Bill Victory After 11 Years of Effort," press release, January 26, 1922, Anti-Lynching File, NAACP Papers, Manuscript Division, Library of Congress, Washington, DC.
[2] W. E. B. Du Bois, *The Crisis*, January 1923, p. 132.

anti-lynching bill by a two-thirds vote. It was a rare moment in early twentieth century America that demonstrated to African Americans they too, could get their voices heard in the national political process.

The fight to secure passage of the Dyer Anti-Lynching Bill in the House of Representatives needs explanation. In less than nine months, leading Republicans went from being apathetic about anti-lynching legislation to actively advocating on its behalf and defending the necessity for such legislation against a determined coalition of southern Democrats. The Dyer Anti-Lynching Bill of 1922 passed the House of Representatives when all previous attempts had failed. More importantly, many House representatives changed their stance and voted favorably on this bill.

The NAACP's turn to the political arena should not be a surprise. As articulated in *The Crisis*, "The Negro himself has regarded loyalty to the nation and to the Republican Party much as a fish regards the water in which it swims – absolutely essential to his well being."[3] Republicans had been on the side of the war to abolish slavery, they bulldozed through critical Civil War amendments to the constitution extending the voting franchise to African American men, and the party actively supported the period of Reconstruction in the South. Thus, in the complete life cycle of African Americans to that point, the narrative of expanding African American freedom was one in which the Republican Party played the leading role. So when the time came for African Americans to mount an attack against lynching, the likely arena for a victory appeared to be in Congress, where Republicans held majorities in both the House and the Senate.

However, just short of a year after its victory in the House, the tide of enthusiasm the NAACP was riding came crashing down. The Dyer bill was never passed into law. The legislation died on the Senate floor as a coalition of southern Democrats and conservative northern Republicans blocked it. The defeat of the anti-lynching bill was deeply frustrating to the NAACP's leadership, many of whom had devoted all of their energies to working on the bill's passage. In the course of one year, the NAACP felt the joy of victory and the stinging blow of political setback. This campaign marked an important turning point in the NAACP's battle against lynching. The organization was forced to face the harsh reality that despite the federal government's previous support of African American rights, the legislative process would no longer be the most productive venue to pursue an agenda focused on the protection of equal citizenship for African Americans.

Though the NAACP did not accomplish its original goal, the NAACP's campaign for Congress to pass anti-lynching legislation provides a window into the frustrating process of pursuing racial equality through the traditional political process in the early twentieth century. The NAACP's failed struggle was instructive in drawing attention to the difficulties associated with pursuing

---

[3] Gustavus Adolphus Steward, "The Negro's Loyalty," *The Crisis*, April 1923, p. 255.

racial change in Congress. This chapter demonstrates the critical role played by the NAACP in the passage of the Dyer Anti-Lynching Bill in the House; it also describes the heart-wrenching downfall of the bill in the Senate. In the rest of this chapter, I detail the NAACP's victory in House passage at length because it is important to understand how much effort the NAACP put into obtaining a legislative victory. Far from being focused solely on the law from the outset, the NAACP was foremost focused on the legislative arena. At a time when it was uncertain about how to best fight for racial equality, it is clear the NAACP relied predominantly on a victory in Congress to protect the rights of African Americans. If the NAACP was able to win Senate passage of the Dyer Anti-Lynching Bill, the NAACP's historic fight for civil rights would have likely been waged in the legislative arena instead of U.S. courtrooms.

The first section of this chapter will contextualize the NAACP's battle in a history of anti-lynching legislation so the reader understands the obstacles the NAACP faced. The second section will describe the remaking of the NAACP into a national anti-lynching lobbying organization. In the next section, the chapter will describe the pressure the NAACP brought to bear on powerful House representatives. The fourth section of the chapter will provide evidence of the NAACP's influence in House passage of the Dyer Anti-Lynching Bill from the Judiciary Committee to floor debates to the final vote. The fifth section will detail the beginning and end of the anti-lynching bill's life in the Senate.

Barriers to Entry

Since the 1890s, members of Congress had tried, unsuccessfully, to gain the support of the federal government in ending mob violence.[4] In January 1900, Representative George White (R-North Carolina) sponsored the first anti-lynching bill in Congress. In 1901, two Massachusetts Republicans, Representative William Moody and Senator George Hoar, introduced an anti-lynching bill designed by Albert Pillsbury, a former Massachusetts attorney general. In hopes of bolstering the anti-lynching bill, Pillsbury wrote a *Harvard Law Review* article, making a case for the constitutionality of the bill.[5] Though the bill did not make it out of committee, it served as the framework for the anti-lynching bill the NAACP would support two decades later.[6] In 1902, Jacob Gallinger (R-New Hampshire) also failed in his attempt to obtain a Senate inquiry into lynching. In subsequent years, numerous bills focused on obtaining the involvement of the federal government against lynchings and mob violence

---

[4] Senators John Mitchell (R-Oregon), William Peffer (Populist-Kansas), and Henry Dawes (R-Massachusetts) brought petitions from their constituents urging federal action against mobs.
[5] Albert Pillsbury, *A Brief Inquiry Into a Federal Remedy For Lynching*, Harvard Law Review 15, no. 9 (1902): 707–713.
[6] James Weldon Johnson to Albert Pillsbury, letter, December 20, 1919, Anti-Lynching File, NAACP Papers, Manuscript Division, Library of Congress, Washington, DC.

were introduced but not one made it out of committee, let alone to a vote in either the House or the Senate.[7]

The NAACP witnessed firsthand the difficulty in gaining passage of legislation as they lent the support of the organization to different anti-lynching legislation measures between 1918 and 1920. In 1918, Representative Leonidas Dyer (R-Missouri) approached the NAACP for support in sponsoring a bill seeking to make lynching a federal crime.[8] Dyer had reasons to be concerned about issues close to African Americans; he served a congressional district that included many African American survivors from the violent East St. Louis race riot in 1917. In April 1918, Dyer and Merrill Moores (R-Indiana) introduced different anti-lynching bills. Despite the NAACP's belief that anti-lynching legislation was important, former American Bar Association president and current NAACP president Moorfield Storey expressed concerns about the constitutionality of the proposed legislation.[9] Fearing it would be too costly to support these bills, the NAACP sent over lynching pamphlets containing statistics and reports of unjust lynchings conducted by NAACP investigators in lieu of an official endorsement. Subsequently, both bills died in committee, but Dyer reintroduced his bill (H.R. 259) in May 1919 and sponsored a resolution (H.R. 319) for an investigation into race riots and mob violence in October 1919. Majority Whip Charles Curtis (R-Kansas) also introduced a resolution (S.R. 189) in the Senate in September 1919 for an investigation into lynchings.[10]

A lot changed over the course of one year. The downturn in race relations led to a reorientation in the NAACP's strategy. The year 1919 marked a grim time for violence in the United States. Despite the NAACP's progress in awakening the public to the prevalence of racist violence as detailed in Chapter 2, Americans seemed to be in quiet acquiescence as the frequency of lynchings continued to increase. It wasn't long before the senior leadership of the NAACP conceded its efforts in raising public awareness would not be enough to stop some of the worst displays of racial violence in the nation. In the wake of the violence, the NAACP placed renewed attention on the political process, and Johnson went to Washington to meet with Dyer to see how the NAACP could be involved. At this meeting, Dyer revealed to Johnson his belief that the House of Representatives could eventually pass anti-lynching legislation,

---

[7] For more on previous anti-lynching bills, see Robert Zangrando, *The NAACP Crusade Against Lynching, 1909–1950*, Philadelphia: Temple University Press, 1980, pp. 16–17.

[8] Leonidas Dyer to John Shillady, letter, April 6, 1918, NAACP Papers, Manuscript Division, Library of Congress, Washington, DC.

[9] BOD Minutes, May 13, 1918, NAACP Papers, Manuscript Division, Library of Congress, Washington, DC; James Weldon Johnson to Leonidas Dyer, letter, August 5, 1918, NAACP Papers, Manuscript Division, Library of Congress, Washington, DC; James Weldon Johnson to Leonidas Dyer, letter, August 12, 1918, NAACP Papers, Manuscript Division, Library of Congress, Washington, DC.

[10] 66th Congress, 1st Session, Senate Resolution 189, September 22, 1919. In previous years, Senator Curtis had introduced similar bills into the Senate without much success.

but it had to be reported out favorably from committee.[11] Cognizant of the obstacles and confident in the organizational capabilities of the NAACP to overcome them, Johnson pledged his support. The NAACP originally backed both Dyer's and Moore's resolutions for a congressional investigation but after reassessing what would be the most promising opportunity to secure a congressional investigation, the NAACP directed the force of the organization's effort behind Dyer's Anti-Lynching Bill and resolution.[12] To aid passage of the legislation, in October 1919 the NAACP encouraged its members to write their congressmen and a delegation including Johnson, attorney and future NAACP president Arthur Spingarn, and Harvard Law–educated Archibald Grimke of the Washington, DC branch represented the NAACP at House Judiciary Committee hearings on the anti-lynching bill.[13] The NAACP exerted a respectable level of effort, but the organization was just beginning to learn the ropes of lobbying, and the bill never made it out of committee before the last session of Congress.[14]

Despite a pattern of congressional inaction when it came to anti-lynching legislation, the NAACP remained hopeful about the ability of Congress to join the fight against lynching and mob violence. The NAACP reasoned it had yet to put the full weight of the organization behind a bill, and if it did, the NAACP could do what seemed to be impossible at the time: persuade members of Congress to enact anti-lynching legislation into law. With the NAACP firmly committed to do whatever it had to do to pass anti-lynching legislation, Dyer reintroduced his anti-lynching bill on the opening day of the Sixty-Seventh Congress, April 11, 1921. The bill, H.R. 13, was read and assigned to the Committee on the Judiciary. The purpose of the bill, as stated in the first sentence, was "to assure persons within the jurisdiction of any state the equal protection of the laws." To fulfill this goal, the Dyer bill provided, first, for the prosecution of lynchers in federal courts instead of state courts and the protection of prisoners by the federal government when a lynching was threatened; second, a fine of $10,000 for any county where a lynching occurred; and third, the making of a federal offense for any law enforcement official that allowed

[11] James Weldon Johnson, *Along This Way: The Autobiography of James Weldon Johnson*, New York: Viking Press, 1933, p. 362.

[12] Leonidas Dyer to John Shillady, letter, September 26, 1919, Anti-Lynching File; John Shillady to the National Office, letter, October 2, 1919, Anti-Lynching File; Leonidas Dyer to James Weldon Johnson, telegram, October 4, 1919, Anti-Lynching File, NAACP Papers, Manuscript Division, Library of Congress, Washington, DC.

[13] "To Learn the Causes of and Provide a Remedy for Present Race Disturbances," NAACP press release, October 8, 1919, Anti-Lynching File; James Weldon Johnson to Local Branches, letter, October 8, 1919, Anti-Lynching File, NAACP Papers, Manuscript Division, Library of Congress, Washington, DC.

[14] Charles Flint Kellogg, *NAACP: A History of the National Association for the Advancement of Colored People*, Baltimore: Johns Hopkins University Press, 1973, p. 237; Robert Zangrando, *The NAACP Crusade Against Lynching, 1909–1950*, Philadelphia: Temple University Press, 1980.

a person to be taken and lynched by a mob.[15] Essentially, the punishments for lynchings would no longer be left up to state governments; if the bill was passed, the federal government would be forced to play a major role.

The NAACP Develops as Lobbyists

The NAACP was now presented with the daunting challenge of helping to pass legislation that had already been denied multiple times in Congress. In hopes of delivering on this goal, the NAACP quickly devised a strategy focused on bringing pressure on two fronts: interacting directly with congressmen and the bringing of pressure through grassroots organizing. The NAACP would meet directly with influential members of Congress, speak in hearings, involve its larger membership in letter-writing campaigns, provide information to the public, and organize public assemblies, the press, and churches to aid in the passage of the Dyer bill. The method, as described by Johnson, was "tact and diplomacy and firm but friendly pressure."[16] This strategy served the NAACP well up until House passage.

The emergence of the NAACP's aggressive lobbying effort is an important part of understanding why H.R. 13 made it out of the House of Representatives. In the past, there was no significant lobbying campaign on behalf of anti-lynching legislation. Members of Congress were not held accountable; even the few congressmen who were in favor of such legislation did not want to create tension with southern members of Congress. As a result, bills about anti-lynching laws were never reported out of committee; there was always another issue that took precedence. To put it simply, the cost-benefit equation did not add up; there was little value added in pushing anti-lynching legislation in which African Americans were perceived as the primary beneficiaries. The NAACP lobbying effort changed this by constantly reminding congressmen of the prevalence of lynchings and pressure was applied to those who stood in the way of passage. Because of the NAACP, the anti-lynching legislation was no longer dead on arrival. As stated by Johnson, in very little time, "the entire machinery of the Association, its full organized strength and all the collateral force it could marshal, were thrown behind the measure."[17] The NAACP proved to be a determined force that members of Congress would have to contend with.

Another strength of the NAACP was the organization's ability to win the support of influential individuals in American politics. Even before the Dyer Anti-Lynching Bill was introduced in Congress, Storey sought out the advice of

[15] H.R. 13, House of Representatives, 67th Congress, 1st Session, Anti-Lynching File, NAACP Papers, Manuscript Division, Library of Congress, Washington, DC.

[16] James Weldon Johnson to NAACP Executive Committee, confidential memo, January 4, 1922, Special Correspondence File, NAACP Papers, Manuscript Division, Library of Congress, Washington, DC.

[17] James Weldon Johnson, *Along This Way: The Autobiography of James Weldon Johnson*, New York, NY: Viking Press, 1933, p. 362.

George Wickersham, attorney general under President William Howard Taft. Over a friendly exchange of letters, they vetted out probable constitutionality concerns in the anti-lynching bill.[18] Though Wickersham still harbored a number of reservations, he eventually became a strong and vocal supporter of the Dyer bill.[19]

As soon as Dyer introduced his bill, Johnson traveled to Washington and spent most of his time there until the summer recess on August 24, 1921. Johnson met and interviewed leaders in the House of Representatives, giving them information regarding lynching and urging upon them the importance of passing the Dyer Anti-Lynching Bill.[20] In particular, Johnson was in close contact with Dyer, who served on the Judiciary Committee and faced the difficult task of convincing members to report favorably on the bill. Johnson quickly became Dyer's key source of information for the anti-lynching bill. There was a collaborative relationship going on between the two men; when concerns surfaced on the Judiciary Committee, Johnson was prepared with necessary information for Dyer to dispel criticisms. Johnson supplied the Judiciary Committee with lynching statistics, and when they had questions about the constitutionality of the bill, Johnson sent Dyer letters from the exchange between Wickersham and Storey, two of America's most respected legal experts, to provide assurances of its constitutionality.[21] Later, when the constitutionality question became a sticking point for some members on the Judiciary Committee, Johnson contacted a number of prominent lawyers across America and arranged for them to provide Representative Dyer with favorable written statements on the constitutionality of the bill.[22]

To augment the work of Johnson, the NAACP began to assemble its organizational strength behind the bill. On July 7, 1921, a letter was sent out from the national office to all the presidents and secretaries of its branches that had

[18] Moorfield Storey to George Wickersham, letter, January 15, 1921, Anti-Lynching File; George Wickersham to Moorfield Storey, letter, January 20, 1921, Anti-Lynching File; Moorfield Storey to George Wickersham, letter, January 22, 1921, Anti-Lynching File; Moorfield Storey to George Wickersham, letter, March 17, 1921, Anti-Lynching File; George Wickersham to Moorfield Storey, letter, March 18, 1921, Anti-Lynching File, NAACP Papers, Manuscript Division, Library of Congress, Washington, DC.

[19] Walter White to Moorfield Storey, letter, August 1, 1921, Anti-Lynching File, NAACP Archives, Library of Congress; Press Release, March 2, 1922, Anti-Lynching File, NAACP Papers, Manuscript Division, Library of Congress, Washington, DC.

[20] Twelfth Annual Report of the NAACP for the year 1921, January 1922, p. 11, NAACP Papers, Manuscript Division, Library of Congress, Washington, DC.

[21] James Weldon Johnson to Leonidas Dyer, letter, May 18, 1921, Anti-Lynching File; Leonidas Dyer to Walter White, May 20, 1921, Anti-Lynching File; Walter White to James Weldon Johnson, letter, May 23, 1921, Anti-Lynching File, NAACP Papers, Manuscript Division, Library of Congress, Washington, DC.

[22] Leonidas Dyer to James Weldon Johnson, letter, July 7, 1921, Anti-Lynching File; James Weldon Johnson to Leonidas Dyer, letter, July 12, 1921, Anti-Lynching File, NAACP Papers, Manuscript Division, Library of Congress, Washington, DC.

members on the Judiciary Committee. The letter called for support, stating, "We must exert every effort, we must bring every pressure to bear on the Committee to secure a favorable report."[23] The national office of the NAACP delegated to its local branches the tasks of grassroots organizing in their respective geographical areas. The letter listed the name of the congressman and steps the NAACP wanted each local branch to apply in order to have the bill voted favorably out of committee; these included: sending of telegrams and letters endorsing the Dyer Anti-Lynching Bill by churches, lodges, fraternal organizations, women's clubs, and other relevant organizations; sending of telegrams and letters by prominent African Americans; appointment of a committee to interview prominent white people and to appear before white organizations to urge them to endorse the bill; and appointment of a committee to interview local newspaper editors, urging them to write editorials recommending federal action against lynching.[24] The aim was to mobilize the constituents of House representatives to create a groundswell of pressure for political support of the Dyer bill.

Back at the national headquarters in New York, NAACP leadership drew on previous experience in working with the press and organized a publicity campaign to bolster public support for anti-lynching legislation. In correspondence with editors, the NAACP made clear the importance of the press in the passage of legislation: "With the cooperation of colored newspapers and colored citizens all over the country, sufficient pressure can be put upon the House of Representatives, there is more hope than ever before that the bill will be enacted into law." Editors were instructed to urge their readers to apply pressure by sending telegrams to their representatives in Congress. The NAACP also reached out to the white press and asked for support in the form of editorials extolling the Dyer Anti-Lynching Bill.

The NAACP's lobbying efforts produced encouraging results. When Congress reconvened in the fall, the Judiciary Committee finished its work on the Dyer Anti-Lynching Bill and favorably reported it out on October 21, 1921.[25] The influence of the NAACP was prominently displayed in the committee's report, which used statistics and tables from the NAACP publication *Thirty Years of Lynching in the United States 1889–1918*.[26] In addition, the Judiciary Committee copied verbatim half of page 7 of *Thirty Years of Lynching in the United States 1889–1918* in making the case that lynching was

[23] Walter White to the Presidents and Secretaries of the Branches, letter, July 7, 1921, Anti-Lynching File, NAACP Papers, Manuscript Division, Library of Congress, Washington, DC.

[24] Walter White to the Presidents and Secretaries of the Branches, letter, July 7, 1921, Anti-Lynching File, NAACP Papers, Manuscript Division, Library of Congress, Washington, DC.

[25] Leonidas Dyer to James Weldon Johnson, telegram, October 21, 1921, Anti-Lynching File, NAACP Papers, Manuscript Division, Library of Congress, Washington, DC.

[26] 67th Congress, 1st Session, House of Representatives, Report No. 452, October 21, 1921; *Thirty Years of Lynching in the United States, 1889–1918*, New York: National Association for the Advancement of Colored People, April 1919.

a problem for the entire nation to reckon with.[27] The NAACP was elated about its role in helping to move anti-lynching legislation favorably out of committee. However, the NAACP spent very little time celebrating, choosing, instead, to focus its energies on gearing up for the next battle in the House.

On the same day the bill was reported out of the Judiciary Committee, the NAACP redoubled its efforts to pressure Congress: the NAACP wired twenty-seven of its largest branches urging them to flood their representatives in Congress with telegrams asking for immediate passage of the bill.[28] Four NAACP representatives were sent out to different parts of the country to rally nationwide support for the bill. In addition, a letter was sent to every local branch with instructions to take up the following steps to help intensify pressure on House representatives: making slides to be shown in movie houses urging viewers to send letters and telegrams to representatives in Congress, large banners to the same effect to be strung across major streets, fliers printed for general distribution instructing individuals to write their congressmen, public education about the Dyer Anti-Lynching Bill in churches, lodge meetings, and other general assemblies, appointment of special committees to interview the editors of white and colored newspapers in order to secure editorial support for the Dyer Anti-Lynching Bill, and sending a delegate to Washington to interview congressmen from each state and impress upon them the need to pass the Dyer bill.[29]

Dyer Begins to Waver and Johnson Flexes His Lobbying Muscle

While the national office was coordinating the grassroots lobbying, Johnson went to Washington to speak directly with Congressmen. His first stop was Dyer, who appeared, for the first time, cautious about the progress of the bill and told Johnson that a favorable report out of the Judiciary Committee was all that could be accomplished in the current session of Congress. Dyer explained the normal course of the bill would be to have it placed on the calendar and then take chances of having it brought up but that such a course would require upwards to a year. Johnson protested that the NAACP was now exerting a significant amount of pressure that it would likely be unable to duplicate. Johnson believed the time was now to gain passage of the Dyer bill and was not in the mood for any possible setbacks. Though his resolve was flagging, Dyer explained the only way to secure prompt action would be to have the Steering

---

[27] 67th Congress, 1st Session, House of Representatives, Report No. 452, October 21, 1921, p. 4; *Thirty Years of Lynching in the United States, 1889–1918*, New York: National Association for the Advancement of Colored People, April 1919, p. 7.

[28] Twelfth Annual Report of the NAACP for the year 1921, NAACP, January 1922, p. 11, NAACP Papers, Manuscript Division, Library of Congress, Washington, DC.

[29] Walter White to Archibald Grimke, letter, October 21, 1921, Anti-Lynching File; James Weldon Johnson to Branches, letter, October 21, 1921, Anti-Lynching File, NAACP Papers, Manuscript Division, Library of Congress, Washington, DC.

Committee place the bill among other measures to be considered and then to have a special rule made on it by the Committee of Rules. Thus, majorities on both committees would need to be in agreement about passing the bill. Doubtful about this chain of events taking place, Dyer had resigned himself about the success of the bill.[30]

It quickly became evident to Johnson that in order for the Dyer bill to pass the House, the NAACP would have to take the lead in securing support for all aspects of House passage. Dyer cared about the bill, but it was apparent he held the bill at a different level of regard than the NAACP: while the issue was expendable for him, the NAACP believed lynching was the most important issue facing the nation. The stakes were too great, and giving up was not an option. After his meeting with Dyer, Johnson decided to do all he could to individually persuade influential Republican members on the Steering Committee and the Committee on Rules to actively support the bill. His first appointment was with the chairman of the Appropriations Committee, Martin Madden (R-Illinois); the meeting went well, and Madden promised to help Johnson by talking with certain party leaders on the same day. Next, Johnson visited the Speaker of the House, Fredrick Gillet (R-Massachusetts), and the majority leader in the House, Frank Mondell (R-Wyoming). Both men listened intently to Johnson as he spoke about the atrocities facing African Americans surrounding lynching and the need for federal government interception; they were responsive and expressed willingness to support the Dyer bill.[31]

Demonstrative of the importance of Johnson's lobbying efforts was a meeting with Nicholas Longworth (R-Ohio), a member of the Steering Committee. In this meeting, Longworth, unsure of where he stood on the Dyer bill and skeptical about anti-lynching legislation, asked Johnson numerous questions concerning the sentiment of African Americans. At the close of the meeting Johnson won over Longworth, who promised that he would do what he could to encourage the Steering Committee to take up the anti-lynching bill.[32]

On the second day of his trip to Washington, Johnson secured additional guarantees of support. He met with the chairman of the House Committee on Rules, Phillip Campbell (R-Kansas), upon whom Johnson impressed the importance of the Dyer bill. At the end of the meeting, Campbell promised that if application were made to the Rules Committee for a special rule on the anti-lynching bill, it would be voted on. His last meeting of the day was with a member of the Committee on Rules, William Rodenberg (R-Illinois). After a brief conversation in which Johnson brought to bear all the force he could,

[30] James Weldon Johnson, Dyer Anti-Lynching Bill, memo, November 1921, Anti-Lynching File, NAACP Papers, Manuscript Division, Library of Congress, Washington, DC.

[31] James Weldon Johnson, Dyer Anti-Lynching Bill, memo, November 1921, Anti-Lynching File, NAACP Papers, Manuscript Division, Library of Congress, Washington, DC.

[32] James Weldon Johnson, Dyer Anti-Lynching Bill, memo, November 1921, Anti-Lynching File, NAACP Papers, Manuscript Division, Library of Congress, Washington, DC.

Rodenberg told Johnson to relay to Dyer that he would vote for a special rule on the bill. From his meetings with senior leadership in the House, Johnson felt confident the bill would pass if it was brought to a vote in the House of Representatives.[33] Johnson's private meetings with leading Republicans and assurances of support for specific legislation indicated the NAACP's considerable influence and command of respect in the corridors of the nation's capitol.

To be clear, the NAACP did not have to convince every legislator lynching was wrong; most northern Republicans were not in the business of defending lynchings. By 1921, a considerable number of northern Republicans thought lynching a terrible blot on America, but it was a controversial issue that greatly irritated southern Democrats. While many Republicans believed it was morally reprehensible, there were no incentives in taking a stand against it; African Americans, whom lynchings impacted the most, had no real voice in the political process. Lawmakers responded to Johnson because he changed the terrain on which the game was played by giving a voice to African American interests in Congress. Johnson was effectively able to persuade legislators that lynching was a humanitarian issue and that by remaining silent they were complicit in the continuance of lynchings. The atrocities of lynching became harder to ignore with Johnson framing the banning of lynching as a matter of "common justice" and bringing to legislators the pressure of the "dissatisfaction, disappointment, and apprehension with which colored people all over the country" are in over the issue of lynching.[34] It is no surprise the NAACP's slogan in the fight to have the Dyer Anti-Lynching Bill enacted into law by the U.S. Congress was "A Vote Against the Dyer Bill is a Vote For Lynching."[35]

Indeed, the NAACP's lobbying efforts paid off. On October 31, 1921, Dyer, now almost assured of a special rule on his bill, took the floor to move to immediate consideration, in hopes that members of the Rules Committee would stay true to their word to Johnson and grant a special rule. The next day, Dyer sent Johnson a telegram informing him the bill would likely come up in the next ten days in the House and suggesting that Johnson "urge colored people all over the United States to get busy in mass meetings, parades, etc. to focus public sentiment and get favorable action."[36] Dyer's enthusiasm for the bill shifted overnight. However, the only major change that had occurred regarding the Dyer bill between the seven days when Johnson visited him and when he sent the telegram to Johnson was the lobbying effort executed by the NAACP. Dyer was ready to give up on the bill on October 24, 1921; only when Johnson took

---

[33] James Weldon Johnson, Dyer Anti-Lynching Bill, memo, November 1921, Anti-Lynching File, NAACP Papers, Manuscript Division, Library of Congress, Washington, DC.

[34] James Weldon Johnson, Dyer Anti-Lynching Bill, memo, November 1921, Anti-Lynching File, NAACP Papers, Manuscript Division, Library of Congress, Washington, DC.

[35] "A Vote Against the Dyer Bill is a Vote For Lynching," press release, August 17, 1921, Anti-Lynching File, NAACP Papers, Manuscript Division, Library of Congress, Washington, DC.

[36] Leonidas Dyer to James Weldon Johnson, telegram, November 1, 1921, Anti-Lynching File, NAACP Papers, Manuscript Division, Library of Congress, Washington, DC.

it upon himself to speak directly to members of Congress and convince them of the necessity of anti-lynching legislation did the tide begin to turn.

Realizing the success of its grassroots lobbying, the NAACP redoubled its efforts to pressure Congress. The NAACP sent 300 letters to selected members of Congress requesting a definite statement in regard to their position on the Dyer bill. The requests were not ignored, and the NAACP received more than 200 letters in response from House representatives stating their position. The majority of letters contained a statement expressing sympathy and an affirmation of a vote in favor of the Dyer bill. The NAACP sent follow-up letters to representatives who did not respond. This method served as an effective way to let congressmen know they were going to be held accountable by African Americans for their vote on this bill.[37]

Unfortunately, Dyer was not finished vacillating on his support for the bill. The NAACP's excitement began to deflate on November 8, 1921, when Johnson received word that amendments were being offered that "would have the effect of robbing the bill of all effectiveness except in cases where prisoners were taken from officers of the law or out of jail, or prison, and lynched."[38] Johnson was outraged, as the majority of lynchings did not occur in this manner. In a telegram to Dyer, Johnson warned that the amendments would make the bill "valueless" and strongly advised Dyer against accepting them. Dyer responded that he did not think there was any chance of passing it unless amendments were made, as the Steering Committee was unwilling to ask for a rule.[39] Upon receipt of this letter, Johnson decided to return immediately to Washington. On November 14, 1921, Johnson visited Dyer, who appeared extremely anxious to get his bill passed and was willing to accept crippling compromises to do so. Johnson, however, was not prepared to concede any ground as he viewed a compromise on the bill as a compromise on the lives of African Americans. He firmly told Dyer, "It would be better to go down to defeat on a strong bill than to have a weak and worthless measure passed under his name."[40] Exasperated with Dyer, Johnson assumed responsibility for convincing the Steering Committee to pass the anti-lynching bill without any amendments.

It was not uncommon for politicians to make false promises about the guarantees of rights to African Americans. The year was 1921, and African Americans were far from being treated as equal citizens. So when Dyer broke the news to Johnson that Representatives Mondell and Campbell, from whom

---

[37] Twelfth Annual Report of the NAACP for the year 1921, p. 14, NAACP Papers, Manuscript Division, Library of Congress, Washington, DC.

[38] Special Report of the Secretary on Washington Trip, November 1921, Anti-Lynching File, NAACP Papers, Manuscript Division, Library of Congress, Washington, DC.

[39] Leonidas Dyer to James Weldon Johnson, letter, November 12, 1921, Anti-Lynching File, NAACP Papers, Manuscript Division, Library of Congress, Washington, DC.

[40] Special Report of the Secretary on Washington Trip, Anti-Lynching File, NAACP Papers, Manuscript Division, Library of Congress, Washington, DC.

Johnson had previously obtained assurances of support, were now opposing the bill, he was not surprised. Though Johnson felt betrayed, he was still confident they could be convinced through pressure from the NAACP grassroots machine. Johnson quickly sent White a telegram directing him to put immediate pressure on Campbell and "to center greatest individual action possible from various parts of country on Mondell."[41] Later that day, White sent overnight telegrams to nine of the organization's largest branches urging them to pressure Representatives Campbell and Mondell. In addition, White sent a letter to the president of the Kansas NAACP branch instructing its members to send as many telegrams as possible by organizations and individuals to Campbell.[42] Johnson did his part as well; in a strongly worded letter sent to Madden, Campbell, and Rodenberg, he warned that "the colored people are no longer in a temper to be played with" and made clear that "if this Congress fails to take action, on this specific piece of legislation, the colored people of this country will regard it as a betrayal."[43] The results were immediate: three days later when Johnson visited Campbell and Mondell, he reported that both were in favor and the outlook of the bill was bright.[44]

An exchange between Campbell and Walter White provides an interesting window to the effectiveness of the NAACP's grassroots lobbying in bringing pressure to bear on national politicians. When White went to visit Campbell in Washington on November 24, 1921, he found that Campbell was on the floor of the House and sent a card in with a messenger. Campbell rushed out to greet White, warmly clasped his hand and called him "Brother White," an unusually friendly greeting that White had never received before from Campbell. Campbell confided to White that he needed his help to tell the people of America (likely the ones that had been flooding his office with letters) that "instead of being opposed to the Dyer bill he was violently in favor of it."[45] Wary of such proclamations from congressmen, White informed Campbell that his future actions would determine how serious he was about this statement. Writing to an ally who helped organize the sending of telegrams and letters to Campbell, White disclosed, "You can see that we have got him on the anxious seat and I think we can safely count on him working hard for the measure."[46]

---

[41] James Weldon Johnson to Walter White, telegram, November 14, 1921, Anti-Lynching File, NAACP Papers, Manuscript Division, Library of Congress, Washington, DC.

[42] Walter White to Moorfield Storey, memo, November 15, 1921, Anti-Lynching File, NAACP Papers, Manuscript Division, Library of Congress, Washington, DC.

[43] Special Report of the Secretary on Washington Trip, November 1921, Anti-Lynching File; James Weldon Johnson to Philip Campbell, form letter, November 12, 1921, Anti-Lynching File, NAACP Papers, Manuscript Division, Library of Congress, Washington, DC.

[44] James Weldon Johnson to Walter White, telegram, November 15, 1921, Anti-Lynching File, NAACP Papers, Manuscript Division, Library of Congress, Washington, DC.

[45] Walter White to Bishop John Hurst, letter, December 1, 1921, Anti-Lynching File, NAACP Papers, Manuscript Division, Library of Congress, Washington, DC.

[46] Ibid.

The necessary representatives were now lined up on the side of the NAACP. When the House returned from Thanksgiving recess, the Committee on Rules made a special rule on the Dyer bill, bringing it up for debate and designated a vote to be taken on December 15, 1921, right before the holiday recess.[47] Closing in on the finish line, the NAACP still faced the obstacle of ensuring that enough congressmen would be present to vote favorably on the bill. Dyer again requested the NAACP's assistance in shoring up its members to place pressure on their representatives to be present and to vote favorably for the bill.[48]

Understanding the importance of having enthusiastic advocates in the House, the NAACP deployed the full extent of its lobbying arsenal. NAACP headquarters immediately wired thirty of the largest branches located in strategic political centers, sent personal letters containing information regarding the Dyer bill to eighty-four friendly Congressmen, mailed personal letters to twenty-nine ministers in New York asking them to urge their congregations to send telegrams to their representatives, and appealed to African American newspapers to instruct readers to send telegrams to their representatives requesting they be present to vote on the Dyer bill. Two days later, the NAACP distributed informational pamphlets containing statistics about lynching to the most influential Republican representatives to prepare them in the House debate where they were sure to face fierce opposition from southern Democrats.[49] The NAACP received another boost from the white press (*The New York Times*, *New York Tribune*, and *The New York Globe*) in the form of editorials voicing support for the anti-lynching bill. White immediately sent them to Dyer, believing the editorials would be of assistance in demonstrating that national sentiment was in favor of the Dyer bill.[50] At this point, the NAACP was trying to assert maximal pressure to achieve House passage.

The Southern Democrats Counterattack

Johnson left for Washington on December 12, 1921, to lobby leading Republicans before December 15, 1921, when the bill was to be brought up for consideration. During this time, Johnson had daily conferences and kept in close contact with Republican leaders who were responsible for fighting for the bill's passage, including Representatives Campbell, chairman of the Committee

---

[47] Press Release, December 10, 1921, NAACP Papers, Manuscript Division, Library of Congress, Washington, DC.

[48] Leonidas Dyer to James Weldon Johnson, letter, December 10, 1921, Anti-Lynching File, NAACP Papers, Manuscript Division, Library of Congress, Washington, DC.

[49] Representatives Dyer, Campbell, Ansorge, Madden, Fess, Longworth, Towner, Burthern, Mondell, and Rodenberg. Twelfth Annual Report of the NAACP for the year 1921, p. 17, NAACP Papers, Manuscript Division, Library of Congress, Washington, DC.

[50] Walter White to Leonidas Dyer, letter, December 17, 1921, Anti-Lynching File, NAACP Papers, Manuscript Division, Library of Congress, Washington, DC.

on Rules; Mondell, Republican majority leader; Madden, chairman of the Appropriations Committee; Andrew Volstead of Minnesota, chairman of the Judiciary Committee; Theodore Burton of Ohio; Simeon Fess of Ohio; Martin Ansorge of New York; Wells Goodykoontz of West Virginia; Merill Moores of Indiana; and Longworth of Ohio.[51] The Republican leaders expressed weariness about bringing the bill for passage before the holiday recess, owing to the absences of forty Republican members who were on a trip to Panama and another twenty who were attending a funeral in California. This reduced the Republican majority to a narrow margin, and the Republican leaders felt the vote would be too close; they were not assured of victory on the bill. Instead of risking defeat by a close vote, after several conferences, it was decided to have a special rule adopted before the recess and leave the debate and vote on the bill until January 1922.

Staying true to his promise to White, on December 19, 1921, Campbell moved the adoption of the rule. Southerners tried with little success to kill the Dyer bill. Their objections mainly centered on the stereotypes that lynching was a direct response to rape. If African Americans wanted lynchings to stop, they reasoned that African American men should stop raping white women. This conviction was articulated by Representative James Aswell (D-Louisiana) when he alleged, "It is fair to state that thinking men recognize that rape or attempted rape is the primary cause of the mob spirit. Remove this cause and other lynchings will cease also."[52] Southern Democrats viewed the Dyer Anti-Lynching Bill as largely a northern attack on states' rights and vehemently argued that Republicans were misled in their support of this bill; Representative James Byrnes (D-South Carolina) voiced this sentiment when he asserted, "It is the criminal Negro and the agitator of the North and East, both black and white, Negroes and white negroettes that mislead you into grievous error on this sort of ignoble legislation." His statement was followed by applause.[53]

Southern Democrats claimed that their stance was not caused by racism or inherent opposition to African American civil rights but by their belief that the federal government did not have jurisdiction over the matter.[54] In hopes of convincing Republicans that their refusal to accept the Dyer bill was principled and did not stem from racial animosity, southern Democrats invoked the mammy stereotype as proof that they were friends of African Americans. Representative

[51] James Weldon Johnson, memo, Re: The Secretary's Trip to Washington, December 12–21, 1921, Anti-Lynching File, NAACP Papers, Manuscript Division, Library of Congress, Washington, DC.

[52] 67th Congress, 2nd Session, Congressional Record, p. 545, December 19, 1921.

[53] 67th Congress, 2nd Session, Congressional Record, p. 546, December 19, 1921.

[54] Elsewhere scholars such as Lisa Miller have discussed how white supremacy was undoubtedly the driving factor behind the legal arguments about federalism and lynching law; see *The Perils of Federalism: Race, Poverty, and the Politics of Crime Control*, New York: Oxford University Press, 2008.

Edward Pou (D-North Carolina) provides an illustrative example of this kind of patronization when he said on the floor,

> There is one other thing that you men from the North can not comprehend, that ineffable, indescribable, unspeakable love that every southern man feels for the old black nurse who took care of him in childhood. [Applause] The sweetest memories of my life go back to my old "mammy" who faithfully and tenderly took care of my brother and myself during those days ... you gentlemen can not comprehend the love and the tenderness that we feel for those black people who cared for us.[55]

Though it may have been true that southern Democrats cared for African Americans, it was not true that so-called innocent and good-natured African Americans were free from the threat of lynching.

Upon hearing these speeches from southern Democrats, Johnson, listening from the gallery, left and called Dyer to come off the floor. When Dyer came out, Johnson made clear the figures the NAACP had gathered about lynching directly contradicted the rape excuse used by the bill's opponents. He provided Dyer with the necessary statistics to counter the rape charges, and Dyer gave the figures to Campbell, who was scheduled to speak on the House floor later that day.[56]

Armed with lynching statistics from the NAACP, Campbell made clear that lynchings happened to innocent, law-abiding African Americans and therefore represented the most serious infringement on their citizenship. Citing NAACP lynching figures and individual stories of lynchings provided by the NAACP, Campbell rebutted rape statements on the floor and reported that rape was the alleged cause in only nineteen percent of lynching cases.[57] By doing so, Campbell was able to undermine southern Democrats' key argument against passage of the Dyer bill. The influence of the NAACP was obvious in the House debate: many Republican supporters used NAACP statistics, news clippings, and arguments in their speeches on the floor.[58] Southerners deeply opposed the bill and attempted not to participate until the chamber doors were locked by order of the House Speaker Gillet and the arrest of members by the sergeant at arms allowed a quorum to be called. Finally, at 8 p.m. the vote upon the special rule was taken and the rule adopted.

The next day witnessed the same tactics by southern Democrats. When an attempt was made to go into Committee of the Whole for consideration of the Dyer bill, southern Democrats filibustered. Following the tactics of the previous day, the Speaker closed the chamber doors and obtained a quorum, which

[55] 67th Congress, 2nd Session, *Congressional Record*, p. 549, December 19, 1921.

[56] James Weldon Johnson, memo, Re: The Secretary's Trip to Washington, December 12–21, 1921, Anti-Lynching File; Report of the Secretary, Board of Directors Meeting, January 6, 1922, Anti-Lynching File, NAACP Papers, Manuscript Division, Library of Congress, Washington, DC.

[57] James W. Johnson to Walter White, telegram, December 19, 1921, Anti-Lynching File, NAACP Papers, Manuscript Division, Library of Congress, Washington, DC.

[58] 67th Congress, 2nd Session, *Congressional Record*, pp. 541–555, December 19, 1922.

allowed the House to go into Committee of the Whole where the Dyer bill was read. Most of the difficult groundwork was now laid for a vote when the House reconvened in January 1922.

It is worthwhile to note that southern Democrats gave credit to the NAACP numerous times during these two days of debates. Brynes attempted to convince Republicans their support was misguided when he said on the House floor, "The National Association for the Advancement of Colored People who are responsible for the presentation of this bill to the House pleaded with the Republican convention for such a declaration in the platform."[59] Later in the House debate, Aswell called the NAACP's magazine *The Crisis* one of "the worst enemies the Negro race has, these agitators are preaching utterly false and impossible theories which unfortunately are deluding some of our Negro leaders, firing the brain of the ignorant and thus arousing suspicion and unrest."[60] Though these sentiments were centered on undermining the work of the NAACP, they served, instead, to provide insight about the forces at work behind the bill.

Triumph in the House

At the beginning of 1922, the NAACP prepared to make its final push of the Dyer bill in the House. In the December debates, the issue of whether anti-lynching legislation was constitutional surfaced. The opposition argued that lynching was murder and thus was a responsibility of the states because the federal government had no jurisdiction in legislating against state crimes. The NAACP had already expended considerable energy proving the constitutionality of the bill but felt it necessary to draft a letter to their supporters to provide them with more ammunition to rebut the constitutional argument. In the letter, the NAACP made clear that lynching was more than murder:

In lynching a mob sets itself up in place of the State and its actions in place of due process of law to mete out death as punishment to persons accused of crime. It is not only against the act of killing that the Federal Government seeks to exercise its power through the proposed law, but against the act of the mob in arrogating to itself the functions of the State and substituting its actions for the due process of law guaranteed by the Constitution to every person accused of crime. In murder, the murderer merely violates the law of the State. In lynching, the mob arrogates to itself the powers of the State and the functions of government. It apprehends, accuses, tries, condemns and executes by meting out death as the punishment – a very different thing from murder. This bill is aimed against lynching not only as murder but as anarchy-anarchy which the States have proven themselves powerless to cope with.[61]

---

[59] 67th Congress, 2nd Session, Congressional Record, p. 543, December 19, 1921.
[60] 67th Congress, 2nd Session, Congressional Record, p. 546, December 19, 1921.
[61] James Weldon Johnson, form letter, January 2, 1922, Anti-Lynching File, NAACP Papers, Manuscript Division, Library of Congress, Washington, DC.

This articulation confirmed more than any other statement from the NAACP that the battle for the Dyer Anti-Lynching Bill was really a fight about the type of criminal justice system many African Americans confronted in southern states. Lynching persisted, the NAACP maintained, because southern criminal justice systems abdicated power to mobs over the handling of African Americans. Mob rule replaced the justice responsibility of the state. Contrary to the NAACP's perspective that these acts were lawless, the organization knew these acts were not viewed as outside the law in southern states – they often operated as an extension of the law. Corroborating this sentiment were southern Democrats who argued in House debates that lynching was simply murder. Thus, in a sinister, backward way, the law of the South protected lawlessness. The NAACP called this "anarchy" and sought to make clear that lynchings were not only murder; they were outside of the law and in desperate need of federal government intervention. This line of reasoning was particularly useful, and the NAACP's stance came to be adopted by influential Republicans who voiced sentiment along these lines in future House debates.

On January 4, 1922, Dyer made a speech on the House floor, stating that he had taken pains to obtain the best possible information regarding lynchings and revealed,

I have one here prepared by the National Association for the Advancement and Protection of Colored People stating that during the period from 1889 up until December, 1919, there were 3,434 known lynchings in the United States. Of that number 570 have been charged with rape or attempted rape – 570 out of 3,434.[62]

In utilizing NAACP statistics on the House floor in support of the anti-lynching bill, Dyer, once again, displayed the prominence of the NAACP's work on this bill. He also cited numerous stories from the NAACP's report *Thirty Years of Lynching in the United States* to demystify the notion that lynchings were motivated by rape.[63] In yet another nod to the NAACP, Dyer quoted verbatim Storey's argument that the bill was constitutional under the Fifth and the Fourteenth Amendments of the Constitution.[64]

Johnson spent most of January 1922 in Washington meeting with Republican leaders and working with them on the strategy they would pursue to secure passage of the Dyer bill.[65] Despite all of their previous lobbying in 1921, victory on the Dyer bill was not a forgone conclusion. Johnson returned to a very hostile Washington. Over the winter recess, southern Democrats had carefully organized opposition to the bill, and northern Democrats no longer seemed anxious

---

[62] 67th Congress, 3rd Session, *Congressional Record*, p. 787, January 4, 1922.
[63] 67th Congress, 3rd Session, *Congressional Record*, pp. 787–790, January 4, 1922.
[64] 67th Congress, 3rd Session, *Congressional Record*, p. 796, January 4, 1922; "Representative Dyer Speaks on Anti-Lynching Bill," press release, January 13, 1922, Anti-Lynching File, NAACP Papers, Manuscript Division, Library of Congress, Washington, DC.
[65] James Weldon Johnson to Walter White, letter, January 6, 1922, Special Correspondence File, NAACP Papers, Manuscript Division, Library of Congress, Washington, DC.

to pass the bill.[66] There was talk of the precedence of the appropriations bill and that the Dyer bill might not make it up to a vote before June. Johnson had met numerous times with Representatives Mondell and Campbell at the beginning of January as they appeared ready to waffle again and left Johnson with the impression "the Republicans were only fooling" and on January 3, 1922, the day Congress reconvened, Johnson had three conferences with Madden. After more meetings, Johnson reported to the NAACP executive committee that he had pressured Mondell to narrow his estimate of time for final action on the bill to two weeks and that in another meeting, Mondell promised that he would attempt to get another special rule setting a date for a vote on the Dyer bill. These assurances were more promising than previous estimates, but Johnson was still weary, writing about the experience, "Of course, I shall keep up my efforts to hold the leaders' feet to the fire."[67]

Johnson stayed true to his word, and everything appeared to be moving in the right direction up until January 25, 1922, when the House went into its final debate on the Dyer bill. African Americans, excited that Congress was deciding upon an issue central to their lives, packed out the galleries. More than 500 African Americans came to watch the House debates.[68] The House fight was contentious as southern Democrats realized they were close to defeat. Using similar arguments in the past, they argued that the Dyer bill was unconstitutional and "a blow at the white people of the South – nothing more and nothing less."[69] However, in a revealing moment, Representative Thomas Sisson (D-Mississippi) gave indication that the fight was still really about racism and the unwillingness of many national politicians to confer equal protection of the law upon African Americans:

The white men of the South are ready for the sacrifice of life itself, if need be, to protect their fair women. Our wives, sisters, and daughters shall be protected from the lust and passion of these black brutes. Before God and high heaven this is the sacred truth. I would rather the whole black race of this world were lynched than for one of the fair daughters of the South to be ravished and torn by one of these black brutes.[70]

It was a comment that prompted Representative Henry Allen Cooper (R-Wisconsin) to announce, "It is the first time that I have heard mob law openly advocated in the Congress of the United States."[71] At this, African Americans in the galleries erupted in applause and shouts. Advocates of the Dyer bill were

[66] Report of the Secretary, Board of Directors Meeting, January 6, 1922, Anti-Lynching File, NAACP Papers, Manuscript Division, Library of Congress, Washington, DC.

[67] James Weldon Johnson to NAACP Executive Committee, confidential memo, January 4, 1922, Special Correspondence File, NAACP Papers, Manuscript Division, Library of Congress, Washington, DC.

[68] James Weldon Johnson to Walter White, telegram, January 25, 1922, Anti-Lynching File, NAACP Papers, Manuscript Division, Library of Congress, Washington, DC.

[69] 67th Congress, 3rd Session, Congressional Record, p. 1703, January 25, 1922.

[70] 67th Congress, 3rd Session, Congressional Record, p. 1721, January 25, 1922.

[71] Ibid.

prepared with arguments, facts, and articles that were supplied to them by the NAACP and effectively countered the claims made by the bill's opponents. Most obvious was Mondell, who used, almost verbatim, the NAACP's argument about the constitutionality of the Dyer bill when he spoke on the House floor: "Mob violence is anarchy; it is anarchy in its most vicious and repulsive form.... It is in my opinion high time that the Federal Government assert its authority, the States having failed to assert theirs."[72] Calling out the NAACP by name, Representative William Driver (D-Arkansas) responded:

This is the stuff which your type of Negro offers his race, and with which the National Association for the Advancement of Colored People and other kindred organizations are circulating over the country, breeding discontent and inviting enough serious trouble.[73]

Anthony Griffin (D-New York) who had lived in the South, made an admission on the floor that was evident of the NAACP's efforts to reach across party lines. He admonished his fellow Democrats, stating, "It is a fatal error on the part of my colleagues on this side of the aisle to take a stand in opposition to this measure."[74] And he went on to use the NAACP's argument about constitutionality of the bill when he made clear, "Lynching is not murder. It may involve murder, but it is more than murder. It is defiance of the law."[75]

The bitter debate lasted fourteen hours, and on January 26, 1922, by a vote of 230 to 119, with only seventeen Republicans opposing and eight northern or border-state Democrats in support, the House made history and passed the Dyer Anti-Lynching Bill. Acknowledging the vital role the NAACP played in keeping the bill alive, Dyer sent Johnson a note and congratulated the NAACP on its work in gaining House passage.[76] In a press release, the NAACP gave credit to the grassroots mobilization and thanked its 400 branches, churches, clubs, and fraternal organizations for working on behalf of the Dyer bill. The NAACP ended the press release with the optimistic assessment, "The passage of the Dyer bill in the House of Representatives conclusively demonstrates that order-loving citizens of the United States can get what they want if they organize for it."[77] The NAACP was justifiably elated and hopeful the federal government would help to eliminate lynching and mob violence.

---

[72] See 67th Congress, 3rd Session, Congressional Record, p. 1700, January 25, 1922; James Weldon Johnson, form letter, January 2, 1922, Anti-Lynching File, NAACP Papers, Manuscript Division, Library of Congress, Washington, DC.

[73] 67th Congress, 3rd Session, Congressional Record, p. 1706, January 25, 1922.

[74] 67th Congress, 3rd Session, Congressional Record, p. 1716, January 25, 1922.

[75] 67th Congress, 3rd Session, Congressional Record, p. 1718, January 25, 1922.

[76] Leonidas Dyer to James Weldon Johnson, letter, January 28, 1922, Anti-Lynching File, NAACP Papers, Manuscript Division, Library of Congress, Washington, DC.

[77] James Weldon Johnson, Dyer Bill Passed by House, January 27, 1922, Anti-Lynching File, NAACP Papers, Manuscript Division, Library of Congress, Washington, DC.

Disillusionment in the Senate

The very next day, the anti-lynching bill was read and referred to the Committee on the Judiciary in the Senate on January 27, 1922. The NAACP began working immediately to apply pressure on the Judiciary Committee to report favorably on the bill.[78] As the NAACP saw it, "If the Judiciary Committee reports the Dyer Bill, its enactment by the senate is almost certain."[79] Dyer added his confident belief that "there is a better chance for success in the Senate in this respect than there was in the House, due to the fact that the rules of the Senate allow unlimited debate."[80] Similar to its strategy in the House, the NAACP focused on direct and grassroots lobbying in the Senate. NAACP leadership played an active role: Storey wrote letters, Johnson visited and personally lobbied senators, and the *Thirty Years of Lynching* pamphlet was mailed to all Republican and northern Democrat senators. In addition, organizing the NAACP's membership in contacting senators was viewed as critical to increasing the Dyer bill's chances of being passed in the Senate. To this end, the NAACP sent a letter detailing a plan of coordinated attack to branches in states from which members on the Judiciary Committee represented. Intensifying the push from NAACP branches, Johnson wrote directly to members on the Judiciary Committee requesting early and favorable action on the bill.[81]

However, the NAACP did not center all of its efforts on the Judiciary Committee – it endeavored to impact the general feeling of the Senate so that members on the Judiciary Committee would feel the urgency to report favorably on the anti-lynching bill from their Senate colleagues. To engineer this public-opinion shift in the Senate, the NAACP listed twenty-four Republican senators "from those states who are friendly toward colored people"[82] and instructed branches in these states to bring all pressure they could to influence their senator. Specifically, the national office of the NAACP instructed each branch to organize an expansive letter-writing campaign composed of ordinary citizens, influential members of society (both white and African American), churches, and fraternal organizations. In addition, the NAACP urged branches

---

[78] Secretary Report, March 1922, Anti-Lynching File, NAACP Papers, Manuscript Division, Library of Congress, Washington, DC.; James Weldon Johnson to Moorfield Storey, letter, February 4, 1922. Moorfield Storey Papers, Manuscript Division, Library of Congress, Washington, DC.

[79] NAACP Branch Letter, February 1, 1922, Anti-Lynching File, NAACP Papers, Manuscript Division, Library of Congress, Washington, DC.

[80] Leonidas Dyer to Moorfield Storey, letter, February 1, 1922, NAACP Papers, Manuscript Division, Library of Congress, Washington, DC. Dyer was optimistic in his assumption that unlimited debate in the Senate would provide for a full discussion of the present state of African Americans and allow NAACP supporters in the Senate a better chance to relay this sentiment than they did in the House.

[81] Secretary Report, February 1922, Anti-Lynching File, NAACP Papers, Manuscript Division, Library of Congress, Washington, DC.

[82] NAACP timeline of Dyer Anti-Lynching Bill, p. 2. Anti-Lynching File, NAACP Papers, Manuscript Division, Library of Congress, Washington, DC.

to secure letters from state, county, and municipal officials. Referring to branch organizing as part of the NAACP's "organizational machine," the NAACP depended greatly on the mass of white and African American citizens that supported its efforts.[83] On February 3, 1922, the NAACP was earnestly reporting, "The machinery of our whole organization has already been put in motion and it will not be long before telegrams and letters will be going in to members of the Senate Committee on the Judiciary and senators at large, from organizations and individuals all over the country."[84] The response from the NAACP's lobbying was prompt. By February 21, 1922, five of the twenty-four senators who the NAACP previously identified in the memo to their branches sent in letters pledging their full support for the Dyer Anti-Lynching Bill: majority leader Henry Cabot Lodge (R-Massachusetts), James Watson (R-Indiana), Howard Sutherland (R-West Virginia), William Calder (R-New York), and George Moses (R-New Hampshire). Senator Lodge wrote assuredly, "I have always been in favor of doing everything possible to put an end to the lawless and hideous business of lynching and expect of course to support the anti-lynching bill when it comes before the Senate." Senator Sutherland affirmed this sentiment, writing, "I expect to support this measure as I am sure all law-abiding citizens want to abolish lynching crimes in this country."[85] But it is a subsequent letter from Representative Dyer that best helps to explain why some senators seemed so eager to respond to the NAACP; he wrote Johnson, "I feel that the Republican Party is under the deepest possible obligation to the people that this legislation be enacted into a law during this Congress."[86] Seeking to capitalize on this sentiment, the NAACP looked for other ways to expand support for the anti-lynching bill.

At the national level, the NAACP put in motion plans for a mass town hall meeting to be held in New York on March 1, 1922.[87] It was resolved that a memorial would be adopted, signed by influential people, and sent to the Senate urging immediate passage of the Dyer bill.[88] The meeting attracted a lot of positive attention and shined a spotlight on the legislation in the Senate. Johnson, Wickersham, Senator Calder, and Representative Dyer addressed the crowd. The memorial was signed by 300 prominent Americans, including

[83] James Weldon Johnson to Branch Secretary, letter, February 8, 1922, Anti-Lynching File, NAACP Papers, Manuscript Division, Library of Congress, Washington, DC.

[84] James Weldon Johnson to Leonidas Dyer, letter, February 3, 1922, Anti-Lynching File, NAACP Papers, Manuscript Division, Library of Congress, Washington, DC.

[85] "Senators Lodge, Calder, Moses, Sutherland, and Watson, Will Support Dyer Bill," February 2, 1922, Anti-Lynching File, NAACP Papers, Manuscript Division, Library of Congress, Washington, DC.

[86] Dyer to Johnson, letter, March 3, 1922. Anti-Lynching File, NAACP Papers, Manuscript Division, Library of Congress, Washington, DC.

[87] James Weldon Johnson to Leonidas Dyer, letter, February 3, 1922, Anti-Lynching File, NAACP Papers, Manuscript Division, Library of Congress, Washington, DC.

[88] Press Release, February 8, 1922, Anti-Lynching File, NAACP Papers, Manuscript Division, Library of Congress, Washington, DC.

two previous United States attorney generals, twenty-five state governors, thirty-eight mayors of large cities, college presidents, archbishops, and editors of major newspapers.[89] Through this memorial, the NAACP endeavored to send a message to the Senate that it was not only African Americans who had a vested interest in this legislation but also influential white men and women in American society. On May 6, 1922, Senate Majority Leader Lodge presented the petition to the U.S. Senate, and the text was printed in the record. The memorial impressed many senators, one of them remarking that to his knowledge, it was the most imposing petition ever presented to Congress.[90]

In addition to the direct and grassroots lobbying, the NAACP reached out to African American newspapers to aid in the effort to pass the anti-lynching bill. In a letter to editors of African American newspapers, Johnson spent two pages explaining the precarious state of the bill in the Judiciary Committee and the need for pressure to encourage passage. Johnson ended his letter with the charge,

No one can do more than the colored editors of the country to drive these facts home to the men in the Senate.... May I suggest that you write as strong an editorial as possible placing these facts before both your readers and the senators from your state?[91]

The NAACP's branches were not in every city, but African American newspapers were in many small towns and big cities in the country and served as one of the most effective mediums to get the word out and to raise the salience of certain issues.

Nevertheless, this effort was not enough to quiet concerns about the bill's constitutionality. In the first week of March 1922, the bill was assigned to a subcommittee composed of two Democrats and three Republicans. William Borah (R-Idaho) was the chairman of the Judiciary Committee, and the NAACP was an early fan of Borah, its members believing they could win him over. However, Borah provided the main pushback, as he was concerned about the constitutionality of the bill. Unconvinced by the NAACP's small army of constitutional scholars and supporting letters vouching that the bill was constitutional, Borah wanted more time to review the bill. The NAACP, however, had different plans. Growing impatient with Borah's increasing demands and eager to move the bill through the Senate, the NAACP attempted to bypass the subcommittee. In May 1922, when the subcommittee had yet to report on the bill, Johnson traveled to the District of Columbia for a nine-day trip to meet with members of Congress. He had private meetings with eleven senators in which he appealed to them on moral ground about the necessity to

[89] Press Release, March 2, 1922, Anti-Lynching File; Press Release, May 5, 1922, Anti-Lynching File, NAACP Papers, Manuscript Division, Library of Congress, Washington, DC.

[90] BOD Minutes, May 8, 1922, Anti-Lynching File, NAACP Papers, Manuscript Division, Library of Congress, Washington, DC.

[91] James Weldon Johnson to Editor, letter, March 23, 1922, Anti-Lynching File, NAACP Papers, Manuscript Division, Library of Congress, Washington, DC.

pass anti-lynching legislation and warned senators that chaotic racial violence would ensue if the bill was not passed into law. Johnson desired for these senators to use their influence on the subcommittee to report the bill out. Johnson also consulted with Lodge about the importance of securing a favorable report from the subcommittee. As the senior Republican in the Senate, Lodge applied pressure to Borah who was none too happy. Concerned about lynching but feeling that his concerns about the bill's constitutionality were not yet adequately addressed, Borah sided with the two Democrats in the subcommittee, breaking rank with the two Republican senators. The bill was reported out on May 22, 1922 to the whole committee with three opposing and two in favor.

Upon finding out the vote count from the subcommittee, Johnson went into damage-control mode. He met with John Adams, chairman of the Republican National Committee, to request his intervention and impressed upon him that an unfavorable report by the committee would be followed by three disastrous conditions: (1) a deplorable psychological effect upon the colored people of the United States growing out of a realization that the federal government had admitted its powerlessness, (2) mobs would feel like they had license to kill, and there would follow a reign of lynching terror too horrible to contemplate, and (3) the political effect of further alienating colored voters from the Republican Party.[92] Chairman Adams assured Johnson that he would immediately contact influential senators to apply pressure to members sitting on the Judiciary Committee. Calder, one of the senators with whom Johnson had previously met, labored behind the scenes and was credited with doing "a great amount of work in bringing about the changed attitude on the part of the Committee which was finally arrived at." The additional commitment of Chairman Adams and Senator Calder was substantial. When Johnson left Washington on May 26, 1922, he reported the bill was in good shape and encouraged the national office of the NAACP and its branches to bring pressure to not only senators on the Judiciary Committee but the whole Senate.

Once again, the NAACP's lobbying strategy produced encouraging results; on June 30, 1922, the Judiciary Committee met and reported the bill favorably to the Senate by a vote of eight to six.[93] Senator Shortridge (R-California) wrote the committee report and was designated to lead the fight on the floor for passage of the bill. Calling Shortridge "a brave fighter," the NAACP was excited to have him lead the charge for passage of the anti-lynching bill. In particular, unlike many other senators, Shortridge had no reservations about the bill's constitutionality and according to Johnson, "never hesitated to meet the stock arguments of the southern members of the Committee with a frontal attack

---

[92] Secretary Report, June 1922, Anti-Lynching File, NAACP Papers, Manuscript Division, Library of Congress, Washington, DC.

[93] U.S. Congress, Senate, Committee on the Judiciary, Report to Accompany H.R. 13, Senate Report No. 837, 67th Congress, 2nd Session.

and demolish them."[94] Immediately after the committee reported the bill out, Johnson went to meet with Shortridge again and determined that he "looks forward with great satisfaction to championing this measure on the floor of the Senate." The NAACP felt good about the progress of the bill, concluding, "With a favorable report on the Bill, the most difficult part of the work for its final enactment by the Senate has been accomplished." Thus, the NAACP began the last stage of Senate passage in hopeful spirits.

The NAACP never expected the fight on the floor of the Senate to be an easy one, but it never imagined that victory would be impossible. On August 30, 1922, the Senate Steering Committee met and placed the Dyer Anti-Lynching Bill on the program for consideration. In September, every attempt to bring the anti-lynching bill to the floor for discussion was thwarted by Democrats. The Senate adjourned on November 20, 1922, but President Harding called for a special session of Congress.[95] The special session lasted from November 20, 1922, until December 4, 1922. On November 27, another attempt was made to bring the bill to the floor, but Democrats, intent on filibustering the bill, outmaneuvered the bill's Republican supporters. During the second week of the special session of Congress, Senator Oscar Underwood (D-Alabama) announced in the Senate that the Democrats proposed "to talk the Dyer Bill to death, even preventing its coming to a vote, and threatened that the entire business of the United States would be held up in the Senate by Southern Democrats unless the Dyer Anti-Lynching Bill were given up by the Republicans."[96] In response to southern interference, the national office of the NAACP redoubled its efforts and directed members to flood Lodge's office with telegrams, contacted branches in eighteen states that had senators deemed important to influence, and encouraged Republicans to stand firm in their support of the anti-lynching bill. Even as late as December 1, 1922, the NAACP remained optimistic about a positive outcome; Walter White wrote, "The situation does look dark but not hopeless from this angle."[97]

The next day, the NAACP's drive to pass a law against lynching and mob violence abruptly ended. On December 2, 1922, a Republican caucus was convened and voted to abandon the anti-lynching bill. Concerned the Democrat filibuster on the anti-lynching bill would prevent the Senate from addressing other important measures on the legislative agenda, the

[94] Secretary Report, July 1922, Anti-Lynching File, NAACP Papers, Manuscript Division, Library of Congress, Washington, DC.

[95] In the aftermath of the November election, a few Republicans lost their seats. Interested in pushing his policy agenda through Congress, President Harding wanted to see what he could get from a lame duck legislature and called for a special session.

[96] "Dyer Bill Made Biggest Issue in U.S. Senate Since Force Bill," press release, December 1, 1922, Anti-Lynching File, NAACP Papers, Manuscript Division, Library of Congress, Washington, DC.

[97] Walter White to James Weldon Johnson, letter, December 1, 1922, Anti-Lynching File, NAACP Papers, Manuscript Division, Library of Congress, Washington, DC.

Republicans determined it was not worth the fight. On December 4, 1922, Lodge conceded on the Senate floor to Underwood, who was leading the filibuster.[98]

The NAACP was understandably furious. NAACP leaders had devoted the majority of the organization's resources over the previous two years to passage of an anti-lynching bill in Congress. Feeling Senate Republicans had abandoned the anti-lynching bill with very little fight, Johnson fired off angry telegrams to Republican leaders and President Harding, admonishing them for not doing more to pass the bill. A few days later, the NAACP attempted to place the blame for mob violence on the cowardice of the Senate. In an open letter addressed to every senator, Johnson penned:

Every United States senator knows that in failing to stand firm for federal protection and guarantee of trial by law to United States citizens within their own country he was acquiescing in the continuing and increasing brutal rule of the mob in America.[99]

With Lodge conceding to Underhill on the floor, the bill was effectively off the table to be considered for the Sixty-Seventh Congress, and in order to be brought up again in the Sixty-Eighth Congress, it would have to go through the same long, grueling battle in the House and the Senate.

Republican senators saw it differently: they viewed the defeat of the anti-lynching as a product of institutional rules in the Senate that made it easy for a minority to prevent business from being conducted in the Senate, and they attempted to relay this sentiment to the NAACP. As far as Republican supporters of the bill were concerned, it was not their ambivalence but the structure of the Senate that forced their hand. Sharing this perspective, Senator George Norris (R-Nebraska) wrote Johnson:

I was in favor of the Dyer Bill and did all that I could to secure its passage. Under the rules of the senate, this was impossible. At the time, let me say that I am in favor of amending the rules of the senate as I do not believe it is possible to pass the Dyer Bill or any Bill of the same nature under our present rules. The South was so bitterly opposed to this bill that they would have tied up all legislation for months before they would have permitted it to pass.[100]

In response to a telegram from Johnson pleading for action, George Christian, secretary to President Harding, wrote Johnson soon after the bill's defeat,

I also feel that our colored citizens will justly place the responsibility for this where it belongs, to wit, upon the Democratic minority whose filibustering under the existing Senate rules would not only prevent the passing of the Anti-Lynching bill but in so

---

[98] 67th Congress, 3rd Session, Congressional Record, Vol. 63, Pt. 1, pp. 288–450.
[99] James Weldon Johnson, Open Letter to Every Senator of the United States, December 13, 1922, NAACP Papers, Manuscript Division, Library of Congress, Washington, DC.
[100] George Norris to James Weldon Johnson, letter, December 15, 1922, Anti-Lynching File, NAACP Papers, Library of Congress, Manuscript Division, Washington DC.

doing defeat the entire legislative program for the session, appropriation bills included, to the benefit of no one but to the detriment of the entire country.[101]

In retrospect, the NAACP appears to be partially correct that the Republicans conceded too easily and could have made more of a push, but in looking back it also appears likely that the institutional design of the Senate, which allows the minority party to exert a considerable amount of power, would have stayed true to its promise and held up all business in the Senate.

The NAACP's drive for an anti-lynching bill speaks volumes about the limits confronting marginalized groups in the American political system in the first half of the twentieth century. There were institutional barriers the NAACP could not surmount. For example, V. O. Key demonstrated that southern Congressmen exhibited little uniformity in their voting behavior, except when it came to race issues.[102] Just as lynchings unified southern whites, race legislation was the one area that unified southern legislators. Thus, it should be little surprise that civil rights legislation served as a catalyst for numerous southern filibusters in the first half of the twentieth century. Tyranny of the minority existed in the area of American race relations; from Reconstruction until 1957, Congress failed to enact one piece of civil rights legislation. The institutional rules of the Senate made it next to impossible for the NAACP to prevail against southern opposition.

However, the NAACP did not view the defeat of the Dyer Anti-Lynching Bill as a complete failure for two important reasons. First, the NAACP's fight for anti-lynching legislation politicized the issue in an unprecedented manner. Writing about the Dyer Anti-Lynching Bill a month after defeat, Du Bois proudly acknowledged this:

Never before in the history of the United States has the Negro population worked more wholeheartedly and intelligently and efficiently toward one end. They made the Republican party do what the Republicans did not, and do not intend to do. They pushed to the forefront a demand for protective legislation, instead of a demand for petty office. They refused to be beguiled by promises and hand-shakes. They said with unusual unanimity that the Anti-Lynching Bill was the price of their political support. All this is a tremendous gain.[103]

The fight for an anti-lynching bill helped to move the issue of racist lynching and mob violence from the periphery of the political debate to the center. In an address at the National NAACP Convention exactly one month after the Republicans convened and decided to give up on pushing the bill, Johnson announced,

<hr>

[101] George B. Christian, Jr. to James Weldon Johnson, letter, December 8, 1922, Anti-Lynching File, NAACP Papers, Manuscript Division, Library of Congress, Washington, DC.
[102] V. O. Key, *Southern Politics in State and Nation*, New York: Vintage Books, 1949.
[103] W. E. B. Du Bois, *The Crisis*, 25, no. 3, January 1923, p. 104.

The Bill has been abandoned.... Nevertheless, the fight for the Dyer Bill was not a defeat; it was not a loss; a great deal has been accomplished. By putting that Bill into Congress and uniting as we did behind it, the preliminary work we have been doing all of these years was spread out before the whole nation. By the fight for the Dyer Anti-Lynching Bill we made lynching a national issue and we have made it also, what is more important, a great political issue. That was accomplishing a great deal.

Second, the fight increased the NAACP's membership base and showed people throughout the nation the possibilities of sustained protest. In particular, the House passage made clear that power in American politics was not always static and could be contested by people on the margins. Johnson continued in his address:

The Bill was brought to this final issue and even though it failed to pass, nevertheless, it was well worth the effort, because for once the colored people have shown and demonstrated a power which they did not before realize, and not only the colored people, but they have brought to their support and in cooperation with them white people who would not have otherwise been attracted.[104]

Though the NAACP was unable to gain passage of the anti-lynching legislation in Congress, it was able to utilize this experience as an effective way to educate the public and politicians about the necessity of reform and at the same time grow its membership. The NAACP rightfully saw these as benefits of the struggle to pass the Dyer Anti-Lynching Bill in Congress.

Conclusion: The Republican Ship Sinks

The Republican Party is the ship; all else is the sea.

– *Frederick Douglass*[105]

The struggle for federal anti-lynching legislation is perhaps one of the most courageous and lesser-known chapters in the NAACP's history. It is impossible to explain the arc of the NAACP's civil rights strategy without reckoning with the tremendous role the NAACP played in working for anti-lynching legislation. Recognizing the extent with which it presumed a victory could be had in Congress is critical in understanding the impact of this defeat on the trajectory of the organization's strategic agenda. The reality that the Republican Party was not going to defend the basic protections of African Americans against racist mob violence sent the NAACP reeling. After the anti-lynching bill was

---

[104] James Weldon Johnson, Address, Annual Meeting of the National Association for the Advancement of Colored People on January 2, 1923, Part 16. Similar sentiment was expressed in a letter from Johnson to Spingarn, December 15, 1922, Series I: C, Box 66, NAACP Papers, Manuscript Division, Library of Congress, Washington, DC.

[105] Booker T. Washington, *Frederick Douglass*, Philadelphia: G. W. Jacobs and Company, 1907, p. 286; James McPherson, "Grant or Greeley? The Abolitionist Dilemma and the Election of 1872," *The American Historical Review*. 71, no. 1 (1965): 50.

abandoned, Johnson released a statement that relayed this disappointment: "The southern Democrats roared like a lion and the Republicans lay down like a scared possum."[106] The defeat of the Dyer Anti-Lynching Bill was a tremendous wake-up call to the NAACP and its supporters that the Republican ship was not going to sail them to victory. In the meantime, they would have to find another vessel.

At this point, the NAACP made a tactical decision about how it would continue to fight mob violence in America, not by choice but out of necessity. From this battle the NAACP learned the U.S. Congress was not going to be the main battleground; it would need to look elsewhere. Johnson alludes to this near the end of his address: "Of course, we are not going to give up the fight. We have just begun to fight. Yet, we must fight along several lines."[107] Indeed, the expansion of the fight to end lynching into different arenas was the most valuable lesson learned. After this battle, the NAACP did not completely abandon the hope of securing federal legislation against lynching but its perspective changed. The defeat in the Senate came three months before the Supreme Court decision in *Moore v. Dempsey* was handed down. Faced with a frustrating loss in Congress and an enormous win in the Supreme Court concerning the similar issue of mob violence, the NAACP decided to focus much more of the organization's resources on litigation in the future.

Despite the NAACP's not securing passage of the Dyer bill, the organization was successful in changing the way national politicians thought about the responsibility of the federal government to protect African Americans from lynchings and mob violence. In this era of American politics, many congressmen did not independently realize the error of their ways – even when confronted with horrible civil rights injustices. It took a large-scale lobbying effort and a full educational campaign from the NAACP for the climate in Congress to shift regarding the acceptability of mob violence. Though unintentional, the NAACP's efforts in gaining the support of members of Congress is an important part of understanding why the Supreme Court ultimately decided in the NAACP's favor in *Moore v. Dempsey*. It wasn't just that the NAACP had mounted an effective legal defense as will be detailed in Chapter 5 – it was also that the surrounding political context was transformed.

[106] "Statement Re: Political Reaction of Colored People on Abandonment of Dyer Anti-Lynching Bill," Series I: C, Box 66, NAACP Papers, Manuscript Division, Library of Congress, Washington, DC.

[107] James Weldon Johnson, Address, Annual Meeting of the National Association for the Advancement of Colored People on January 2, 1923, Part 16, NAACP Papers, Manuscript Division, Library of Congress, Washington, DC.

5

Defending the Right to Live

The states are indifferent or helpless, so that federal action is necessary to protect the citizenship rights of individuals and to maintain law and order in the case of Negroes accused either of crimes or infractions of what would be regarded by white people as improper actions.
– NAACP Anti-Lynching Committee, November 14, 1919

The year 1923 is not usually considered to be part of the civil rights movement timeline. It is not etched into our collective memory, like the landmark *Brown v. Board of Education* Supreme Court decision of 1954, the courage of the Little Rock Nine in 1957, or the March on Washington in 1963. But if the U.S. civil rights movement is understood as an effort to secure the full social, political, and legal rights of citizenship, then 1923 marks a significant event. That year, the NAACP fundamentally changed the operation of Jim Crow courtrooms in the South when the Supreme Court of the United States directly responded to the NAACP's appeal and handed down a landmark decision in *Moore v. Dempsey*, 261 U.S. 86, which reversed the death sentences of six African American men in Phillips County, Arkansas, on the grounds that these defendants had their Fourteenth Amendment rights violated by a hostile white mob. As one of the NAACP's leaders would write afterward, "The Supreme Court decision in this notable case thus becomes one of the *milestones* in the Negro's fight for justice – an achievement that is as important as any event since the signing of the Emancipation Proclamation."[1]

For many, *Moore v. Dempsey* was shocking – mob-dominated trials and hastily issued death sentences for African American defendants had been widely accepted practices in the South ever since the legal end of slavery. In this context, state criminal trials were typically considered to be immune from federal court oversight. Thus, *Moore v. Dempsey* marked a turning point in legal

[1] Walter White, "The Defeat of Arkansas Mob Law," in *The Crisis*, April 1923, p. 261.

discourse about constitutional rights, due to the Supreme Court's willingness to intervene in unjust state criminal court proceedings.[2] Even more remarkable, the U.S. Supreme Court would continue to narrow the power of individual states in the area of criminal law and broaden federal court power through a string of groundbreaking criminal procedure decisions in the following decades.[3] |

The U.S. Supreme Court's ruling in *Moore v. Dempsey* is especially noteworthy because it departed from the precedent set in *Frank v. Mangum*, 237 U.S. 309 (1915), a decision concerning mob violence handed down only eight years prior. In that case, Leo Frank, a Jewish man, was on trial for the murder of a thirteen-year-old Christian girl in Atlanta where anti-Semitic sentiments ran feverishly high. His trial was dominated by a violent mob threatening to hang Frank if he was not convicted and sentenced to die. Subsequently, his guilty verdict was upheld by the Georgia Supreme Court and the U.S. Supreme Court. In its decision, the Supreme Court broadly interpreted what constituted "due process" in the conduct of state criminal proceedings and determined that by providing opportunities to review the case in a higher state court, the state of Georgia had provided a sufficient "corrective process" for Frank and thus did not deny him due process of law. The Supreme Court made clear that its determination of constitutionality rested not on the presence of the mob but on the availability for subsequent review by a state appellate court. By deferring

---

[2] *Moore v. Dempsey* was not the first time the Supreme Court delivered a surprise ruling in a case that touched on issues of race and criminal justice. *United States v. Shipp*, 203 U.S. 563 (1906), was a case originally involving Ed Johnson, an African American man who had been convicted in Hamilton County, Tennessee, for the rape of a white woman and sentenced to die. Johnson filed a petition for a writ of habeas corpus arguing that his Fourteenth Amendment rights to due process had been violated due to a myriad of familiar Jim Crow trial features: exclusion of black jurors, denial of counsel, and mob intimidation. The Supreme Court allowed his appeal, which stayed his punishment until his appeal could be heard. On the day that word reached Johnson about the Supreme Court's decision to hear his appeal, Sheriff Joseph Shipp and the jailer opened the door to his jail cell and allowed a mob to beat and then lynch Johnson. The Supreme Court ruled that Shipp's actions constituted contempt of court. This case is notable for being the only criminal trial heard by the Supreme Court. However, while some of the circumstances between this case and *Moore* were similar, there were also considerable differences. Among the differences: *United States v. Shipp* addressed the question whether the actions of sheriff Shipp constituted contempt whereas in *Moore*, the question before the court was whether mob domination was a violation of due process. In fact, it seemed the court ruled so decisively in *United States v. Shipp* not because Johnson was being railroaded to death (the Supreme Court heard petitions of cases citing violation of due process by mobs but did nothing; see for example *Frank v. Mangum*, decided years after *United States v. Shipp* in 1915) but because its authority was challenged. It was not a clear statement about growing federal court power nor did this case mark a new direction in the Supreme Court's jurisprudence because Johnson died before his petition could be heard. For more on *United States v. Shipp*, see Mark Curriden and Leroy Phillips Jr., *Contempt of Court*, New York: Faber and Faber, 1999.

[3] *Powell v. Alabama*, 287 U.S. 45 (1932); *Hollins v. Oklahoma*, 295 U.S. 394 (1935); *Brown v. Mississippi*, 297 U.S. 278 (1936); *Johnson v. Zerbst*, 304 U.S. 458 (1938); *Chambers v. Florida*, 309 U.S. 227 (1940).

to the state court ruling, the Supreme Court affirmed earlier decisions that the protection of minority rights would be left to the province of states, not to the federal government.[4]

Because of the holding in *Frank v. Mangum*, the NAACP faced considerable obstacles in litigating *Moore v. Dempsey*. Before arguing the case in front of the Supreme Court, NAACP president Moorfield Storey admitted, "I am very much afraid that under the decision of the Supreme Court in the case of *Frank*, whom you will remember was tried under very bad circumstances in Atlanta, we shall not be able to win the case, but I am going to try."[5] But the NAACP ultimately succeeded and convinced the highest court in the nation to address the impact of mob influence on a defendant's right to a fair trial. In *Moore v. Dempsey*, the Supreme Court determined that even if the state "corrective process" was carried out, mob domination made "the trial absolutely void" and provided grounds for federal judges to step in and correct the wrong. Louis Marshall, the attorney for Leo Frank, congratulated the NAACP on the decision in *Moore v. Dempsey*, writing, "I regarded it as a great achievement in constitutional law. Due process of law now means, not merely a right to be heard before a court, but that it must be before a court that is not paralyzed by mob domination."[6] Through constitutional litigation, the NAACP finally won its greatest victory against racist violence in America.

The connection that I have laid out between the NAACP and the Supreme Court's decision in *Moore v. Dempsey* offers a theoretical lens that helps to make better sense of why the Supreme Court decided to wrestle power away from state courts in this instance. This perspective challenges the broader discourse of American political and constitutional development that usually treats civil rights groups as irrelevant. Unfortunately, as they exist right now, our theoretical frameworks have failed to properly account for the role of civil rights groups in the period of political and constitutional development before the 1940s. We have too often ignored their agency in our research, and I believe our analyses of development suffer because of this constrained scope. The stories of state building and constitution building we tell are not ones in which civil rights organizations carry significant weight; I suggest in this chapter that this needs to change.

Of course, to argue that the NAACP was an engine behind the Supreme Court's decision making and consequently was an essential cog to the growth of federal court power is to address a problematic gap in the literature. Existing scholarship has oversimplified how the Supreme Court became an

---

[4] *The Slaughterhouse Cases*, 83 U.S. 36 (1873); *Giles v. Harris*, 189 U.S. 475 (1903).

[5] Moorfield Storey to Mary White Ovington, letter, November 13, 1922, Arthur Waskow Papers, Wisconsin State Historical Society, University of Wisconsin, Madison. Hereafter, material in this collection, which is contained in two boxes, is referred to simply as Waskow Papers. Additional information about the location and origin of this archival collection is located in the Appendix.

[6] Louis Marshall to NAACP, letter, March 12, 1923, NAACP Papers, Manuscript Division, Library of Congress, Washington, DC.

interventionist in state court trials. In line with public law scholars who have linked expansions in court power to elected officials as well as public opinion, experts tend to see the federalization of power in criminal law as a product of the changing political and social environment.[7] Scholars who analyze *Moore v. Dempsey* tend to do so from a Hartzian perspective and propose that the Supreme Court could not ignore the racist facts of this case in the context of a changing and more egalitarian America.[8] Focusing specifically on early criminal procedure cases, Michael Klarman argues that though these cases were somewhat surprising – they were instances of "obvious injustices" – and that changes in the broader political-social context explain the Supreme Court's decision making.[9] The variables Klarman cites are indisputably significant, but stating that landmark Supreme Court decisions depend on changes in the political-social environment does not fully tell the story. The important and too-often overlooked question seems to be: How do the political and social conditions change so as to permit a case like *Moore v. Dempsey* to be decided the way it was? What drove this shift in public opinion? How did this case encourage individuals to shift their view concerning the responsibility of federal courts versus state courts? What propelled changes in the larger political environment? These are all questions for which the current literature is without adequate answers. Indeed, one crucial development this political-social argument tends to miss is the independent role the NAACP played in bringing to the fore the issues that would transform the public, political, and legal environments. My research makes clear that without the NAACP's campaign against racial violence, the Supreme Court would not have interfered in this case. This is so because both measures that scholars point to as responsible for the Supreme Court's decision in *Moore v. Dempsey* – public opinion and the political climate – would not have shifted without the NAACP's previous work in the political environment (executive and legislative branches) and the organization's efforts focused on publicizing the Arkansas injustice to the nation. Indeed, this chapter will show that the Supreme Court was responding not

---

[7] Mark Graber, "The Nonmajoritarian Difficulty: Legislative Deference to the Judiciary," *Studies in American Political Development* 7 (1993): 35–73. According to Graber, courts offer "opportunities for pushing unwanted political fights off the political agenda" and are encouraged by legislators to engage in "judicial policymaking." Paul Frymer, "Acting When Elected Officials Won't: Federal Courts and Civil Rights Enforcement in U.S. Labor Union, 1935–85." *American Political Science Review* 97, no. 3 (2003): 483–499; Barry Friedman, *The Will of the People: How Public Opinion has Influenced the Supreme Court and Shaped the Meaning of the Constitution*, New York: Farrar, Straus and Giroux, 2009.

[8] Michael Klarman, *From Jim Crow to Civil Rights: The Supreme Court and the Struggle for Racial Equality*, New York: Oxford University Press, 2004; Malcolm Feely, *The Black Basis of Constitutional Development* in *Earl Warren and the Warren Court: The Legacy in American and Foreign Law*, edited by Harry N. Scheiber, Lanham: Lexington Books/Rowman & Littlefield Publishers, 2007.

[9] Michael Klarman, "The Racial Origins of Modern Criminal Procedure," *Michigan Law Review* 99, no. 1 (2000): 49.

simply to the changing political-social environment but also to the actions of the NAACP.

In this chapter, I chart the emergence of federal court power in criminal law by describing the constellation of forces that led to the Supreme Court's decision in *Moore v. Dempsey*, including the central role of the NAACP. In the first section, I discuss the broader context of mob violence that set the tone for *Moore v. Dempsey* and the sentencing of the men accused of murder. The second section explores the NAACP's efforts to influence the case in three ways: through publicity, fundraising, and the acquisition of legal counsel. In the third section to demonstrate the connection between its overall litigation strategy and the final outcome of the case, I document the NAACP's attempts to keep the case alive through legal battles in the local and state courts. Finally, this chapter links the Supreme Court's decision in *Moore v. Dempsey* to a shift in the NAACP's strategy about how to wage a successful war for civil rights in the United States: after *Moore* the organization would shift its focus from a primary emphasis on political lobbying to a range of litigation tactics.

The Geography of Racial and Economic Tension

By the summer of 1919, Phillips County, Arkansas, was in a state of nervous transformation. The racial makeup of rural Phillips County was predominately African American (of the 44,530 residents, only 11,601 were white).[10] However, World War I had helped to spark the "Great Migration" of African Americans from the South to the North in search of better work opportunities. This migration had devastating financial consequences for the economy of Phillips County because its main industry, cotton farming, was largely dependent on African American labor. Alarmed by the loss of cheap labor, many white planters tried to trap African American tenant farmers in a system called sharecropping or peonage. Under these conditions, African American tenants were provided supplies for living based on credit until the cotton crop was harvested. Afterward, tenants were given a statement telling how much they owed for supplies, how much the crop was worth, and the amount of the balance due. Planters almost always refused to provide itemized accounts of their workers' debts but continually maintained that the tenant still owed money and could not leave. There was very little recourse for African American tenant farmers against this exploitation; instead, there was an unwritten law that no African American could leave until his or her debt was paid off. This was often enforced through physical violence.[11]

[10] Fourteenth Census, III, Washington, DC: Government Printing Office, 1922, p. 96.
[11] For description of the sharecropping system in Arkansas, see U. S. Bratton, Arkansas, to Frank Burke, Assistant of Division and Chief of Bureau of Investigation, Department of Justice, Washington DC, letter, November 6, 1919, Waskow Papers; Answer by W. E. B. Du Bois, Editor of *The Crisis* to article by Claire Kenmore in *New York World*, November 23, 1919, Waskow

In this context of economic exploitation, a small group of African American tenant farmers, calling themselves the Progressive Farmers and Household Union of America (PFHUA), began strategizing about how to free themselves from this coercive system. They contracted the services of Ulysses Bratton, a sympathetic white lawyer from Little Rock, to help in their efforts of getting the market price for their cotton and began meeting in a small church in Elaine, Arkansas, at the southern part of Phillips County, to plot strategy. Having become aware of this gathering, a small group of white law-enforcement officials and landowners went by car to the church, arrived at around 11 p.m., turned off their headlights, and fired gunshots into the building to break up the gathering. The lights in the church went out, and a small group of African Americans fired back in defense. Amid the confusion and disorder, one white man was killed, but it was not clear if it was by a member of his group or by the African Americans. The number of African Americans that were murdered in the crossfire was never determined, as the church was set on fire the next day to destroy any evidence of the ambush.

Surprised and frightened that African Americans had actually defended themselves, Phillips County law enforcement, along with other concerned whites, quickly concocted a story they knew would draw sympathy from local residents: armed and dangerous African Americans were organizing a plot to kill the white planters of Phillips County. The leading newspaper in Arkansas, the *Arkansas Gazette,* reported that Elaine had become "a zone of negro insurrection." Arkansas governor Charles Brough was pressured to ask for federal troops, and neighboring states were encouraged to send white men over to Phillips County to help quell the "uprising." The response was tremendous: more than 600 white men from the Arkansas Delta, Mississippi, and Tennessee, along with more than 500 U.S. militia men immediately rushed to Phillips County.[12]

The chaos that ensued over the next two days resulted in a massacre of the African American population of Phillips County. According to one description of the violent events, by a long time African American resident:

When the morning had come, I saw about 200 white men in cars shooting down the Negroes and sent us word that they were going to "kill every nigger" they could find in the county. And at 11:30 that day we saw near 300 white armed white men coming and

---

Papers; Walter White, "Massacring Whites in Arkansas," *The Nation,* December 6, 1919, Waskow Papers.

[12] *Arkansas Gazette,* October 2, 1919, "500 Camp Pike Soldiers sent to Quell Riot," *Arkansas Gazette,* October 4, 1919; Richard Cortner, *A Mob Intent on Death: The NAACP and the Arkansas Riot Cases,* Middletown: Wesleyan University Press, 1988. Governor Brough initially requested federal troops from nearby Camp Pike, but the commanding officer recused without orders from the War Department. However, the two Arkansas senators quickly got involved, and 583 troops from the Fifty-Seventh Infantry arrived early in the morning of October 3, 1919.

we all ran back of the field and when we got back of the field there was a big crowd of white men shooting and killing Jim Miller's family.[13]

Despite the widely circulated propaganda that African Americans were armed and dangerous, only five whites lost their lives. The death toll of African Americans was staggering by comparison: though there is no official death toll, one estimate is 856;[14] meanwhile the NAACP's more conservative estimate cited 250 fatalities.[15] African Americans reportedly fled to the woods for shelter as their homes and businesses were being burned and destroyed. By the time the angry mobs had departed on October 2, 1919, hundreds of African Americans were trapped in makeshift stockades, awaiting employers who could vouch for their innocence to be set free. Set in the context of the violence that occurred in the summer and fall of 1919, the Phillips County riot, while extreme, was not an anomaly. During the "Red Summer of 1919," as it is now known because of the bloodshed during this time, at least twenty-five race riots occurred in response to rising economic tensions in cities throughout the United States.[16]

Even after the violence had finally subsided, the line separating members of mob violence from law enforcement officials remained blurry. A group of seven prominent white men, representing the white-power establishment in Phillips County and calling themselves the "Committee of Seven," convinced Governor Brough to allow them to carry out a formal investigation of the race riot.[17] Contributing to the group's claims of legitimacy, the Committee of Seven members included the sheriff (F. F. Kitchens) and the county judge (H. D. Moore). The organization publicly stated that it was "authorized to carry on the investigation both by the municipal and county authorities." The committee conducted an investigation and delivered its report on October 7, 1919. It

---

[13] Ida B. Wells, *The Arkansas Race Riot*, pamphlet, 1920. Archives and Special Collections, University of Central Arkansas Library.

[14] L. S. Dunaway, *What A Preacher Saw Through a Keyhole in Arkansas*, Little Rock: Parke-Harper Publishing Company, 1925.

[15] Brief for the Appellants, *Moore v. Dempsey*, 261 U.S. 86 (1923). On p. 37, the brief cites evidence proving that between 200 and 300 black people were killed. In his oral argument before the Supreme Court in *Moore v. Dempsey*, Bratton told the court that "some 200 innocent negroes" had been killed in the riot. There is no exact number of black people killed, but White's estimates after his investigation are viewed as being on the conservative side. See Walter White to Thomas Mufson, letter, The Teachers Union, New York City, December 9, 1921, Waskow Papers.

[16] Arthur Waskow, *From Race Riot to Sit-in, 1919 and the 1960s*, New York: Doubleday, 1966; Cameron McWhirter, *Red Summer: The Summer of 1919 and the Awakening of Black America*, New York: Henry Holt and Company, 2011.

[17] The seven members: H. D. Moore (county judge), Frank Kitchens (sheriff), J. C. Knight (mayor of Helena), E. M. Allen (planter and president of the Helena Business Men's League), Sebastian Straub (owner of wholesale and retail grocers and cotton), E. C. Hornor (planter and founder of West Helena), and T. W. Kessee (a planter and Allen's brother-in-law).

announced that the initial fight at the church had prematurely set off a planned insurrection by members of the PFHUA, originally set for October 6, 1919, and that specific white planters were marked to be killed. In its report to the press, Committee of Seven member E. M. Allen offered a shocking summary of the events:

The present trouble with Negroes in Phillips County is not a race riot. It is a deliberately planned insurrection of the Negroes against the whites, directed by an organization known as the "Progressive Farmers and Household Union of America," established for the purpose of banding negroes together for the killing of white people.

According to the official report based on literature of the PFHUA and "stenographic copies of testimony and from evidence taken from numerous prisoners," many African Americans all over Phillips County were tricked into joining the union. The mastermind of the insurrection was identified as the leader of the PFHUA, Robert Hill, who "told the darkies that he was an agent of the government ... and that it would be necessary for all members of the Union to arm themselves in preparation for the day when they should be called upon to attack their white oppressors." The report read as a damning indictment of everyone involved in or who sympathized with the PFHUA.[18]

The courts wasted no time in interrogating African Americans and assigning charges. The accused were taken before the Committee of Seven; if the prisoners did not tell what the Committee of Seven wanted to hear, they would be taken to the torture room of the jail. Two men, T. K. Jones and H. F. Smiddy, who participated in the interrogations, stated almost two years after the initial trial that they had misgivings about what happened and gave sworn statements of the events as they remembered them.[19] H. F. Smiddy, one of the white men involved in the torture, reported:

After they [Committee of Seven] would get through with him I would take him back to the jail and would take him upstairs on the third floor to the whipping room and where the electric chair was located, where the Negro would be stripped naked and whipped from his head to his feet with a seven-pound leather strap. The Negroes were whipped unmercifully. Every time the strap was applied it would bring blood. I have personally applied the lash to a great number of these Negroes. We whipped them to make them tell what we wanted them to tell. We wanted them to tell facts that would convict

---

[18] *Moore v. Dempsey*, Transcript of Record, Supreme Court of the United States, Number 595, Filed October 24, 1921, Exhibit A: E. M. Allen's statement to the press, p. 11–15. See also *The Atlanta Constitution*, "Not a Racial Riot but Insurrection," October 7, 1919, p. 8.; *The New York Times*, "Says Negro Union Plotted Uprising," October 7, 1919, p. 2; *Chicago Daily Tribune*, "The Harebrained Plot of a Negro Wallingford," October 7, 1919, p. 14.

[19] A number of African Americans had already given sworn statements of the circumstances of their interrogation, but the NAACP's counsel was looking for whites to corroborate these statements and found Jones and Smiddy willing to testify in September 1921. Their sworn affidavits, which became part of the official appeal to the Supreme Court, offer a rare window into the operation of Jim Crow court trials.

themselves and others under arrest.... In addition to the whipping, and frequently during the course of the whipping, formaldehyde was put to the nose of the Negroes to further torture and frighten them and compel them to give damaging evidence against themselves and others. In addition to this, there was an electric chair in the same room on the third floor of the Phillips County jail in which a great many Negroes were stripped naked and put and the current turned on to frighten and torture them into giving damaging statements against themselves and others.[20]

The beatings stopped when the jailed African American men were willing to confess or testify against others. Those who refused to provide incriminating statements, such as Frank Moore (who received three brutal whippings) faced much harsher sentences. All of the evidence the state of Arkansas acquired against the twelve men charged with murder (the Phillips County 12) was collected in this manner.[21]

However, it wasn't just the manner in which the so-called evidence was gathered that was contrary to the constitutional guarantee of a fair trial – the selection of the grand and petit juries also raises flags. T. W. Kesse and Sebastian Straub were members of the Committee of Seven and placed on the grand jury. The choice of Straub in particular is perplexing: he was the chairman of the Committee of Seven and responsible for hiring an African American man to infiltrate the PFHUA. On the petit jury was E. M. Allen, who took command of the Committee of Seven investigation and had full knowledge of the torture inflicted on the African American men in custody.[22] In addition, a number of the individuals on the grand and petit juries were part of the posse of white men who hunted down and killed African Americans in the days directly following the shooting in Elaine.[23] Thus, it was little surprise that between the end of October and beginning of November that year, the Phillips County grand jury quickly began to return indictments against those who were alleged to have participated in the riot. Not a single white person was indicted. Overall, 122 African Americans were indicted by the grand jury, and 79 were charged with crimes ranging from murder to night riding.

Frank Moore, along with five other African American men (Ed Coleman, Paul Hall, Ed and Frank Hicks, and J. E. Knox), was tried for the first-degree murder of Clinton Lee, who had been shot under the left arm while riding in a car. A raucous, bloodthirsty mob had packed the courtroom and an even

---

[20] H. F. Smiddy, Affidavit, *Moore v. Dempsey*, Transcript of Record, Supreme Court of the United States, Number 595, Filed October 24, 1921.

[21] There would be no constitutional protection against the use of confessions extracted by torture in state trials until a later NAACP case, *Brown v. Mississippi*, 297 U.S. 278 (1936).

[22] For list of grand jury and petit jury members see *Moore v. Arkansas*, Transcript of Record, Supreme Court of the United States, Number 360, Filed May 24, 1920. Kesse was later excused for unknown reasons.

[23] *Moore v. Dempsey*, Transcript of Record, Supreme Court of the United States, Number 595, Filed October 24, 1921, p. 98.

larger crowd surrounded the courthouse. It was so bad, reported a white observer, that:

No man could have sat upon any jury in Phillips County at these trials and have voted for an acquittal, and have continued to live in Phillips County. Large crowds attended the trials, thronged the courthouse and round, all of whom so far as I was able to observe were unfriendly to the petitioners and all of whom were bent upon their conviction and death. If any prisoner had by any chance been acquitted by a jury he could not have escaped the mob.[24]

The mob was not a new phenomenon in Phillips County. Four days after African Americans were rounded up, a mob was formed and gathered around the jail and courthouse with the intention of lynching a number of those in jail. The mob only dispersed when promised that if they did not harm anyone, the African Americans would be put to death through the law. The mob at the actual trial simply came to make sure that promise was kept.

Frank Hicks was tried first, on November 3, 1919, as he was accused of firing the shots that killed Lee. Seven witnesses testified on behalf of the prosecution. One of the two PFHUA witnesses, George Green, alleged he saw Frank Hicks shoot in the direction of Lee's car, but under cross-examination admitted that there were a number of men around Hicks and he could not be certain it was Hicks or if his gunfire even hit anyone. Four of the white witnesses called to testify could not identify the shooter but the last to testify, S. S. Stokes, was the prosecution's star witness. Stokes was part of a group of five white men who tortured Hicks in jail. When asked who interrogated Hicks, Stokes replied defensively,

There wasn't much interrogating, it was a volunteer statement to us.... He didn't answer the questions, he made a statement; when he got started he just told us the story right there, straight through; we didn't have to question him very much.

According to a lengthy rendering by Stokes, Hicks confessed that he was with Frank Moore, Ed Ware, Paul Hall, and Ed Coleman when they heard shots ring out in Elaine and decided to go toward the shooting to surround the white people with their guns. Stokes then testified that Hicks borrowed Coleman's rifle and shot into the crowd. The State of Arkansas rested its case at this point, and the court-appointed defense counsel declined to cross-examine or even to bring Hicks to testify. As a result, Stokes's hearsay account was treated as an accurate account, and, after an eight-minute deliberation, the jury convicted Hicks of first-degree murder.[25]

The five remaining men (Moore, Hall, Coleman, Knox, and Ed Hicks) were tried together on the same day as accessories to the murder of Lee. The state of Arkansas called four white witnesses and three African Americans to testify in

---

[24] *Moore v. Dempsey*, Transcript of Record, Supreme Court of the United States, Number 595, Filed October 24, 1921, pp. 86–99.

[25] *Frank Hicks v. State of Arkansas*, Transcript of Record, Supreme Court of the United States, Number 361, Filed May 24, 1920, pp. 1–30.

this case. One white witness, R. L. Brooks, was riding with Clinton Lee in the car but when asked who fired the shot, he testified, "I haven't the least idea." The second white witness, the doctor whose residence Lee's body was brought to after he suffered the gun shot, said that he had not even seen the bullet hole. A third witness, Tom Faulkner, was friends with Lee and testified that he saw "three Negroes" fire the shots that killed Lee, but when asked which of the defendants on trial were the shooters, he admitted, "I couldn't identify any of them." John Jefferson, a PFHUA member, identified Frank Moore, Ed Hicks, and Joe Knox as the responsible parties, but the veracity of his testimony was put into question when cross-examination revealed that he had also been arrested and interrogated for first-degree murder and thus likely forced to go along with the prosecution's story to protect his own life. A second PFHUA witness, Walter Ward, testified that Frank Moore was the shooter, but upon further questioning from defense counsel stated that he was also indicted for the murder of Clinton Lee and confessed that as far as he knew, the defendants had not done anything to anyone. The last African American witness, Dave Archer, reported that he overheard Frank Moore and Ed Hicks saying they were going to kill white people but that he did not hear anything inflammatory from Paul Hall, Joe Knox, or Ed Coleman. The final witness called by the state was Judge Graham Burke, an individual who was used to corroborate the story that the proper procedures were followed. Judge Burke testified that he asked the defendants questions while they were in jail, but that no coercion was used in his presence. The defendants were not called to the stand to testify, and the defense rested without bringing any witnesses.[26] As it stood after all the witnesses were called, it could not be determined who was actually involved in the shooting. Nevertheless, the jury deliberated for seven minutes and determined that all five men were guilty.

The next day, in similarly questionable trial proceedings, five more African American men were sentenced to death for the murder of two white men (Albert Giles and Joe Fox for the murder of James Tappan; and John Martin, Alf Banks, and Will Wordlow for the murder of W. D. Adkins). Ed Ware, secretary of the Progressive Farmers Union, was sentenced to the same fate for the murder of Adkins on November 18, 1919, after being apprehended in New Orleans. In all of the trials, the jury (of which E. M. Allen was still a member) deliberated for fewer than ten minutes. The execution of the Phillips County 12 was set to take place by electrocution a mere two months after the trial on December 2, 1919, and January 2, 1920. Once these twelve men were sentenced to capital punishment, the remaining sixty-seven imprisoned rushed to plea-bargain and were sentenced to lesser jail terms of one to twenty-one years.[27]

---

[26] *Moore v. Arkansas*, Transcript of Record, Supreme Court of the United States, Number 360, Filed May 24, 1920, pp. 5–29.

[27] Arthur Ocean Waskow, *From Race Riot to Sit-In, 1919 and the 1960s; A Study in the Connections Between Conflict and Violence*, Garden City: Anchor Books, 1967; Richard Cortner, *A Mob Intent on Death: The NAACP and the Arkansas Riot Cases*, Middletown: Wesleyan University Press, 1988.

NAACP Responds

To appreciate the novelty of the NAACP's role in this incident, it is necessary to understand that in 1919, the NAACP had not yet identified litigation as a worthwhile strategy to advance the organization's goals of racial equality in American society. A 1915 report to the board of directors from the first NAACP secretary, Mary Childs Nerney, documenting her observations after travel to eight cities, revealed surprising insight: "The majority of the whites do not regard the struggle for civil rights by legal measures as practical now except in spectacular instances, and the majority of colored people are not interested in legal disabilities as much as in securing an economic opportunity."[28] Though the NAACP established a legal committee early on, this division functioned primarily as an information bureau, as the 1916 NAACP Annual Report specified:

> It is the belief of the Chairman of the [Legal] Committee that it can do no single service of greater value than to collect accurately and exhaustively all the laws relating to discrimination and the like and to act as a clearinghouse for organizations and their attorneys who have not the time nor facilities for obtaining this information.[29]

The NAACP attributed its limited focus in the legal arena to the complexity and costs associated with litigation, noting that the legal committee was "seriously handicapped by the fact that it has to depend entirely upon the gratuitous services of already over-busy lawyers."[30] As a result, the legal committee was small, constrained by lack of funding, and tasked mainly with managing small, local cases of racial discrimination.[31] Throughout its first decade, the NAACP devoted most of its resources and energies to working for racial equality through the changing of public opinion and through lobbying for anti-lynching legislation in Congress.[32]

---

[28] Mary Childs Nerney to NAACP Board of Directors, travel report letter, December 6, 1915, NAACP Papers, Manuscript Division, Library of Congress, Washington, DC.

[29] Seventh Annual Report for the National Association of Colored People, 1917, NAACP Papers, Manuscript Division, Library of Congress, Washington, DC.

[30] Seventh Annual Report for the National Association of Colored People, 1917, NAACP Papers, Manuscript Division, Library of Congress, Washington, DC.

[31] For information about the beginning of the local cases pursued by the NAACP's first legal committee see Seventh Annual Report for the National Association of Colored People, 1917, NAACP Papers, Manuscript Division, Library of Congress, Washington, DC.; Tenth Annual Report for the National Association of Colored People, 1920, NAACP Papers, Manuscript Division, Library of Congress, Washington, DC; Susan Carle, "Race, Class, and Legal Ethics in the Early NAACP (1910–1920)," *Law and History Review* 20, no. 1 (2002): 115–116.

[32] Charles Flint Kellogg, *NAACP: A History of the National Association for the Advancement of Colored People*, Baltimore: Johns Hopkins University Press, 1973; Robert Zangrando, *The NAACP Crusade Against Lynching, 1909–1950*, Philadelphia: Temple University Press, 1980; Patricia Sullivan, *Lift Every Voice: The NAACP and the Making of the Civil Rights Movement*, New York: New Press, 2009.

Of course, the NAACP was involved in two previous cases that reached the Supreme Court, but the decision to get involved in litigation efforts in the NAACP's early years appears to be ad hoc instead of constitutive of a larger litigation master plan. The NAACP participated in *Guinn v. United States,* 238 U.S. 347 (1915) by filing an amicus brief attacking Oklahoma's use of the grandfather clause to disenfranchise African American voters, and the organization successfully attacked municipally mandated residential segregation in a test case started by the Louisville, Kentucky, branch in *Buchanan v. Warley,* 245 U.S. 60 (1917). Parting ways with a literature that extols the transformative nature of these cases, focused research reveals they did little to change the NAACP's strategic orientation and failed to generate additional funding.[33] On the contrary, litigation was understood as laborious and a strain on resources. In the Annual Report for 1919, the NAACP gave an account of its legal defense work, revealing that "Despite many requests for legal assistance of the most appealing character, the Association, up to the latter part of the year, was able to handle only such cases as required no considerable expenditure nor the engagement of special counsel." To complicate matters further, in the same report the NAACP revealed, "Advice was too often ineffective. Money was needed and funds had to be conserved."[34] Thus, in 1919, with limited success in the legal arena and dwindling financial resources, it seemed unlikely the NAACP would take up what was obviously a thorny and difficult case. Nevertheless, while litigation did not appear to be the organic extension of its work at the time, the NAACP considered the case of the Phillips County 12 to be "the most important" of all the legal cases handled by the organization to date.[35] As a result, the NAACP quickly constructed a litigation plan that would serve them well throughout the long legal campaign that eventually resulted in the successful *Moore v. Dempsey* decision.

Focusing on how marginalized groups use the law as a tool to fight for justice, scholars who study the relationship between law and social movements have stressed the importance of identifying the specific factors that contribute to the success of groundbreaking legal struggles. Particularly notable is the work of Charles Epp, who argues that the Supreme Court decisions that formed the rights revolution from 1961 through the mid-1970s were largely influenced by well-organized advocacy groups whose work was made possible because of a "support structure" consisting of financial resources, organizations committed to establishing rights, and competent lawyers.[36]

33 Susan Carle, "Race, Class, and Legal Ethics in the Early NAACP (1910–1920)," *Law and History Review* 20, no. 1 (2002), 97–146.

34 Tenth Annual Report for the National Association of Colored People, 1920, p. 50, NAACP Papers, Manuscript Division, Library of Congress, Washington, DC.

35 Eleventh Annual Report for the National Association of Colored People, 1921, p. 14. NAACP Papers, Manuscript Division, Library of Congress, Washington, DC.

36 Charles Epp, *The Rights Revolution: Lawyers, Activists and Supreme Courts in Comparative Perspective*, Chicago: The University of Chicago Press, 1998.

Epp's support-structure hypothesis places sustained funding and the strategic efforts of lawyers front and center because it is his belief that properly positioned, financed, and mobilized groups can engineer a significant amount of change from the Supreme Court. Similarly, Michael McCann describes the critical role of litigation groups in the movement for pay equity reform.[37] McCann's empirical study compares media coverage of different social movement tactics in the movement for pay equity and found that publicity was an important factor to effective legal mobilization.[38] Likewise, in the case of *Moore v. Dempsey*, three factors stand out as significant: publicity used to raise awareness about the important issues and to transform public opinion, fundraising to finance the lengthy litigation, and a tenacious legal defense that was able to outmaneuver the State of Arkansas's attorneys and compel resistant judges to respond, even when the accused's legal options looked bleak.[39]

A Battle for Hearts and Minds

News of the rioting in Phillips County reached the offices of the NAACP on October 1, 1919. As told by NAACP assistant secretary Walter White, "Throughout the nation, newspapers published alarming stories of Negroes plotting to massacre whites and take over the government of the state."[40] While the press painted the PFHUA as a lawless and roguish group, the leadership at the NAACP's national office emphasized a different aspect of the story: the plight of tenant farmers trying to organize by legal means. Well aware of the exploitative peonage system in the South, the NAACP was very skeptical about reports that the riot broke out as part of the unionizing activities. After they contacted a local NAACP branch in nearby Memphis, their suspicions were confirmed.[41] The letter made clear the real issue at stake was a dispute over the price of cotton between white planters and African American tenants, and that the propaganda published about the uncover-

---

[37] Michael McCann, *Rights at Work: Pay Equity Reform and the Politics of Legal Mobilization*, Chicago: University of Chicago Press, 1994.

[38] Michael McCann, *Rights at Work: Pay Equity Reform and the Politics of Legal Mobilization*, Chicago: University of Chicago Press, 1994, pp. 59–61.

[39] For additional scholarship that highlights the importance of lawyers as independent actors in the judicial decision making process, see Marc Galanter, "Why the 'Haves' Come Out Ahead: Speculations on the Limits of Legal Change," *Law and Society Review* 9 (1974): 95–160; Robert Kagan, *Adversarial Legalism: The American Way of Law*, Cambridge: Harvard University Press, 2001.

[40] Walter Francis White, *A Man Called White, The Autobiography of Walter White*, New York: Viking Press, 1948, p. 47.

[41] Mary White Ovington, *The Walls Came Tumbling Down*, New York: Harcourt Brace, 1947, pp. 154–155.

ILLUSTRATION 5.1 The twelve members of the Progressive Farmers and Household Union of America who were sentenced to death. "Elaine Massacre Defendants."
Source: Photographer unknown. Courtesy of the Butler Center for Arkansas Studies, Central Arkansas Library System, Little Rock.

ing of a plot to kill whites was "too ridiculous to be given any thought"[42] (Illustration 5.1).

Immediately after the riot, while things were still in disorder and before the court trials, White undertook the first investigation by an outside entity of the racial violence in Phillips County, Arkansas. Eager to figure out the truth, on October 7, 1919, White wrote NAACP secretary John Shillady, "In view of the critical situation which existed in Arkansas during the past week, it appears to me that this is a matter which needs careful investigation."[43] The next day, in the midst of the turmoil, White appeared on the scene in Phillips County to conduct an official inquiry into the alleged African American uprising for the NAACP. With his blond hair, fair skin and blue eyes, White could easily "pass" as a white man. Disguising himself as a sympathetic reporter from the *Chicago Daily News* (he went so far as to obtain an official press badge), White was able to secure a meeting with Governor Brough and talk to other local residents who provided additional reason to doubt the validity of press reports about a planned African American insurrection.

White's trip to Phillips County, while courageous, would be the most dangerous investigation of his career, and he would barely escape with his life. In

---

[42] Walter White to Robert Church, letter, October 4, 1919, Series 1: C, Box 349 NAACP Papers, Manuscript Division, Library of Congress, Washington, DC.; Robert Church to Walter White, letter, October 6, 1919, Waskow Papers.
[43] Walter White to John Shillady, letter, October 7, 1919, Waskow Papers.

his memoir, White writes that after he had been there a few days, an African American man who knew his identity came up to him and whispered under his breath that the whites of Phillips County were looking for him and he needed to leave immediately. Wasting no time, White rushed to the train station and was lucky to jump on the only train leaving before nightfall. However, when he went to pay for his ticket, the train conductor told him, "But you're leaving, mister, just when the fun is going to start, there's a damned yellow nigger down there passing for white and the boys are going to get him." When White asked what they would do if they found him, the conductor assured White, "When they get through with him he won't pass for white no more!"[44] The train ride out of Phillips County was the longest ride of White's life.

Surprisingly, the most valuable part of White's trip occurred outside of Phillips County in Little Rock, where he was introduced to Bratton. Bratton was a partner in the law firm that the PFHUA had contacted directly before the riot and was forthcoming with details about the economic exploitation experienced by African Americans. From Bratton, White began to understand the real reasons behind the riot and immediately notified the NAACP of his findings.[45]

Even after White completed his investigation, there was still no alternative narrative to explain the violent events that occurred in Phillips County in any national, local, or African American newspaper. The national media outlets had blamed the violence on unruly African Americans: *The New York Times* front page headline read "Planned Massacre of Whites Today" and the *Los Angeles Times* declared on its front page "Whites Battle with Negro Gangs."[46] Upon White's return to New York, the NAACP held a press conference on October 11, 1919, and released a press report with White's findings. Determined to expose the cover-up orchestrated by the Committee of Seven, White published the results of his investigation in the *Chicago Daily News* on October 18, 1919. In this article, White explained the PFHUA was not formed to murder white planters but to hire a lawyer to work on behalf of settlements for African American sharecroppers who had been cheated out of their wages by greedy white landowners who were trying to replicate slavery in the post-emancipation South. Referencing the accusations in the Committee of Seven's report, White confidently stated, "The reports sent about a general massacre seem to be only a figment of the imagination of Arkansas whites and not based on fact."[47] White viewed the falsified reporting of the rioting as a blatant example of the depths southern whites would go to protect their economic and racial status, and he

---

[44] Walter Francis White, *A Man Called White, The Autobiography of Walter White*, New York: Viking Press, 1948, pp. 50–51.

[45] Walter Francis White, *A Man Called White, The Autobiography of Walter White*, New York: Viking Press, 1948, p. 48.

[46] "Planned Massacre of Whites Today," *The New York Times*, October 6, 1919, p. 1; "Arkansas Riot-Torn: Whites Battle with Negro Gangs," *Los Angeles Times*, October 2, 1919, p. I1.

[47] Walter White, "Arkansas Race Riots Laid to Bad System," *Chicago Daily News*, October 18, 1919.

wanted other Americans to know the truth. E. M. Allen, spokesman for the Committee of Seven and treasurer of the Gerald B. Lambert Company, which owned a 21,000-acre cotton plantation near Elaine that employed 750 African American sharecroppers, was a symbol of this type of exploitation. White continued writing and submitted a separate article of his investigation to *The Nation*. In this article, White boldly declared that the rioting in Phillips County started when angry whites retaliated, and subsequently, African Americans:

> were being hunted and 250 shot down like wild beasts, in the Arkansas cane breaks, because they had organized to employ a lawyer in an endeavor to obtain settlements and statements of account from their landlords under the share-cropping system.[48]

The Nation article received a lot of praise and 5,000 copies were later reprinted and distributed by the NAACP.[49]

The Crisis, which had its largest readership in 1919, was another medium the NAACP utilized to spread the results of White's investigation.[50] Du Bois, editor of *The Crisis,* was very interested in attacking the class and economic obstacles that African Americans faced and saw this as a stark example of labor exploitation. *The Crisis* published a scathing critique of the Phillips County incident, charging that local authorities had purposely hunted and shot down African Americans who wanted to protest peacefully against the farm owners who exploited their labor as sharecroppers.[51]

White's articles led to a snowballing in the public mind. The articles represented the first time that many in the nation (including Phillips County) had heard another side of the story. Until the NAACP publications, most of the nation had uniformly accepted the story that African Americans had planned an insurrection against white planters in Phillips County, and the twelve guilty perpetrators had been found and justifiably sentenced to death. No one had come forward with another account. Afterward, newspapers, including the *Pittsburg Dispatch, Boston Chronicle,* and *Buffalo Express* began to repeat the NAACP's version of events.[52] Outraged by the violence reported by White, the *Baltimore Herald* called the violence a "butchery of Negroes."[53] A testament to the NAACP's success in getting people to accept its story, as early

---

[48] Walter White, "Massacring Whites in Arkansas," *The Nation,* December 6, 1919.
[49] Prince Edwoods to Walter White, letter, December 23, 1919, Waskow Papers.
[50] *The Crisis* was the official publication of the NAACP. Its circulation increased from 1,000 copies per month in 1910 to a peak of 100,000 copies per month in 1919. In June 1919, circulation increased to 104,000. BOD Minutes, July 11, 1919. Average monthly circulation during 1919 was 94,908. See Twelfth Annual Report for the Year 1921 for *The Crisis* circulation from 1911 to 1921, NAACP Papers, Manuscript Division, Library of Congress, Washington, DC.
[51] Walter White, "Hell Breaks Out in Arkansas," *The Crisis,* no date recorded, Waskow Papers.
[52] BOD Minutes, Part 7, Series A, Reel 21, January 14, 1925, NAACP Papers, Manuscript Division, Library of Congress, Washington, DC; "Arkansas Race Riots Laid to Bad System," *Chicago Daily News,* October 18, 1919; "Hell Breaks Out in Arkansas," *The Crisis,* Anonymous report, no date, Waskow Papers.
[53] "If There is One Infamy," *Baltimore Daily Herald,* November 8, 1919, Waskow Papers.

as December 1919 the NAACP was able to hold public rallies in New York and Philadelphia against the Phillips County trials.[54] By offering a different account, the NAACP provoked people to ask whether a different institution, like the federal government, might be necessary to protect African Americans from state violence at the local level.

At a time when most Americans trusted print media as the best source for reliable news information, the Arkansas press felt compelled to address the NAACP's findings. The day after White's article was published in the *Chicago Daily News*, the *Arkansas Gazette* argued that the NAACP's investigation was severely misleading. Reiterating the story of a planned African American insurrection, the *Arkansas Gazette* asserted, "The authorities of Helena and of Phillips County should have a reckoning with the National Association for the Advancement of Colored People over this matter."[55] Though Governor Brough praised Phillips County law enforcement for its handling of the riot, he was also aware that the trial had now come under the scrutiny of the national media.[56] And the prevailing view of the white-power establishment in Arkansas was not favorable. Concerned that the speed of the trial had translated into the widespread perception of impropriety, and tired of receiving flack from northern newspapers, Governor Brough devised a plan he hoped would silence his critics: he announced a Commission on Race Relations to be composed of nine whites and eight African Americans. As its first order of business, the commission passed a resolution recommending the appeal of the Phillips County 12 on death row to the Arkansas Supreme Court. The commission argued that,

Publicity [had] given the fact that it required only a few minutes for the juries to reach verdicts in some of the cases ... and if the higher tribunal should affirm the verdicts, the newspapers of the North and East could no longer "harp" on that point.[57]

While the commission had no formal legal role in appealing the decision, its recommendation carried weight with Governor Brough and likely influenced the trial judge, who ultimately stayed the executions. As a result, the executions of the Phillips County 12 were temporarily suspended.

Evidence of the NAACP's effectiveness in countering the dominant narrative of the Phillips County race riots was the commission's use of "negative publicity" as one of its reasons for recommending an appeal for the Phillips County 12. By examining the NAACP's publicity work, we see the pivotal role

---

[54] John Muilholland to Mary White Ovington, letter, December 4, 1919; John Muilholland to Mary White Ovington, letter, December 17, 1919, NAACP Papers, Manuscript Division, Library of Congress, Washington, DC.

[55] *Arkansas Gazette*, October 19, 1919, p. 2.

[56] *Arkansas Gazette*, November 24, 1919; *Arkansas Gazette*, November 25, 1919, p. 8.

[57] Richard Cortner, *A Mob Intent on Death: The NAACP and the Arkansas Riot Cases*, Middletown: Wesleyan University Press, 1988, pp. 47–48; see also *Arkansas Gazette*, November 25, 1919.

this organization would come to play in addressing legal issues that would ultimately motivate the Supreme Court to get involved.

Funding

Upon learning about the Phillips County 12, the NAACP got involved and launched a fundraising campaign to raise money for their legal defense in late November 1919. Unlike *Guinn* and *Buchanan*, the NAACP viewed this case as directly linked to their lynching and mob violence–reduction campaign, which was the NAACP's top agenda concern since they were formed in 1909. Through the NAACP's investigation, it became clear that mob justice was being carried out under the veneer of law in Arkansas, and the law-enforcement officials were no different than mob members. This was not extralegal mob violence; this was the legitimization and institutionalization of mob rule in Arkansas's legal structure. Thus, if the NAACP was going to have any chance at winning the fight against mob violence, it was necessary to target the legal system. Though they initially balked at the costs associated with litigation, members of the NAACP board of directors were confident they could make a powerful appeal to the court and that most Americans would be aghast at the circumstances surrounding the case because it involved the twin evils of racial violence and labor exploitation. The NAACP's narrative was that twelve African American men would be put to death for peacefully assembling in hopes of securing money owed to them from their landlords. Essentially, the NAACP's theme was economic exploitation and the devastating repercussions of trying to achieve justice.[58]

In the beginning, the NAACP could not publicize its fundraising campaign because aiding the legal defense would have to be concealed, as the organization did not want to damage the chances of the appeal for the Phillips County 12.[59] A negative backlash could develop if it were discovered that the NAACP, an outside organization, was financing the defense. Understanding the sensitivity of the incident in Arkansas, NAACP secretary Johnson made clear that success in the case depended on NAACP secrecy when he wrote in a letter:

> We feel certain that if the people of Arkansas knew that we were raising funds to set aside the verdicts already rendered by the courts of Arkansas, there would be aroused opinion on the part of the public, if not on the part of the courts, which would be prejudicial to the cases of the men on trial.[60]

---

[58] Mary White Ovington, *The Walls Came Tumbling Down*, New York: Harcourt Brace, 1947, p. 157.

[59] Walter White to Hugh T. Fisher, County Attorney, Topeka, KS, letter, January 28, 1920, NAACP Papers, Manuscript Division, Library of Congress, Washington, DC.

[60] James Weldon Johnson to Robert R. Church, letter, Memphis, TN, December 2, 1919, NAACP Archives, Waskow Papers.

Though the NAACP could not make public its fundraising efforts, by 1919 the growing NAACP had 220 local branches and 56,345 members scattered across the United States whom they could solicit for funds. Immediately, the board of directors, including Walter White, John Shillady, Mary White Ovington, Moorfield Storey, and James Weldon Johnson, became involved in identifying and contacting potential sources of funding. The urgency of this case was apparent to everyone involved. Details of the circumstances leading up to the arrests and the sentencing of the Phillips County 12 were sent out to prominent funders, local affiliates were called upon to help in the fundraising effort, and larger branches were asked to contribute $25, and smaller branches were asked to contribute $10.[61]

Indeed, part of the NAACP's success in this case came from its expertise in generating funds in previous instances when the organization fully mobilized its members in support of an issue. Since 1909, the NAACP had been fundraising on behalf of the civil rights of African Americans. By 1919, the NAACP had developed strong relationships with numerous wealthy people in the North – many of whom were already financing its anti-lynching campaign when it began in 1916. As described by Ovington, "The labor slant made the case at once a success [to their funding base]."[62] The wife of a wealthy publisher and a close friend of Eleanor Roosevelt convened the first NAACP fundraising meeting for the Phillips County 12 in her home. As a result of the organization's efforts, in the course of only a few months, the NAACP reported receiving $3,194 in general contributions; adjusted for inflation today, the amount would be $35,922.76.[63]

However, in December 1920, the NAACP needed to quickly raise another $5,000 to continue funding the defense team's work, so the organization decided to go public about its involvement in the case and launched a more expansive fundraising drive.[64] Once public, the anti-lynching committee issued an announcement for a campaign to raise $50,000 to defray the costs for defense of the twelve men sentenced to death and the sixty-seven others who had received unjust prison sentences. At the time, this fundraising campaign was the largest the NAACP had ever undertaken. To raise the funds, meetings were held in supporters' homes, money was solicited from friends, letters were written to past supporters, and lectures were held to raise awareness. Individuals contributed anywhere from $1 to $500 to support the NAACP's legal defense efforts. At the end of the trials, the NAACP reported it had

---

[61] Mary White Ovington, form letter, November 26, 1919; James Weldon Johnson to George Bell, letter, December 3, 1919, NAACP Archives, Waskow Papers.

[62] Mary White Ovington, *The Walls Came Tumbling Down*, New York: Harcourt Brace, 1947, p. 158.

[63] BOD Minutes, January 1920, p. 3, NAACP Papers, Manuscript Division, Library of Congress, Washington, DC.

[64] *The Crisis*, "Funds Needed to Fight Arkansas Cases," December 1920, pp. 65–66.

raised and spent over $15,000 on the Arkansas case ($168,704.25 adjusted for inflation).[65]

Acquisition of Counsel

Ulysses Bratton, the Little Rock attorney who spoke frankly with Walter White during his investigation in Arkansas, would become an invaluable asset to the NAACP in the construction of the legal defense. Bratton was a strong Republican who served as an assistant U.S. attorney in Little Rock during the Taft and Roosevelt administrations, during which time he sued planters for violation of federal peonage laws. Bratton had gained a reputation among African Americans as a trustworthy white attorney who could effectively defend them. When he was contacted by the PFHUA, he decided to send his son, Ocier Bratton, to investigate on October 1, 1919, but Ocier was arrested before he made it to Phillips County and held without cause for a month. Disillusioned with the criminal justice system in Arkansas, Bratton felt that something had to be done to prevent further injustice in Phillips County.

In early November, Bratton traveled from Little Rock to New York City where he met with the NAACP leadership at the national headquarters and made a statement at the monthly board of directors meeting about the underlying causes of the situation in Arkansas.[66] He also committed himself to work with the NAACP to raise awareness about the real source of racial violence in Phillips County. Believing the Phillips County incident to be a grave miscarriage of justice, the NAACP's board approved that "all practical methods that could be devised for bringing out the facts, correcting the evils and mitigating the sentences of men whose trials have been held."[67] The Anti-Lynching Committee met four days later and similarly agreed to do all that was possible to aid those convicted in Phillips County.[68] Together, these meetings began the formal commitment of the NAACP to work on freeing the men arrested in response to the Phillips County incident. With time running out, the NAACP board of directors convened a special meeting to decide to what extent they would become legally involved in the case. Previously, Bratton had identified Colonel George Murphy of the Little Rock law firm Murphy, McHaney & Dunaway, as a reliable and respected lawyer to work on the case. At the special meeting, the board voted in favor of employing Murphy for a one-time fee of $3,000 to defend the seventy-nine men sentenced arising from the Arkansas

---

[65] "Arkansas Case is Ended," special NAACP news release, January 14, 1925, NAACP Papers, Manuscript Division, Library of Congress, Washington, D.C.

[66] BOD Minutes, November 10, 1919, NAACP Papers, Manuscript Division, Library of Congress, Washington, DC.

[67] BOD Minutes, November 10, 1919, NAACP Papers, Manuscript Division, Library of Congress, Washington, DC.

[68] Minutes of the Anti-Lynching Committee, November 14, 1919, NAACP Papers, Manuscript Division, Library of Congress, Washington, DC.

riots.[69] This represented the largest amount the NAACP had ever disbursed in a single payment.

The NAACP was not alone in arranging legal defense for the Phillips County 12. Around the same time, a number of prominent African Americans in Phillips County formed a separate organization, Citizens Defense Fund Commission (CDFC), to raise money and employ legal counsel for the Phillips County 12.[70] After the Governor's Commission on Race Relations approved of an appeal of the cases to the Arkansas Supreme Court in December 1919, a well-known African American lawyer, Scipio Jones, was brought on board to help free the Phillips County 12.[71]

The CDFC sent a request for funding to the NAACP's national office at the end of November 1919 as the NAACP was considered the central organization in America fighting against racial injustice.[72] Because of the secret nature of the NAACP's involvement, none of the CDFC members knew that the NAACP was already involved. Upon receipt of their letter, the NAACP informed the CDFC they had already retained the services of Murphy.[73] However, because the NAACP's funds were limited to some extent, they found it beneficial to work with Jones, the talented lawyer appointed by the CDFC.[74] Through Bratton, the NAACP was able to establish a joint legal defense team of Jones and Murphy.[75] Though it wasn't immediately evident, Jones was a godsend to the NAACP. After Murphy passed away a year later due to a heart attack and

[69] BOD Minutes, November 24, 1919, NAACP Papers, Manuscript Division, Library of Congress, Washington, DC.

[70] Organization Statement of Citizens Defense Fund, Little Rock, Ark., March 2, 1921, Waskow Papers.

[71] Scipio Jones was born a slave in 1863, attended rural schools in Tulip, Arkansas, and went to Little Rock to attend Philander Smith College. Denied entrance to the University of Arkansas law school because of his skin color, Jones acquired his legal education on his own while studying law at a prominent white Little Rock law firm. In 1889 he was admitted to the bar. He became a prominent African American in Arkansas, running unsuccessfully for state representative in 1892, and was a delegate to the Republican National Convention a few times. For more, see Tom Dillard, "Scipio A. Jones," *Arkansas Historical Quarterly* 31 (1972): 201–219.

[72] Thomas J. Price, Attorney in Little Rock, to Walter White, letter, November 26, 1919, Waskow Papers.

[73] Walter White to Thomas J. Price, letter, December 1, 1919, Waskow Papers.

[74] The CDFC's involvement is notable: during the first year of the legal battle, the CDFC would raise and spend more money than the NAACP in the legal defense of the Phillips County 12. However, the CFDC had no spending plan, and all but $1,000 of its money was used up by June 1920. In the end, the NAACP spent more money on legal defense than the CDFC and was able to sustain the legal defense in this case until the victory in front of the Supreme Court. If left in the CDFC's hands, the case would have died in 1920 and never reached the Supreme Court. See Report of J. H. McConico, Secretary of the Citizens Defense Fund Commission, April 7, 1920, Waskow Papers; J. H. McConico to John R. Shillady, letter, June 10, 1920, Waskow Papers.

[75] Thomas Price to Walter White, letter, November 26, 1919, Waskow Papers. Though not realized initially, Jones was a godsend to the NAACP. After Murphy passed away a year later and his law firm refused to honor Murphy's commitment to the case, Jones became the sole head counsel for the Phillips County 12.

his law firm refused to honor Murphy's commitment to the case, Jones became the NAACP's lead counsel for the Phillips County 12.[76] The NAACP worked closely with Jones, providing him with white co-counsel when he needed it and with funds to support the subsequent appeal of the case to the Supreme Court of the United States.[77]

The NAACP's influence in the legal defense was further displayed by the watchdog role it played in this case. This was the greatest legal battle the NAACP had ever undertaken, and its leadership influenced every important decision. Not content with simply disbursing money, the NAACP wanted a direct hand in monitoring the litigation activities. After securing Murphy and Jones as counsel, the director of the Memphis NAACP branch was contacted to keep tabs on Murphy and Jones for the national leadership in New York.[78] Furthermore, NAACP board members were constantly in touch with defense counsel, and reports on the progress of the Arkansas cases were delivered at the monthly board of director meetings; these monthly updates began as soon as the NAACP pledged its commitment, and they continued until all the men were free in 1925.

The Legal Struggle in Local and State Courts

To understand the importance of the NAACP's role in *Moore v. Dempsey*, it is necessary to first examine the legal battles in the local and state courts. Through a relentless legal defense and sustained NAACP organizational oversight, the lives of the Phillips County 12 were eventually spared. A close look at the events leading up to the Supreme Court decision in *Moore* reveals that the NAACP's influence was evident at every step along the road to victory.

The litigation plan developed by the NAACP's defense counsel was a reflection of the tremendous obstacles they faced in taking up these cases. From the outset, Jones and Murphy were realistic that the courts in Arkansas were unlikely to set the Phillips County 12 free. At the time, Phillips County was a very hostile environment as most of the white residents were still incensed about the riot. It seemed the only plausible prospect for success would be taking the case of the Phillips County 12 outside of Arkansas. Murphy and Jones therefore decided to pursue a legal strategy that focused on the exhaustion of all local and state possibilities. They planned to file motions for new trials in the Phillips County Circuit Court, the Arkansas Supreme Court, and would go so far as the U.S. Supreme Court. However, if the U.S. Supreme Court was to deny review, it was determined that a petition for a writ of habeas corpus be

---

[76] Mary White Ovington to G. L. Beer, letter, October 8, 1921, NAACP Papers, Manuscript Division, Library of Congress, Washington, DC.

[77] NAACP Board Chairman to Arkansas Contributors, letter, October 7, 1922, NAACP Papers, Manuscript Division, Library of Congress, Washington, DC.

[78] James Weldon Johnson to Robert Church, letter, December 2, 1919, Waskow Papers.

filed in the U.S. Federal District Court on the ground that the twelve African American men had been denied due process of law in violation of the due process clause of the Fourteenth Amendment of the U.S. Constitution. This strategy, combined with the persistence of the NAACP's defense, would prove to be effective throughout the course of the legal battle.[79]

First Attempt: Court Error Leads to the Saving of Six Men

With the execution dates fast approaching, Murphy and Jones filed a motion for a new trial in the Phillips County Circuit Court on the grounds that mob domination over the court and jury was a constitutional violation of the right to a fair trial. While Murphy and Jones did not expect the Phillips county court to grant a new trial, they provided a detailed account about why the verdicts of death were contrary to law and the available evidence. In their motion they argued that

> The trials of the accused occurred during a period of great excitement; that the accused were given no opportunity to consult with friends or to employ counsel, and, while they were confined awaiting trial, a mob composed of several hundred armed white men surrounded the jail and courthouse and that the excitement and feeling against the accused among the white people of the county was such that it was impossible to obtain an impartial jury.[80]

In subsequent appeals, the NAACP would use the same argument developed here to establish that the defendants' due process rights were violated. On December 18, 1919, its motion was heard in court, yet it was denied that same day. The next step was an appeal to the Arkansas Supreme Court.

The appeal of the Phillips County 12 to the Arkansas Supreme Court would mark an important turning point in this case. Before the cases were set to be argued in the court they were formally divided into two groups, though from all accounts there was no particular reasoning to the separation into two groups: the first group, *Ed Ware et al.* (Alf Banks Jr., Joe Fox, Albert Giles, John Martin, William Wardow, and Ed Ware) and the second group, *Frank Moore et al.* (Ed Coleman, Frank Hall, Ed Hicks, Frank Hicks, Joe Knox, and Frank Moore).[81] In arguing the cases, NAACP counsel raised a new issue that, in accordance with Arkansas law, the jury was required to specify if the offense was for murder in the first or second degree when rendering the decision. In its apparent haste, the jury in the *Ed Ware et al.* cases did not specify the degree of murder, and in the *Frank Moore et al.* cases, the jury had made the same mistake although the presiding judge had later corrected it.[82] NAACP counsel based its appeal in the *Ed Ware et al.* case on the error of the jury in specifying the degree of murder, while in the *Moore et al. case*, it focused on the complete

[79] U. S. Bratton to Walter White, letter, October 15, 1920, Waskow Papers.
[80] *State v. Martineau*, 149 Ark. 237 (1921).
[81] *Arkansas Gazette*, March 23, 1920, p. 7; NAACP 12th Annual Report.
[82] *Arkansas Gazette*, March 21, 1920, p. 20.

exclusion of African Americans from the grand or petit juries.[83] Because the questions pertaining to each set of men were similar, the Arkansas Supreme Court said the cases could be tried in two groups. From this point further, the NAACP legal defense would be working on two separate (yet obviously related) cases.[84]

On March 29, 1920, the Arkansas Supreme Court announced its decision to overturn the death sentences handed down by the Phillips County Circuit Court in the *Ed Ware et al.* case. The law in Arkansas mandated that a verdict not specifying the degree of murder be considered "defective."[85] The Arkansas Supreme Court had no choice but to reverse the verdict of the lower court in order to maintain the appearance of impartiality, once the NAACP legal defense team had identified this error. Though the cases of the men in *Ed Ware et al.* were sent back for retrial, the defendants' safety was temporarily secured.[86]

However, the six men in the *Moore et al.* case were not so lucky; the court quickly dismissed the defense's claim that the jury did not specify the degree of murder, pointing to the fact that the judge had corrected for the error in the verdict before he approved and signed it. On the allegation that African Americans were systematically excluded from jury service, the court pointed to Arkansas law which clearly states that this issue must be raised from the outset of the trials to be considered by the court, and that it could not be retroactively raised in a motion for a new trial.[87] In response to the NAACP's argument

---

[83] There were precedents for federal courts overturning trial verdicts in cases where African Americans were excluded from grand and petit juries, going back to *Strauder v. West Virginia*, 100 U.S. 303 (1880) and *Neal v. Delaware*, 103 U.S. 370 (1881). Both were cases where a jury in which African Americans were excluded convicted an African American man. The Supreme Court ruled in both cases that the trials violated the equal protection clause of the Fourteenth Amendment.

[84] Mary White Ovington, *The Walls Came Tumbling Down*, New York: Harcourt Brace, 1947, p. 159.

[85] *Banks v. State*, 143 Ark. 154 (1920). "[A] verdict of conviction in a case of murder, which does not find the degree of murder, is so fatally defective that no judgment can be entered upon it," pp. 155–156.

[86] While all six men in *Ed Ware et al.* would face new trials for murder, with legal counsel in place, it was assured that their trials would be handled more fairly than the first trial. Subsequently, a heated litigation back-and-forth would take place between the NAACP legal defense team and the State of Arkansas (including another reversal of a death sentence on conviction, the granting of a change of venue, and an agreement to a continuance). However, once the Supreme Court agreed to review *Moore v. Dempsey*, it became clear that Arkansas was waiting on the court's decision to gauge how forcefully it would continue to push this case; in this way the fate of the men in *Ed Ware et al.* were inextricably tied to *Frank Moore et al.* With the Supreme Court decision in *Moore v. Dempsey*, the state of Arkansas decided not to pursue the case against the men in *Ed Ware et al.* They were eventually discharged in 1923. See *Banks v. State*, 143 Ark. 154 (1920); *Ware v. State*, 146 Ark. 321 (1920); *Ware v. State*, 159 Ark. 540 (1923); *Martin v. State*, 162 Ark. 282 (1924); *Arkansas Gazette*, June 26, 1923; James Weldon Johnson, Secretary Report for the March Meeting of the Board, March 9, 1923, NAACP Papers, Manuscript Division, Library of Congress, Washington, DC.

[87] *Hicks v. State*, 143 Ark. 158 (1920).

that a mob-dominated atmosphere prevented the carrying out of a fair trial, the court disagreed: "The trials were had according to law, the jury was correctly charged as to the law of the case, and the testimony is legally sufficient to support the verdicts returned."[88] Thus, despite NAACP legal arguments to the contrary, the Arkansas state court saw nothing wrong with the way the trial was carried out. The death sentences of the six men in *Moore et al.* were all affirmed.

Anticipating defeat in the state court, the NAACP's legal defense team prepared to take the case of the Phillips County 6 to the U.S. Supreme Court on a writ of certiorari, filed on October 5, 1920.[89] However, the U.S. Supreme Court was no more helpful in this matter than the courts of Arkansas and declined to review the Arkansas Supreme Court decision on October 20, 1920, finding that it did not present substantial federal questions.[90] As a result, a new date of execution was arranged.

Second Attempt: Habeas Corpus Pleadings Delay Executions

NAACP board members were closely watching the developments and were concerned about an execution date that was fast approaching. Two days before the scheduled execution of the Phillips County 6, the governor of Arkansas denied the NAACP's request for a stay of execution. At the same time, the NAACP planned to file a petition for a writ of habeas corpus in the U.S. District Court in Little Rock.[91] Ordinarily, the writ of habeas corpus represents an important safeguard against the infringement of civil liberties from lawless state action. A defendant can challenge constitutional violations by filing a habeas corpus petition, which demands that an official holding an individual in custody be made to explain the legal authority and the factual basis for holding the individual. If the court determines that the incarceration is unlawful, it can order the official to release the prisoner.[92] Thus, the writ of habeas corpus has historically stood as a fundamental instrument for safeguarding individual freedom and liberties from abusive state power.

Unfortunately, no judge was available to hear the case until after the execution date in Little Rock's Federal District Court. The situation appeared grim: the Arkansas governor refused to interfere, and the court in which the NAACP filed the habeas petition was not hearing cases. The NAACP defense refused to give up, notwithstanding the bleak chances of obtaining court intervention a mere two days before the planned execution. Though it was a long shot, to

---

[88] *Hicks v. State*, 143 Ark. 158 (1920).

[89] NAACP BOD Minutes, Report of the Secretary, April 1920, NAACP Papers, Manuscript Division, Library of Congress, Washington, DC.

[90] *Hicks*, cert. denied 254 U.S. 630 (1920).

[91] Scipio Jones to Walter White, letter, May 20, 1921, Series 1: C, Box 349 NAACP Papers, Manuscript Division, Library of Congress, Washington, DC.

[92] James Liebman and Randy Hertz, *Federal Habeas Corpus Practice and Procedure*, 5th ed., LexisNexis Michie, 2005.

stall for more time, NAACP defense counsel filed another petition for habeas corpus in which it repeated the same allegations of mob domination before Little Rock's Pulsaki Chancery Court, a state court that is authorized to apply principles of equity, not law, to cases.[93] The brief stated:

> The entire trial, verdict and judgment against them was but an empty ceremony; that their real trial and condemnation had already taken place before said "Committee of Seven" … the program laid out by said committee was carried through, and the verdict against petitioners was pronounced, not as the independent verdict of an unbiased jury, but as part of the prearranged scheme and judgment of said committee.[94]

Persistence finally produced a breakthrough before the state court: Chancellor John Martineau was sympathetic to the NAACP's claims and ordered the warden of the state penitentiary, E. H. Dempsey, to appear in court to explain why the men had received the death sentence.[95] Dissatisfied with his explanation, Chancellor Martineau issued an injunction staying the executions until the habeas hearing could be held.

The victory was short-lived. As soon as the verdict was rendered, Arkansas authorities applied to the Arkansas Supreme Court for a writ of prohibition. They alleged that the chancery court, a court of equity, did not have appellate jurisdiction in criminal trials. The Arkansas Supreme Court agreed and quashed the writ of habeas corpus. In doing so, the Arkansas Supreme Court not only affirmed that the chancery court was out of line in ruling in this case, but issued a warning to NAACP counsel about pursuing federal review in its opinion:

> "Due process of law" does not mean that the operation of the State government shall be conducted without error or fault in any particular case, nor that the Federal Courts may substitute their judgment for that of the State courts, or exercise any general review over their proceedings, but only that the fundamental rights of the prisoner shall not be taken from him.[96]

Undeterred, the NAACP appealed the decision to the U.S. Supreme Court on August 4, 1921, in another attempt to postpone the date of the executions. But the case did not present a federal question: the U.S. Supreme Court had no jurisdiction to decide whether under Arkansas law, a chancery court had habeas corpus jurisdiction over a criminal conviction. The writ was quickly

---

[93] The chancery court is an English institution that is a separate court to deal with equity proceedings. The Pulsaki Chancery Court was the first chancery court created in Arkansas and was legislated into existence in 1855 to resolve a banking dispute. Today, Arkansas is one of only four states to have separate chancery courts (Mississippi, Tennessee, and Delaware are the others). For more on this, see Morton Gitelman, "The First Chancery Court in Arkansas," *The Arkansas Historical Society* 55, no. 4 (1996): pp. 357–382.

[94] *State v. Martineau*, 149 Ark. 237 (1921), pp. 244–245.

[95] A chancellor is someone that serves in an official judicial role, similar to a judge but in a chancery court.

[96] *State v. Martineau*, 149 Ark. 237 (1921).

dismissed, not even denied on its merits by the U.S. Supreme Court.[97] Once again, a new date of execution was set, this time for September 23, 1921.[98]

Third Attempt: The State Court's Machinery
of Correction Needs Repair

With a bit more time on its hands, the NAACP filed a motion for a writ of habeas corpus in the proper court, the U.S. District Court for the Eastern District of Arkansas, on September 21, 1921.[99] Similar to the previous defense appeals, the petition for a writ of habeas corpus was based on White's investigation of the Phillips County riot, in which he discovered that African Americans had peacefully assembled against the economic exploitation of the peonage system but had been attacked by angry whites, and that their imprisonment and death sentences were the result of a conspiracy by leading whites of Phillips County. Referencing resolutions calling for the execution of the defendants by prominent whites in Phillips County, Jones stated in the petition for a writ of habeas corpus:

Said resolutions further and conclusively show the existence of the mob spirit prevalent among all the white people of Phillips County at the time petitioners and the other defendants were put through the form of trials and show that the only reason the mob stayed its hand, the only reason they were not lynched was that the leading citizens of the community made a solemn promise to the mob that they should be executed in the form of law.[100]

Furthermore, Jones claimed the defendants were "denied the equal protection of the law, and have been convicted, condemned and are about to be deprived of their lives without due process of law."[101] The filing of the petition on September 21, 1921, again delayed the executions of the men in the *Moore* case.

New cracks were appearing in the state of Arkansas's case. The federal judge appointed to the U.S. District Court for the Eastern District of Arkansas recused himself because he had previously been a resident of the city of Helena in Phillips County. His replacement was an outsider, U.S. district judge J. H. Cotteral from Oklahoma. This was welcome news to the NAACP, who had long doubted the sharecroppers could receive a fair trial in the state of Arkansas given that the racial violence of 1919 had created significant tensions and tainted many

---

[97] *Martineau*, cert. dismissed with costs, 257 U.S. 665 (1921).
[98] Twelfth Annual Report, NAACP, for the year 1921, p. 21, NAACP Papers, Manuscript Division, Library of Congress, Washington, DC.
[99] BOD Minutes, Report of the Secretary, August 1921, NAACP Papers, Manuscript Division, Library of Congress, Washington, DC.
[100] From the brief prepared by Scipio Jones for the writ of habeas corpus, reprinted in the Twelfth Annual Report, NAACP.
[101] From the brief prepared by Scipio Jones for the writ of habeas corpus, reprinted in the Twelfth Annual Report, NAACP.

in the white-power structure of the state. In response to the NAACP's motion for a writ of habeas corpus, the attorney general for Arkansas simply demurred and did not dispute any of the NAACP's allegations. The demurrer was sustained, and Judge Cotteral dismissed the petition on September 27, 1921.[102] In legal pleading, a demurrer was a responsive filing in federal court that admitted the alleged facts of the opponent's argument but denied that they entitled the petitioner a legal basis for relief.[103] The demurrer by the state of Arkansas meant that moving forward, federal courts would have to treat the allegations in the NAACP's petition as true.

The same day that the habeas petition was dismissed, but in a separate proceeding before Judge Cotteral, the NAACP appealed and filed an assignment of errors, claiming that "the court erred in holding that the facts stated in the petition for the writ of habeas corpus and the exhibits filed there with, are insufficient to entitle them to any relief."[104] But Judge Cotteral stated "that there exists probable cause for an appeal in this cause," providing encouragement for the NAACP's defense team to appeal to the U.S. Supreme Court.[105] On the NAACP's third attempt, the Supreme Court finally gave the defendants a hearing, and the NAACP began preparing for its most important legal battle yet in the organization's history.[106]

The U.S. Supreme Court and a Breakthrough in Constitutional Law

After a three-year struggle, the NAACP's litigation efforts reached the highest court in the nation in *Moore v. Dempsey*.[107] However, the NAACP faced

---

[102] Scipio Jones to James Weldon Johnson, telegram, September 27, 1921, Part I, Series C: Box 349, NAACP Papers, Manuscript Division, Library of Congress, Washington, DC.

[103] The demurrer was abolished by Rule 7(c) of the Federal Rules of Civil Procedure when those rules went into effect in 1938. Today, lawyers no longer "demur," but they file motions to dismiss for failure to state a claim upon which relief can be based, known as a Rule 12(b)(6) motion under the Federal Rules of Civil Procedure. The thrust of that type of motion is that, even taking the alleged facts as true, they do not establish a claim for which the law provides relief.

[104] Assignment of Errors, Transcript of Record, *Moore v. Dempsey*, 101–103.

[105] Court Order, Transcript of the Record, *Moore v. Dempsey*, 101–102; Mary White Ovington to F. E. Pinson, letter, October 26, 1921, Part 7, Series A, Reel 20, NAACP Papers, Manuscript Division, Library of Congress, Washington, DC.

[106] Of particular significance, Frank Moore and his four codefendants had been tried as a group up to this point. Frank Hicks, whose case was originally heard separately, was not tried with Frank Moore and the others on subsequent appeals. However, because both cases were so closely related, the NAACP lawyers filed similar appeals and briefs for *Moore v. Dempsey* and *Hicks v. Dempsey* from 1919 up until this case. Finally, with the appeal to the Supreme Court granted in the U.S. District Court for the writ of habeas corpus in both cases, the Supreme Court consolidated *Hicks v. Dempsey* with *Moore v. Dempsey* and reported both in its opinion found at *Moore v. Dempsey*, 261 U.S. 86 (1923).

[107] Historical circumstances explain why this case skips from the U.S. District Court for the Eastern District of Arkansas to the Supreme Court of the United States. In 1921, the Judiciary Act or Judges Act of 1925 (43 Stat. 936) had not yet been passed. The act would eliminate

a number of obstacles before it could succeed: (1) the organization needed to make a believer out of NAACP president Moorfield Storey, who was scheduled to argue the case in front of the Supreme Court, and (2) the organization had to overcome the troublesome legal precedent of *Frank v. Mangum*,[108] described at the beginning of this chapter.

In determining who would argue the case in front of the Supreme Court, Moorfield Storey emerged as the obvious choice. A prominent Boston lawyer with a deep commitment to furthering the goals of the NAACP, Storey agreed to argue the case before the Supreme Court after much prodding from other NAACP officers.[109] Close to retirement, however, Storey wished to be exempt from researching and preparing the briefs, and in October 1922, Jones sent a copy of the record over to the NAACP offices so Storey could be properly informed and prepare himself to argue the case. Storey knew his chief obstacle was the *Frank* case. If the NAACP were to win this case, it would have to prove that the state of Arkansas did not provide a proper corrective process. However, this was a daunting task since the Arkansas Supreme Court had produced a six-page opinion denying relief. Thus, the NAACP would have to show that review by the Arkansas Supreme Court was inadequate to correct the flaws of the original trial.

The NAACP couched its legal arguments for federal court intervention in the Fourteenth Amendment. Citing violation of the due process clause of the Fourteenth Amendment by the state of Arkansas, the NAACP brief in the Supreme Court made a strong case that the influence of the mob on the court and jury prevented the defendants from receiving a "fair and impartial trial before a white jury."[110] Once again discrediting the story of a planned African American insurrection and utilizing the results of White's initial investigation in Phillips County, the brief argued that the reasons behind the violence stemmed from the exploitative sharecropping system and the bitterness of white landlords upon finding out that African American farmers were organizing to procure better settlements. The brief further stated that "a great many innocent Negro men and women, many of whom were picking cotton in the fields, were

direct appeals from the district courts in all but a select number of cases, creating the certiorari system in order to decrease the volume of the Supreme Court's caseload. Ever since, the Supreme Court has picked its caseload, and the U.S. Circuit Court of Appeals has had the final say in a great many appellate cases. However, before the Judiciary Act of 1925, writs of error or appeal could go directly from the district court to the Supreme Court for obligatory review. Thus, because the district court of the Eastern District of Arkansas granted the NAACP's appeal to the U.S. Supreme Court, the NAACP did not have to go through the Court of Appeals.

[108] *Frank v. Mangum*, 237 U.S. 309 (1915).

[109] Conference of Scipio Jones with the Secretary, regarding the Arkansas Cases, September 14, 1922, NAACP Papers, Manuscript Division, Library of Congress, Washington, DC.

[110] *Moore v. Dempsey*, Brief for the Appellants, Supreme Court of the United States, October Term 1922, No. 199, Filed on January 8, 1923, p. 8.

killed in cold blood"[111] in the violence that ensued, and their subsequent trials were dominated by a mob whereby

the feeling against petitioners was such that it overawed the Judge on the bench, the jury, the attorney appointed to defend them and everyone connected with said court; that all, Judge, jury, and counsel, were dominated by the mob spirit that was universally present in court and out, so that if any juror had had the courage to investigate said charge with any spirit of fairness, and vote for an acquittal, he himself would have been the victim of the mob.[112]

The NAACP tried distinguishing its case from *Frank*, arguing that the facts of mob domination prevented any subsequent process from sufficiently correcting for the errors in the original case. In a bold move, the NAACP made clear that the Supreme Court needed to do more to protect the constitutional guarantee to a fair trial: "It would be preposterous to say that the requirements of the 14th Amendment are satisfied by giving one seeking a new trial an 'empty right' to another trial in the same hostile environment."[113] By virtue of mob domination of the court, counsel, and jury, the NAACP argued the court in Arkansas "lost its jurisdiction ... and the result was but an empty ceremony, carried through in the apparent form of law, and that the verdict of the jury was really a mob verdict, dictated by the spirit of the mob and returned because no other verdict would have been tolerated, and that the judgment against them is therefore a nullity."[114] Upholding the conviction, the NAACP's brief reasoned, would be committing "judicial murder."[115]

But it was not just the NAACP's legal arguments that influenced the court. As, the rest of this book aims to make clear, by the time *Moore v. Dempsey* was before the Supreme Court, the political climate had changed as a result of the NAACP's activism. During the journey of *Moore v. Dempsey* through the different courts in the U.S. legal system, the NAACP had obtained a presidential denouncement of lynching, and an anti-lynching bill had passed the House of Representatives. Highlighting the importance of the NAACP's involvement in the political sphere, Colonel Murphy, one of the organization's attorneys in the *Moore* case, wrote to the organization in 1919 that he believed the hearings on the anti-lynching bill would "be of great value in

---

[111] *Moore v. Dempsey*, Brief for the Appellants, Supreme Court of the United States, October Term 1922, No. 199, Filed on January 8, 1923, pp. 3–4.

[112] *Moore v. Dempsey*, Brief for the Appellants, Supreme Court of the United States, October Term 1922, No. 199, Filed on January 8, 1923, p. 8.

[113] *Moore v. Dempsey*, Brief for the Appellants, Supreme Court of the United States, October Term 1922, No. 199, Filed on January 8, 1923, p. 40.

[114] *Moore v. Dempsey*, Brief for the Appellants, Supreme Court of the United States, October Term 1922, No. 199, Filed on January 8, 1923, p. 9.

[115] *Moore v. Dempsey*, Brief for the Appellants, Supreme Court of the United States, October Term 1922, No. 199, Filed on January 8, 1923, p. 33.

the habeas corpus proceedings which are to be brought in the United States Court."[116]

The most obvious example of the way the NAACP's activism in the political sphere translated into an impact on the Supreme Court is the shifting position of William Howard Taft. In 1911, while president, he ignored NAACP requests to take a stand on a particularly gruesome lynching that had taken place in Livermore, Kentucky, telling the group that it was not a federal matter.[117] However, in 1919 when the NAACP convened its first national conference on lynching at Carnegie Hall in New York City to raise public awareness about the need for federal involvement, Taft became one of the prominent signatories of the *Address to the Nation on Lynchings*, a public statement that called for congressional inquiry into the lynching menace in the South.[118] Even more surprising, Taft, while being confirmed as chief justice of the Supreme Court in 1921, made it known to the NAACP through Representative Leonidas Dyer that he thought the anti-lynching bill was constitutional.[119] Though this information was strictly confidential and only made available to the ranking leadership in the NAACP, Taft's affirmation that it was indeed constitutional for the federal government to get involved in meting out punishments to those responsible for lynchings indicated that he might vote in favor of the *Moore* defendants (Illustration 5.2).

The oral argument was presented before the U.S. Supreme Court on January 9, 1923. The NAACP would not be disappointed. On February 19, 1923, the Supreme Court handed down its decision, which agreed with NAACP claims that the defendants' rights to due process were violated by an impassioned mob. In the 6–2 opinion, Justice Oliver Wendell Holmes wrote,

But if the case is that the whole proceeding is a mask – that counsel, jury and judge were swept to the fatal end by an irresistible wave of public passion, and that the State Courts failed to correct the wrong, neither perfection in the machinery for correction nor the possibility that the trial court and counsel saw no other way of avoiding an immediate outbreak of the mob can prevent this Court from securing to the petitioners their constitutional rights.[120]

---

[116] Johnson to Storey, letter, December 17, 1919, Series I: C, Box 66, NAACP Papers, Manuscript Division, Library of Congress, Washington, DC.

[117] An African American man had been accused of killing a white person and had been taken out of custody by a mob to an opera house where spectators bought tickets and shot his body into pieces. A delegation of citizens from Washington, DC presented Taft with the NAACP resolution denouncing lynching, and he demurred that it was not a federal matter. (*The Crisis* January/February 2002, p. 43).

[118] Tenth Annual Report for the year 1919, p. 13, NAACP Papers, Manuscript Division, Library of Congress, Washington, DC.

[119] James Weldon Johnson to Oswald Villard, letter, August 1, 1921, Anti-Lynching File; Walter White to Louis Marshall, letter, August 2, 1921, Anti-Lynching File; James Weldon Johnson to William Walling, letter, August 3, 1921, Anti-Lynching File, NAACP Papers, Manuscript Division, Library of Congress, Washington, DC.

[120] *Moore v. Dempsey*, 261 U.S. 86 (1923). The total number of justices who heard *Moore v. Dempsey* was eight instead of the usual nine. On the day *Moore v. Dempsey* was decided, Justice Edward Sanford was sworn in to replace Justice Mahlon Pitney who had suffered a stroke.

ILLUSTRATION 5.2 Justices of the Supreme Court of the United States who decided *Moore v. Dempsey*. Back row (left to right): Pierce Butler, Louis Brandeis, George Sutherland, and Edward Sanford (did not vote). Front row (left to right) William Van Devanter, Joseph McKenna, Chief Justice William Howard Taft, Oliver Wendell Holmes, and James McReynolds. "The U.S. Supreme Court 1924."
Source: Photographer Unknown. Courtesy of the Library of Congress, Prints and Photographs Division, LC-USZ62–91090, LOT 11520.

And so with this case, the wall of precedent insulating state criminal court proceedings came crashing down. Two members of the Supreme Court remained unconvinced. A dissent written by Justice James Clark McReynolds, joined in by Justice George Sutherland, concluded, "I find nothing in this statement which counsels lawlessness or indicates more than an honest effort by upstanding men to meet the grave situation."[121] Citing liberally from *Frank v. Mangum*, the minority argued that the law had been carried out and a proper corrective process applied by Arkansas. The majority, on the other hand, determined that the state of Arkansas did not provide a sufficient corrective process to correct for the presence of the mob and remanded the case to the district court in Arkansas (for a breakdown of all the justices and how they voted, see Table 5.1).[122]

[121] *Moore v. Dempsey*, 261 U.S. 86 (1923).
[122] Curious to some readers is why I have not addressed the well-regarded attitudinalist model to explain the Supreme Court's decision making in *Moore*. The short answer is that it has

TABLE 5.1 Supreme Court justices in *Moore v. Dempsey*

Supreme Court Justices	President Appointed By	Vote on *Moore*
William Howard Taft (C.J.)	Harding	Majority
Joseph McKenna	McKinley	Majority
Oliver Wendell Holmes	T. Roosevelt	Majority
Willis Van Devanter	Taft	Majority
James McReynolds	Wilson	Dissent
Louis Brandeis	Wilson	Majority
George Sutherland	Harding	Dissent
Pierce Butler	Harding	Majority
Edward Sanford (Justice Pitney)	On the day *Moore v. Dempsey* was decided, Justice Edward Sanford was sworn in to replace Justice Mahlon Pitney	

Though it had been a long journey, the NAACP secured a huge victory and was justifiably jubilant. White wrote soon afterward, "Only by the carrying of these cases to the highest tribunal in the land could justice or, rather, the prevention of gross injustice be secured," and Ovington added in her memoir, "Of the many favorable decisions that we have obtained from the Supreme Court, this is the most far-reaching, affecting as it does colored and white alike, forbidding that 'legal lynching' that Walling feared."[123] After the Supreme Court decision, the NAACP continued to work with Jones on the release of all the men connected with the violence in Phillips County. Finally, on January 13, 1925, Jones sent a telegram to White notifying him that the last of the prisoners convicted in conjunction with the violence of 1919 had been freed. It had taken

severe limitations in terms of explanatory power for this case. Attitudinalists assume judges are self-interested decision makers who will maximize their utility by deciding in accordance with their ideological preferences. Under an attitudinal framework, Supreme Court justices are expected to follow whoever appoints them. Therefore, deviations in the Supreme Court's jurisprudence would be explained by changes in the composition of justices on the high court. However, in considering the Supreme Court's criminal procedure jurisprudence, the attitudinal approach meets some critical difficulties. First, when it comes to *Moore v. Dempsey*, the justices did not vote along partisan lines. Though the bench changed a bit since it had ruled against *Frank v. Mangum*, the changes were not necessarily favorable to the NAACP. Under Chief Justice Taft, the court was more conservative than it had been under the tenure of Chief Justice White, and furthermore, justices appointed by the same president voted differently in this case. For more on the attitudinal model, see Glendon Schubert, "From Public Law to Judicial Behavior." In *Judicial Decision-Making*, edited by Glendon Schubert, New York: Free Press, 1963; Jeffery Segal and Harold Spaeth, *The Supreme Court and the Attitudinal Model*, New York: Cambridge University Press, 1993; Harold Spaeth and Jeffrey Segal, *Majority Rule or Minority Will: Adherence to Precedent on the U.S. Supreme Court*, New York: Cambridge University Press, 1999.

[123] Walter White, "The Defeat of Arkansas Mob Law," in *The Crisis*, April 1923, p. 259; Mary White Ovington, *The Walls Came Tumbling Down*, New York: Harcourt Brace, 1947, p. 163.

more than five years, but the NAACP triumphed by securing the freedom of Ed Coleman, Paul Hall, Ed Hicks, Frank Hicks, J. E. Knox, and Frank Moore.

Conclusion: Law As a Resource

Upon hearing that all the men were released, the Reverend J. R. Maxwell likened the NAACP's work on this case to a miracle, writing, "It was like a thunder bolt from a clear sky. Had it not been for the masterly work done by the Association, long before this, those men would have answered the roll call in judgment."[124] *The Dallas Express*, self-proclaimed as "The South's Oldest and Largest Negro Newspaper," reported that the NAACP's struggle to free the men in Phillips County "ends one of the most sensational struggles ever recorded in America and its victory is one of greater significance to the race than can now be imagined."[125] *The Washington Post* carried news of the verdict in an article titled "Supreme Court Halts Riot Execution," and almost a year after the verdict was returned, the African American newspaper *The Chicago Defender* concluded, "Riot Cases Big Legal Victory."[126] The reactions from the white and African American press were in agreement that this decision was extraordinary.[127]

The NAACP's victory in *Moore v. Dempsey* is critical to understanding how and why the NAACP became a massive and successful litigation engine a few decades later. In the aftermath of *Moore*, the NAACP quickly began to ride the momentum from its victory toward a greater focus on litigation. The February 1923 board meeting minutes provide evidence of the NAACP's heightened interest in litigation as a strategy to achieve its goals: in preparation for discussion at this meeting, the NAACP drafted three pages of proposed activities it was interested in pursuing in the near future. After the section on anti-lynching, the proposal contained a section on legal defense, which stated that in addition to the fight for the men on trial in Arkansas, "The scope of our defense work should be widened so as to include the giving of aid to branches that have undertaken the defense of cases too costly or too important for them to handle alone.... For comprehensive and effective legal defense work, a defense fund from $25,000 to $50,000 is necessary."[128] The NAACP wasted little time

---

[124] Rev. J. R. Maxwell to NAACP, letter, January 22, 1925, NAACP Papers, Manuscript Division, Library of Congress, Washington, DC.

[125] "Justice at Last For The Elaine Rioters," *The Dallas Express*, January 24, 1925.

[126] "Supreme Court Halts Riot Execution," *The Washington Post*, February 20, 1923; "Riot Cases Big Legal Victory," *The Chicago Defender*, February 9, 1924.

[127] For more on press reaction, see *St. Louis Post-Dispatch*, Editorial, February 25, 1923; *Toledo Times*, Editorial, February 22, 1923; "The U.S. Supreme Court Saves Eleven in Ark. Riot Cases," *The Chicago Defender*, March 3, 1923; "US Supreme Court reverses Conviction," *The New York Amsterdam News*, February 28, 1923.

[128] BOD Minutes, February 5, 1923. NAACP Papers, Manuscript Division, Library of Congress, Washington, DC.

in using this case as leverage for fundraising for its legal department: from 1923 to 1924, the NAACP legal defense fund grew from $120.01 to $1,068.[129] While this figure does not seem much today, it represents a near 600 percent increase in one year. However, it wasn't just the NAACP's leadership that was affected; the supporters of the NAACP became acutely aware of the impact of this case. In the year after *Moore v. Dempsey* was decided, the NAACP noted, "In 1924 there came from all parts of the United States and in some instances from without the country, appeals for legal aid. In the twelve months ending December 31, these cases reached a total of 476."[130] The NAACP reported taking action in most of the cases. To put this figure in context, in the Annual Report for 1919, the year the NAACP took on *Moore v. Dempsey*, the NAACP reported involvement of the national office in only three other legal cases.[131] The dramatic increase of individuals making rights claims through the law, along with the NAACP's growing attention to the legal arena after *Moore v. Dempsey*, marks a critical moment in the making of American civil rights in the twentieth century.

Of course, all did not seamlessly change in the aftermath of *Moore v. Dempsey*. Many questions about resources and strategies remained unanswered, and the NAACP was too disorganized internally to fully capitalize on this victory. The NAACP had achieved a remarkable degree of national success in a relatively short period of time and was not fully prepared to transition from a fledgling civil rights organization to one with prominence and national standing. Specifically, with multiple competing interests about how the organization should move forward in the future and capitalize on *Moore*, internal tension erupted in the next decade and threatened to derail the organization. The NAACP would misstep egregiously in the near future – most famously in its disastrous handling of the Scottsboro cases in the 1930s.[132]

[129] Fourteenth Annual Report for the Year 1923, p. 48, NAACP Archives, Fifteenth Annual Report for the Year 1924, p. 59. NAACP Papers, Manuscript Division, Library of Congress, Washington, DC.

[130] Fifteenth Annual Report for the Year 1924, p. 7, NAACP Archives, Widener Library Stacks, Harvard University.

[131] Tenth Annual Report for the Year 1919, pp. 50–56, NAACP Papers, Manuscript Division, Library of Congress, Washington, DC.

[132] The Scottsboro tragedy involved nine young African American men who were dragged off a train in 1931 and arrested for the alleged crime of rape of two white women. In rushed Jim Crow court trials without adequate representation, the young men were convicted and sentenced to death. The NAACP and the International Labor Defense (legal arm of the American Communist Party) got in a heated struggle over which organization would represent the young men in the appeal. Due to numerous issues, the International Labor Defense ultimately prevailed in representing the men in two landmark Supreme Court cases (*Powell v. Alabama* [1932], which established that defendants in capital cases have a right to state appointed counsel and *Norris v. Alabama* [1935], which established that exclusion of African American jurors is unconstitutional). The NAACP was critiqued for its handling of the cases at the early stage; prominent among the accusations was the charge it was an elitist organization and that it spoke down to the families of the men. For more, see Dan Carter, *Scottsboro: A Tragedy of the American South*, Baton Rouge: Louisiana State University Press, 1969.

Even with these setbacks, *Moore v. Dempsey* is of particular importance for putting litigation on the table of available strategies in a way that had never been done before. The NAACP had realized, for the first time, the utility of litigation to weaken the operation of institutional racism in U.S. courtrooms. It marked the beginning of the crumbling of the constitutional legal structure upholding Jim Crow – not just *Guinn* or *Buchannan*, as others have argued. *Moore* took the more harrowing aspects of Jim Crow head-on in ways that *Guinn* and *Buchannan* did not.

6

Civil Rights Bound

> *Government is instituted for the common good; for the protection, safety, prosperity and happiness of the people; and not for the profit, honor, or private interest of any one man, family, or class of men: Therefore the people alone have an incontestable, unalienable, and indefeasible right to institute government; and to reform, alter, or totally change the same, when their protection, safety, prosperity and happiness require it.*
> *– John Adams, Samuel Adams, and James Bowdoin, 1780*

Late in the evening of March 30, 1934, Arthur Ellington, an African American farmer, was accused of murdering a white planter. He denied committing the crime, only to have a white mob surround him, place a rope around his neck, and hang him from the branch of a tree. Maintaining his innocence while gasping for air, he was released from the noose, beaten until blood flowed, then returned to the tree until he was near death – but released again. After the spectacle, Ellington was let go for a day but then picked up at his residence and formally arrested by the deputy. While transporting Ellington to the county jail, the deputy pulled to the side of the road to unleash another excruciating beating on the already bruised body, declaring that the whipping would not stop until Ellington confessed, which he eventually agreed to do. The deputy likewise rounded up two more African American tenant farmers, Ed Brown and Henry Shields, as coconspirators in the murder. Once in custody, Brown and Shields were forced to strip naked and then beaten with leather straps with buckles until their backs were badly cut. The merciless punishment stopped only when they ended their pleas of innocence and agreed to go along with the deputy's version of events.

These three men were swiftly convicted by an all-white jury, based exclusively on their coerced confessions and sentenced to die by hanging. On appeal, the Mississippi Supreme Court affirmed the lower court's ruling. However, the U.S. Supreme Court disagreed, and in *Brown v. Mississippi* (297 US 278) – a landmark criminal procedure case decided on January 10, 1936 – the Supreme Court ruled that confessions obtained through torture violate the due process clause of the Fourteenth Amendment. Noting the importance of *Moore v. Dempsey*, the court relied on this case twice in its rationale, even quoting directly from Justice Holmes's 1923 opinion. Writing for a unanimous court in *Brown v. Mississippi*, Chief Justice Charles Evan Hughes, explained,

> The rack and torture chamber may not be substituted for the witness stand. The State may not permit an accused to be hurried to conviction under mob domination – where the whole proceeding is a mask – without supplying corrective process. *Moore v. Dempsey* 261 US 86, 91

Chief Justice Hughes added that the failure of the defendants' counsel to move to exclude the coerced confessions was "not mere error, but a wrong so fundamental that it made the whole proceeding a mere pretense of a trial and rendered the conviction and sentence wholly void," citing *Moore v. Dempsey*. The case marked the first time the Supreme Court declared coerced confessions unconstitutional. This development evinced an increased willingness on behalf of the Supreme Court to look behind the mere forms of state court proceedings to discern whether criminal defendants had actually been afforded a fair trial.

Brown v. Mississippi was made possible in part through the precedent established in *Moore v. Dempsey*. The political-legal context in which *Moore* was won represented an opportunity to redirect both U.S. constitutional development and the future of civil rights struggles. Prior to the 1920s, the federal government had no role in local or state criminal trials. Since then, the government has been involved like never before, laying down new standards of fairness while expanding the numbers of crimes deemed federal. *Moore v. Dempsey* made clear that states could not always be trusted to properly deal with matters of criminal procedure and that, when state courts acted as a menace to equal rights, federal courts could intervene. In the process, the Supreme Court eradicated the widespread idea that the boundaries of state criminal court trials were impervious to outsiders and set new rules for the relationship between local and federal courts. In the decades that followed, the Supreme Court used the precedent established in *Moore* to expand its reach through a string of landmark decisions that scholars would consequently call "the criminal procedure revolution."[1] During this revolutionary moment, federal courts power-grabbed from state courts, which helped to invent a stronger central state apparatus during the course of the twentieth century. While some scholars might argue the NAACP's victory in *Moore v. Dempsey* and the entrenchment of a federal civil rights agenda refer to unrelated moments, this book suggests that the latter cannot be understood without the former.

---

[1] Michael Klarman, *From Jim Crow to Civil Rights: The Supreme Court and the Struggle for Racial Equality*, New York: Oxford University Press, 2004.

How *Moore* Built *Brown*

The NAACP's efforts to end racist violence fundamentally shifted the relationship between civil rights and the federal government. However, there has been a deafening silence around the NAACP's movement against lynching and mob violence in existing political science scholarship. The greater attention given to studies that locate the U.S. civil rights movement in the timeframe 1954–1965 while ignoring the NAACP's work in the executive and legislative branches of government, is misleading. So are accounts of political development that focus exclusively on institutions and political elites to explain the growth of federal court power. In the voluminous literature that has been written about civil rights and constitutional law there exists not one account that has detailed at length the theoretical and political stakes of the NAACP's campaign against racial violence. This neglect means that casual explanations focused on describing constitutional and civil rights development are often incomplete.

The structure and expertise of the NAACP, which allowed it to play the role it did during the *Brown* era of civil rights, was determined by a series of earlier events that set it down that path. It has been the claim of this book that portions of the civil rights state were erected before the NAACP's infamous education desegregation campaign of the 1930s-1950s and that we must understand how this happened to properly account for the formation of federal court power in criminal law and the expansion of civil rights. Whereas the accepted logic in the civil rights literature is that the NAACP through *Brown v. Board of Education* helped to grow the federal government's commitment to racial equality, I believe there are several limitations to this snapshot view of civil rights development. First and foremost, it misses the opportunity to understand why public opinion and political lobbying strategies were abandoned in this period in favor of litigation. Second, it treats the heyday of civil rights activism and the numerous Supreme Court decisions during this period as a jarring and dramatic break from the norm. In this version of events, civil rights breakthroughs emerge from nationwide sit-ins and marches (social history and sociology) or from national security concerns (political science). As a result, we know much about the big political-social events and far too little about the in-between period that made these changes possible. To help fill in the gaps, more emphasis needs to be placed on the mechanisms for social change that preceded these landmark breakthroughs. Finally, a longer historical perspective reveals that the central moments that have figured so prominently in research on the civil rights movement were path-dependent on earlier campaigns against racist violence, and that the ability of the Supreme Court to siphon power away from southern states in the 1950s and 1960s was connected to its criminal procedure revolution that was set in motion by *Moore v. Dempsey*. Indeed, if *Brown* was the spark, as a legion of scholars have argued – and if we can trace a straight line from *Moore v. Dempsey* to *Brown v. Board of Education*, as I have argued we can – then it seems logical to consider this case the foundation for the civil rights state.

Mark Tushnet, in the seminal book *The NAACP's Legal Strategy Against Segregated Education*, traces the litigation campaign that would culminate in the 1954 victory to a 1930 grant from the American Fund for Public Service, most often referred to as the Garland Fund after its benefactor Charles Garland.[2] The Garland Fund, established in 1922, was a progressive philanthropy, with a board of directors that amounts to a roster of notable American radicals (including Roger Baldwin, Morris Ernst, Elizabeth Gurley Flynn, William Foster, Freda Kirchwey, and Norman Thomas). The stated purpose of the Garland Fund was to provide money for the following movements:

Those in the economic field closest to the interests of the producing classes – namely the industrial workers and farmers; Those which deal with the interests of minority groups, particularly industrial or racial, disadvantaged under present conditions; Experimental movements in the field of education.[3]

Important for those interested in the development of civil rights in the United States is the $100,000 grant awarded to the NAACP in November 1929 to fund a coordinated legal campaign. Although by 1937, when the last installment of the grant was disbursed, the NAACP had received less than $30,000 (the fund reportedly lost money during the Great Depression), this charitable gift still marked the largest grant the NAACP had ever received and thus "the first time the NAACP had enough money to proceed in a planned, sustained fashion" to address the constitutional structure of Jim Crow.[4] Reflecting on that moment, Walter White confessed, "The grant from the Garland Fund permitted us to alter our entire method of operation.... It enabled us to make the most complete and authoritative study of the legal status of the Negro which had ever been conceived or executed."[5]

The Garland Fund came with specific directives. Its internal committee on "Negro Work" had formulated a plan to commit the money for NAACP court cases aimed at achieving equal rights for African Americans. The committee recommended a "dramatic large-scale campaign to give Negroes equal rights in the public schools, in the voting booths, on the railroad, and on the juries"

[2] Mark Tushnet, *The NAACP's Legal Strategy Against Segregated Education, 1925–1950*, Chapel Hill: University of North Carolina Press, 1987.

[3] Statement of Policy in Dealing with Applications for Assistance, August 10, 1922, Reel 2, American Fund for Public Service Records, Rare Books and Manuscripts Division, Schwarzman Building, New York Public Library.

[4] Richard Kluger, *Simple Justice: The History of Brown v. Board of Education and Black America's Struggle for Equality*, New York: Knopf, 1975, p. 133; Gloria Samson, *The American Fund for Public Service: Charles Garland and Radical Philanthropy, 1922–1941*, Westport, CT: Greenwood Press, 1996, p. 214.

[5] Walter Francis White, *A Man Called White, The Autobiography of Walter White*, New York: Viking Press, 1948, p. 142.

in every state.[6] The significance of the Garland Fund's proposal was the focus on "public schools." By 1929 the NAACP had been working on weakening the constitutional structure in the other recommended areas, but education was a new issue.[7] What emerged in the next three years, after being vetted by senior NAACP officials, was an implementation plan with a solitary focus on education and a three-pronged strategy of attacking the separate-but-equal doctrine. Between 1933 and 1950, the NAACP would handle three different types of education desegregation suits connected with the Garland grant: suits against segregated higher education, suits to equalize teacher salaries, and suits against unequal facilities in primary and secondary education. Charles Hamilton Houston, former dean of Howard University Law School, accepted a position with the NAACP as full-time legal counsel and spearheaded the effort. This is the litigation campaign that led directly to the landmark *Brown v. Board of Education* decision.

While scholars of the NAACP are well aware the litigation strategy that produced *Brown* would not have been possible without the funding from the Garland grant, they have failed to fully appreciate how it directly connects with the NAACP's anti-lynching campaign. If the NAACP had not engaged in a national struggle to end lynching, there may have been no *Brown* – the relationship that led to this grant was established much earlier, when the NAACP was working against racist violence. The first grant and the second grant from the Garland Fund occurred in 1922 and 1923 to support the NAACP in its anti-lynching campaign. In other words, the publicity the NAACP garnered from its national work in the anti-lynching campaign drew the attention of the Garland Fund and led to a grant of $2,500 and an additional appropriation of $865.50 to provide publicity to assist in passing the Dyer Anti-Lynching Bill in Congress.[8] Subsequently, ads were taken out in major newspapers across the United States to urge readers to contact their senators in support of the Dyer bill. A typical ad filled a full page and called lynching "The Shame of America." The Garland Fund acknowledged that the NAACP's "anti-lynching campaign in 1922 was successful beyond anticipation."[9] A few months after the bill died in the Senate, the importance of

---

[6] Memo, October 18, 1929, American Fund for Public Service Records, Rare Books and Manuscripts Division, Schwarzman Building, New York Public Library.

[7] Mark Tushnet, *The NAACP's Legal Strategy Against Segregated Education, 1925–1950*, Chapel Hill: University of North Carolina Press, 1987, p. 20.

[8] Appropriation of $2,500 was voted on October 11, 1922 for an educational campaign in connection with the Federal Anti-Lynching Campaign. Additional appropriation of $865.50 was voted on and approved on January 24, 1923, Reel 10, Box 15, American Fund for Public Service Records, Rare Books and Manuscripts Division, Schwarzman Building, New York Public Library.

[9] Report of the Committee on Negro Work, October 13, 1929, Reel 4, Box 7, American Fund for Public Service Records, Rare Books and Manuscripts Division, Schwarzman Building, New York Public Library.

litigation was impressed upon the Garland Fund after the NAACP's victory in *Moore v. Dempsey*.

What the NAACP had done in a short time that attracted the attention of the Garland Fund was to push the political system in a direction it was not initially willing to go – not through lobbying but through litigation. In appealing to the Garland Fund for a large sum of money to support the establishment of a legal defense fund, the NAACP wrapped its request for increased funding in the afterglow of its *Moore v. Dempsey* legal victory:

Outstanding in its defense work is the defense of the Arkansas peons, in which case twelve innocent Negro farmers, hastily condemned to death after a farcical trial lasting a few minutes and sixty-seven others sentenced to long prison terms, were absolutely acquitted and freed by the efforts of this Association for five years through the courts of the State of Arkansas and up to and through the United States Supreme Court.... Indeed, the main work of the Association is the combating of forces which are baneful not alone to the Negro but to American law and free institutions.[10]

The NAACP's legal work had not gone unnoticed. After drafting the contours of a strategy to help African Americans achieve equal rights in 1929, the Garland Fund's board of directors surveyed the landscape of civil rights organizations and determined, "It seems to all so obvious that the only organization which would effectively carry out the brunt of such a campaign is the NAACP."[11] In making a case for gifting the NAACP with this grant instead of the American Civil Liberties Union (who was referred to as "a spendthrift bunch of wastrels") or any other left-leaning organization, the Garland Fund's board of directors used *Moore v. Dempsey* in their rationale. Writing to supporters, they reasoned:

Compare for instance, the costs and results of the Arkansas cases with 12 men twice condemned to die – carried through to a victory in the Supreme Court. The NAACP has been more effective per dollar spent. It has a personnel, a record, and a proven technique that justify more confidence than any other organization in the entire racial field with which we are acquainted.[12]

Without the successes of the NAACP in the political and legal arenas around the issue of racial violence, it is unlikely the relationship with the Garland Fund would have been forged. By extension, without the Garland Fund, it is unlikely the NAACP would have focused on education or had the funding structure necessary to secure legal victories against something as entrenched as racism in the U.S. education system.

---

[10] Memo, 1929, NAACP, Series IC, Box 196, NAACP Papers, Manuscript Division, Library of Congress, Washington DC.

[11] Committee on Negro Work to the Directors of the AFPS, Memo, October 18, 1929, Series IC, Box 196, NAACP Papers, Manuscript Division, Library of Congress, Washington DC.

[12] Board of Directors, letter, 1930. Reel 4, American Fund for Public Service Records, Rare Books and Manuscripts Division, Schwarzman Building, New York Public Library.

Hollowed Strategies

The door to remedy injustice through constitutional litigation that was cracked with *Moore* swung open in the following decades. As a result, most civil rights scholarship paints the NAACP as singularly focused on legal victories. One of the contemporary political leaders who echoed this sentiment, Barack Obama, during his tenure as an Illinois state senator, remarked on a radio show about what he called "one of the … tragedies of the civil rights movement":

Because the civil rights movement became so court focused, I think that there was a tendency to lose track of the political and community organizing activities on the ground that are able to put together the actual coalitions of power.[13]

According to Obama, the courts are "poorly equipped" to address the "basic issues of political and economic justice in this society."[14] Obama's comments reflect a common perspective of many in the legal and political community that the civil rights movement would have achieved greater success if organizations focused more energy and resources on obtaining political instead of legal victories.[15] This critique implicitly assumes that civil rights organizations privileged legal tactics over political tactics from the outset and largely ignored the political arena in their quest for racial equality.

A powerful strain of the scholarship in political science considers courts hollow hopes to civil rights activists. Focusing on the NAACP's struggle against education desegregation in the U.S. Supreme Court, this research determines that courts are largely incapable of bringing about meaningful social change and chastises groups like the NAACP for ignoring political lobbying and grassroots mobilization. Yet this scholarship does not demonstrate how litigation became identified as a viable and prominent strategy in the NAACP. By taking a step back and focusing on the period of the NAACP's emergence, this book shows how the political process proved even more hollow than courts to the NAACP in the early part of the twentieth century. It wasn't that the association ignored the political arena; on the contrary this book details that the political arena was the NAACP's first point of entry in fighting against racist violence in the federal government. If African Americans ultimately came to focus more on litigation than on any other political strategy it is because when faced with the most flagrant violations of African American citizenship, lynching and mob violence, it was the courts and not the president or Congress that responded to their appeals. To understand this, we need to view the political-legal landscape from the lens of the NAACP in 1923. As the NAACP saw it, there was a block of southern senators committed to filibustering any piece of legislation that

---

[13] On January 18, 2001, then–state senator Barack Obama appeared on a public radio chat show (WBEZ-FM's "Odyssey") to discuss the courts and civil rights.
[14] Ibid.
[15] Gerald Rosenberg, *The Hollow Hope: Can Courts Bring about Social Change?*, Chicago: The University of Chicago Press, 1991.

hinted at racial equality, a presidency grown increasingly standoffish to civil rights organizations, and a landmark Supreme Court decision that provided African Americans with substantive protection from racial violence. Given this perspective, it is little wonder the NAACP viewed litigation as its best chance at breaking the back of Jim Crow.

At the same time, it is important to recognize that protests aimed at the legislative and executive branches of government were not for naught. While the NAACP did not achieve all its goals in these branches, the organization was still able to win significant victories – symbolic presidential denouncements of lynching and House passage of the anti-lynching bill – that attracted national attention. Its work in both branches was critical to creating a political climate that was more receptive to the idea of federal involvement in the area of racial violence. The NAACP leveraged these victories as evidence it was having an impact and built up an advanced network of support, including sympathetic media and financial resources. In addition, minor victories showed the public that political power was not static and through sustained protest, it was possible to shift. As a result, NAACP membership rolls expanded; between 1912 and 1919, NAACP membership increased more than 280 percent (from 321 to 91,203), and the number of branches grew from 3 in 1912 to 310 in 1919.[16] Even more remarkable, while the NAACP was long thought to be a force in the North and had strong branches in New York, Washington DC, and Boston, the membership numbers of those in the South finally outpaced the North in 1919, when it was reported that 42,588 of its members were from southern states and 38,420 of its members were from northern states. Also, by this time it was estimated that about 90 percent of the members were African American. The increases in resources and membership were all helpful in growing the organization's operations and positioning the NAACP for future action. Indeed, part of the reason the Supreme Court interfered in a state criminal trial in *Moore* was because the political climate in 1923 surrounding the acceptability of mob violence was not what it was in 1915 when *Frank v. Mangum* was decided.

Organizations, Rights Claiming, and a Fragmented Agenda

The NAACP's efforts in shifting the political climate are even more striking when compared to those of other social movement organizations. Unlike the vibrant 1950s and 1960s when different civil rights groups often came together and united behind a common agenda, the first quarter of the twentieth century was a time when the NAACP was relatively alone in making the case against racist violence. During this period, there were a small number of African American organizations and surprisingly, no organization was focused

---

[16] *The Crisis*, Vol. 19, no. 5, March 1920, pp. 240–245.

on addressing racist violence in the manner of the NAACP.[17] Over the timespan of the NAACP's struggle against mob violence and lynching covered in this book, there were four prominent organizations working to improve the rights of African Americans: the National Association of Colored Women (NACW), the United Negro Improvement Association (UNIA), the National Urban League (NUL), and the Tuskegee Institute.[18] To underscore the nascent state of civil rights organizations and the solitary issue sphere in which the NAACP was operating, I would like to briefly discuss the organizational landscape.

The NACW formed in 1896, actively fought for civil rights, and was involved in advocating women's suffrage and the repeal of Jim Crow laws.[19] Paula Giddings considered the NACW "watershed in the history of black women."[20] The NACW was a predecessor of the African American women's club movement, and its motto was "lifting as we climb," which reflected its belief that African American club women played a critical role in the advancement of the race. The NACW focused most of its energies on charitable pursuits such as setting up kindergartens, nurseries, and homes for the elderly.[21] The organization was also involved in the anti-lynching effort; for example, in 1922 under NACW president Mary Talbert, they formed the "anti-lynching crusaders" and set out to fundraise on behalf of the fight against lynching.[22] However, efforts to counter lynching were coordinated by the NAACP. Writing about African American club women's involvement in the anti-lynching struggle, Deborah Gray White reveals:

Until the 1920's black women's organizations were basically devoted to self-help uplift and community development. This meant that although NACW women lobbied

---

[17] There were, of course, black radicals who spoke out against racial violence and who were members of other left-leaning organizations (e.g., the African Blood Brotherhood and the Liberty League) but there was no independent black left organization besides the NAACP that focused on this issue during this time period. For an excellent discussion of black radicalism, see Michael Dawson, *Blacks In and Out of the Left*, Cambridge: Harvard University Press, 2013.

[18] A. Philip Randolph's Brotherhood of Sleeping Car Porters was founded in 1925 and thus falls outside of the time period in question.

[19] For more on the NACW, see Paula Giddings, *When and Where I Enter: The Impact of Black Women on Race and Sex in America*, New York: Morrow, 1984, pp. 95–117; Elizabeth Davis, *Lifting As They Climb*, New York: G. K. Hall, 1996; Deborah Gray White, *Too Heavy A Load: Black Women in Defense of Themselves, 1894–1994*, New York: W. W. Norton, 1999; Mary Jane Davis, *Eradicating This Evil: Women in the American Anti-Lynching Movement, 1892–1940*, New York: Garland, 2000; Melissa Harris-Perry, *Sister Citizen: Shame, Stereotypes, and Black Women in America*, New Haven: Yale University Press, 2011.

[20] Paula Giddings, *When and Where I Enter: The Impact of Black Women on Race and Sex in America*, New York: Morrow, 1984, p. 95.

[21] Beverley Jones, "Mary Church Terrell and the National Association of Colored Women 1896–1901," *The Journal of Negro History* 67, no. 1 (1982): 20–23; John Hope Franklin, *From Slavery to Freedom: A History of African Americans*, 8th ed., New York: A. A. Knopf, 2000.

[22] Robert Zangrando, *The NAACP Crusade Against Lynching, 1909–1950*, Philadelphia: Temple University Press, 1980, pp. 77–79.

nationally for antilynching legislation, and used a national platform to defend black women, their fundamental approach was to create or support local institutions.[23]

Though the NACW played an important role in the struggle to end lynching and mob violence, its role was auxiliary to the NAACP.

The fastest growing and most popular organization during this time period was the UNIA, with a membership of more than 2 million by 1919.[24] Jamaican-born Marcus Garvey formed the UNIA in New York in May 1917 to spread the message of black nationalism. Believing that racial equality between blacks and whites would never happen, Garvey championed a "back to Africa" movement in which he hoped to return all people of African descent to Africa.[25] The UNIA promoted racial unity and pride, and Garvey made famous the notion "black is beautiful" long before it was popularized in the 1960s. While path-breaking, the mission of the UNIA was not focused on addressing the structures of oppression such as lynching on a national level. Its concentration was insular, focusing on developing racial pride among the black community and preparing black peoples to return to Africa.[26]

Similarly inward looking, the NUL was founded in 1910 with a focus on strengthening structures of support in the African American community.[27] The NUL aimed to improve conditions of black migrants in cities and directed

[23] Deborah Gray White, *Too Heavy a Load: Black Women in Defense of Themselves, 1894–1994*, New York: W. W. Norton, 1999, p. 146. See also Mary Jane Davis, *Eradicating this Evil: Women in the American Anti-Lynching Movement, 1892–1940*, New York: Garland, 2000, pp. 10, 95.

[24] Garvey was inconsistent in his estimate of global UNIA followers. For example, in August 1924, Garvey wrote that the UNIA movement had at least 55,000 followers between the United States and Great Britain. However, in September 1923, Garvey claimed that the UNIA's membership had risen from 2 million members in 1919 to 6 million members in more than 900 branches worldwide. "Negroes: Garvey Again," *TIME*, Vol. 4, issue 6, (August 11, 1924): pp. 5–6; Marcus Garvey, "The Negro's Greatest Enemy," *Current History* 18, no. 6 (1923): pp. 951–957.

[25] For more on the UNIA and Garvey, see Tony Martin, *Race First: The Ideological and Organizational Struggles of Marcus Garvey and the Universal Negro Improvement Association*, Westport, CT: Greenwood Press, 1976; Lawrence Levin, "Marcus Garvey and the Politics of Revitalization," *Black Leaders of the Twentieth Century*, edited by John Hope Franklin and August Meier, Urbana: University of Illinois Press, 1982; Judith Stein, *The World of Marcus Garvey: Race and Class in Modern Society*, Baton Rouge: Louisiana State University Press, 1986; Colin Grant, *Negro with a Hat: The Rise and Fall of Marcus Garvey*, New York: Oxford University Press, 2008; Alvin Tillery, *Between Homeland and Motherland: Africa, US Foreign Policy, and Black Leadership in America*, Ithaca, NY: Cornell University Press, 2011.

[26] This is not to say that Garvey and the UNIA ignored the issues of lynching and mob violence. Garvey spoke out about lynching and the East St. Louis Riot of 1917, but this was not a top agenda issue for the UNIA.

[27] Guichard Parris and Lester Brooks, *Blacks in the City: A History of the National Urban League*, Boston and Toronto: Little Brown and Company, 1971; Nancy Weiss, *The National Urban League 1910–1940*, New York: Oxford University Press, 1974; John Hope Franklin, *From Slavery to Freedom: A History of African Americans*, 8th ed., New York: A. A. Knopf, 2000.

the majority of its efforts to finding employment, housing, and sponsored job training and other programs for youth.[28] While the NUL acknowledged the menace of lynching, it preferred to deal with issues of philanthropy and social economy in the African American community rather than fight for political and civil rights on a national platform.[29]

Finally, Booker T. Washington's Tuskegee Institute, discussed in Chapter 2, supported an accommodationist strategy, advocating the path to greater equality would come through hard work and patience – not political protest and active rights claiming. Thus, the Tuskegee Institute, the most influential African American organization in the early part of the twentieth century did not actively address the host of social ills crippling the African American community on the national political scene. For the most part, Washington believed lynching was too controversial an issue to address in public settings and did not want to antagonize his white allies.[30]

Thus, in the first quarter of the twentieth century, the NAACP was among a small handful of organizations rethinking the relationship between race and American democracy and one of the few that placed racist violence at the crux of citizenship. If individuals could be lynched by a mob, they were not free and equal. This book has deliberately sidestepped the peak of the civil rights movement, choosing instead to focus on the beginning – when the seeds of civil rights were being sowed and staggering losses were incurred next to astonishing victories. The NAACP, working in a relative silo, endured setbacks in the legislative and executive branches but was able to shine a national spotlight on the violent spectacle of mob violence and secured federal protection in the form of a landmark Supreme Court case. It wasn't a steady march forward for the NAACP, but it was a necessary one that helped position the organization to have a greater impact on the federal government in the years to come.

Citizen Activism and American Political Development

The NAACP's movement against racist violence shaped the type of government we have as well as society as a whole. Democracy no longer meant unbridled violence toward one group of people. Of course, all did not immediately

---

[28] Meeting Minutes, Committee on Urban Conditions Among Negroes, New York, September 29, 1910, National Urban League Collection, Library of Congress.

[29] Nancy Weiss, *The National Urban League 1910–1940*, New York: Oxford University Press, 1974, p. 65.

[30] August Meier, *Negro Thought in America, 1880–1915: Radical Ideologies in the Age of Booker T. Washington*, Ann Arbor: The University of Michigan Press, 1963; Cary Wintz, ed., *African American Political Thought, 1890–1930: Washington, Du Bois, Garvey, and Randolph*, Armonk, NY: M. E. Sharpe, 1996; Wilson Jeremiah Moses, *Creative Conflict in African American Thought: Frederick Douglass, Alexander Crummell, Booker T. Washington, W.E.B. Du Bois, and Marcus Garvey*, New York: Cambridge University Press, 2004.

change, but it was a critical first step in showing that marginalized citizens could impact the sacred boundaries of state power. Just how this feat was accomplished magnifies the feedback process between state and society – specifically, it shows how civil rights organizations can mediate between the state and black civil society. I have grounded the analysis in this book between two areas of research: social history, which tends to focus on individuals and organizations, and political science which tends to emphasize the way existing institutional arrangements and state elites shape political development. From a methodological perspective, the thrust of this book has been to show that a fuller picture emerges when we combine insight from both disciplines and treat the interaction between state and citizens as dynamic. I believe much is to be gained in empirical political science analyses by paying closer attention to non-elite citizen presence in state development as well as institutional constraints in the political environment.

The NAACP's campaign to end racial violence provides compelling evidence that political institutions can sometimes reflect the expressions of society's preferences. Put simply: institutional development derives from the tension between powerful actors and those who contest and critique the projects they seek to implement. The NAACP made a strong case for the growth of federal government authority by drawing attention to the persistence of racial violence and the inability of states to appropriately punish those responsible. The effort that culminated in the landmark Supreme Court decision *Moore v. Dempsey* in particular, exemplifies how the NAACP created opportunities for black civil society to challenge Jim Crow (via criminal court trials) and how the organization ultimately pushed the federal government in a new direction. These were ordinary African American citizens – sharecroppers and teachers and domestic workers and storeowners – unwilling to sit idly by and watch the escalation of injustice, but equipped with an unrelenting belief that the United States' best days were ahead. These citizen actors contested the boundaries of what it meant to live in a democracy in which government purports to care for all citizens. The Supreme Court's decision in *Moore* chipped away at an enshrined system of white supremacy, disrupting the presumption that southern states ought to be the sole architects of policies involving the intersection of race and justice.

This has not been simply an account about how the NAACP influenced the federal government in a particular direction but also about how its victory in the Supreme Court began to inscribe litigation in the NAACP's advocacy and social change strategies. The arrow of influence did not merely flow one way as extant studies have too often uncritically assumed. Just as the NAACP's organizational priorities were influenced by political dynamics, the organization would in turn reshape the political landscape. A telling example of the change in perspective about how to fight racial injustice came from W. E. B. Du Bois, who, in 1903, wrote, "Negroes came to look upon courts as instruments of injustice and oppression." His tone became more hopeful after the Arkansas cases, which he called "notable fights for justice."[31] Du Bois went even further in his praise in acknowledging the legal aid provided by Moorfield Storey, who argued *Moore v. Dempsey* in front of the Supreme Court: "Moorfield Storey has rendered a service which makes him immortal in the struggle for full justice to the Negro."[32] This dramatic shift in understanding law as an oppressive institution to one that could operate as a vehicle of change for African Americans over a twenty-year timespan was not just personal – it was also organizational. In drafting out a tentative program of future activities in February 1923, the NAACP wrote:

> The fight for the Arkansas peons should be continued. The scope of our defense work should be widened so as to include the giving of aid to branches that have undertaken the defense of cases too costly or too important for them to handle alone. The inability to give such aid has always been a source of deep regret and often embarrassment. For comprehensive and effective legal defense work, a defense fund from $25,000 to $50,000 is necessary.[33]

Indeed, mirroring the general feeling of many African Americans in the wake of *Moore v. Dempsey*, Du Bois and the NAACP readjusted their perspective of the utility of a litigation-centered strategy in the effort to bring about equal citizenship rights.

This feedback loop between state and society is not limited to the NAACP and federal courts. The argument I make in this book is part of a burgeoning body of literature that is explicitly concerned with this intersection. Increasingly, scholars take as a starting point the notion that residents of a polity and the state are joint players in the construction of American society and politics. Deliberation is understood to happen at institutional sites in addition to less formal venues in civil society. Deviating from established traditions in political science and history, this means that there is not an autonomous state in which citizens are simply made to respond to, nor are the actions of the social sphere prioritized; it means that the preferences of each often converge, and what we get in the end is a symbiosis of both. Certain transformations in the sphere of American politics remain understudied, for example: What led to the growth of state police power at the end of the nineteenth century? How did protections for homosexuality become ensconced in law? What explains the pre–New Deal growth of disaster relief? Why did state constitutions include provisions for labor rights at the beginning of the twentieth century? Scholars in American political development, legal history, and political history have started to tread this path, and their research reveals exciting insight.[34] In a sweeping analysis,

---

[31] W. E. B. Du Bois, *The Souls of Black Folk*, Chicago: A. C. McClurg & Co., 1903, p. 118; "Opinion of W. E. B. Du Bois," *The Crisis* Vol. 25, no. 5 (1923), p. 200.

[32] "Opinion of W. E. B. Du Bois," *The Crisis* Vol. 25, no. 5 (1923), p. 200.

[33] Tentative Draft of Proposed Activities of the NAACP, February 5, 1923, Part 1, NAACP Papers, Manuscript Division, Library of Congress, Washington DC.

[34] Alan Brinkley, *Voices of Protest: Huey Long, Father Coughlin and the Great Depression*, New York: Random House, 1982; Elizabeth Sanders, *Roots of Reform: Farm Workers and*

Marie Gottschalk argues that the building of the "carceral state" has deep historical and institutional roots and details the impact of four social movement struggles (victims', women's, prisoners', and death penalty activists') in making the criminal justice system more punitive.[35] In Gottschalk's hands, the rise of the carceral state was a confluence of state policy objectives and citizen groups. In a similar vein but on a separate topic, James Sparrow focuses on World War II and chronicles how the federal government greatly enlarged its powers over many aspects of American life.[36] At the same time, Sparrow's analysis details how citizens were making counterclaims and clamoring for an expanding vision of citizenship rights. Sparrow's work shows how this moment was every bit about the redefinition of American citizenship as it was about the expanding power of the federal government during wartime. Gottschalk and Sparrow explore areas that have been mined before but by taking seriously the agency of the state and the social arena, they are able to present a reinterpretation of important facets of American politics.

We Can't Be Silent! We Got to Fight Back!

While parts of this book draw from distinct moments in which the practices and aspirations discussed were cultivated, it is designed to address long-standing questions central to the development of the U.S. political system, such as: How is American democracy contested and restructured over time? How have marginalized individuals in our polity challenged what it means to be a U.S. citizen? Can social protest shift governmental institutions? To revisit the NAACP's campaign to end racial violence a century later is to celebrate the role of citizen activism but also to acknowledge the fragility of citizenship and the complicated process of institutional change.

The narrative of the NAACP documented throughout the pages of this book provides a window in how groups far outside of the political mainstream can get their voices heard in the national political process. The NAACP, during a

---

the American State, 1877–1916, Chicago: University of Chicago Press, 1999; Julie Novkov, *Constituting Workers, Protecting Women: Gender, Law, and Labor in the Progressive Era and New Deal Years*, Ann Arbor: University of Michigan Press, 2001; Paul Frymer, *Black and Blue: African Americans, the Labor Movement, and the Decline of the Democratic Party*, Princeton: Princeton University Press, 2008; Margot Canaday, *The Straight State: Sexuality and Citizenship in Twentieth Century America*, Princeton: Princeton University Press, 2011; Michele Landis Dauber, *The Sympathetic State: Disaster Relief and the Origins of the American Welfare State*, Chicago: University of Chicago Press, 2012; Tomiko Brown-Nagin, *Courage to Dissent: Atlanta and the Long History of the Civil Rights Movement*, New York: Oxford University Press, 2012; Emily Zackin, *Looking for Rights in All the Wrong Places: Why State Constitutions Contain America's Positive Rights*, Princeton: Princeton University Press, 2013.

[35] Marie Gottschalk, *The Prison and the Gallows: The Politics of Mass Incarceration in America*, Cambridge: Cambridge University Press, 2006.

[36] James Sparrow, *Warfare State: World War II Americans and the Age of Big Government*, New York: Oxford University Press, 2011.

low point in the state of U.S. race relations, forced its way into the Oval Office, congressional hearings, and eventually into the Supreme Court. This was not the result of fortuitous timing or deep pockets of funding but the workings of a social movement organization that engaged in protest directed at the three branches of government. Subsequently, the NAACP chose to focus its attention on the legal arena not due to some intrinsic power of the law to create social change but because the Supreme Court was the one branch of government where the organization secured a substantive breakthrough.

The NAACP's campaign shares many characteristics with contemporary movements for social change in American society. In particular, two dramatic events occurred in 2011 for which my research provides greater context. First is the campaign to prevent the execution of Troy Davis in September 2011. Troy Davis, an African American man, had spent twenty-two years on death row for the killing of a white police officer. He sat on Georgia's death row, a state notorious for racial bias in its criminal justice system.[37] Support for his plea of innocence grew as seven of the nine witnesses recanted their testimony. No DNA or physical evidence could be produced that Davis was even at the scene of the crime. Davis's supporters, who included politicians, activists, and social media users worldwide, called for the execution to be delayed because of "too much doubt," a phrase that became the slogan for the campaign in support of a stay in the execution. The leading rights organizations in the country, including the American Civil Liberties Union (ACLU), Amnesty International, and the NAACP, mobilized on behalf of Davis. Millions of citizens signed petitions, carried makeshift signs in demonstrations, and wrote letters. While successful in shifting the narrative and raising public awareness about the issue of the death penalty and the disproportionate number of minorities behind bars, the protest was not successful in stopping Davis's execution. In the swirl of questions that arose in the moments after he was executed one looms large: Did the protest matter? Was there any chance for this organized protest to make a difference against something as formidable as the U.S. criminal justice system?

Following closely on the heels of the Troy Davis protests were those of the Occupy Movement that began in Zuccotti Park in New York City but quickly spread across the country and even around the world. Rallying against the growing gap between rich and poor, corporate greed, and political policies that protect these corporations, men, women, and children took to the streets in huge numbers to protest. The protesters' slogan "We are the 99%" refers to the growing income and wealth inequality in the United States between the wealthiest 1 percent and the rest of the population. Frequent and at times well organized demonstrations were conducted across the country, and protesters took up residence in city parks. During the protests, House majority leader Eric Cantor dismissed the Occupy protests as "growing mobs." Later, in March

---

[37] See *McCleskey v. Kemp*, 481 U.S. 279 (1987).

2012, New York City Mayor Michael Bloomberg justified the arrest of seventy Occupy protesters, arguing:

Just trying to cause chaos doesn't do anything to advance anybody's cause. It doesn't make society better. If you have something really to say that would be a great contribution, nobody can hear you when everybody's yelling and screaming and pushing and shoving. But it makes great theater.

Bloomberg's flippant dismissal of the protests as "theater," while not surprising, does call into question the effectiveness of this mass movement: can citizens use widespread protest to transform politics or is government impenetrable?

What the Troy Davis and Occupy protests have in common is a question about how social movements can engage with powerful political institutions. Can citizens shift the operation of the criminal justice system? Can citizens work in the political process against an entrenched and privileged 1 percent? These questions can be asked because the relationship between citizen activism and the development of federal institutions and policy is viewed in this book as dynamic. This book helps to show that citizens matter in ways critical to the development of U.S. politics and that, similar to the Troy Davis and the Occupy protests, they can shift the narrative, but protest must also be connected to shifting multiple institutional structures to create entrenched disorganization in the system. After the apex of social movement activism in the 1960s and 1970s, an emphasis has been placed on public demonstrations and rights litigation, but this focus may be misguided. For example, the scholarship of Steven Teles has been instrumental in explaining how conservative legal organizations, following and expanding upon the model set forth by their liberal forebears, have upended legal institutions and used the law to institutionalize their agenda.[38] This does not mean that litigation is no longer a viable strategy to social movements seeking policy transformations – just that it is no longer the panacea it has long been thought to be.

Building successful movements means that we must revisit lessons of the past while critically rethinking the present. Proving tactics from the NAACP's struggle against racist violence may have import today. A silent protest march was held along Fifth Avenue in New York City on June 17, 2012. Modeled after the Silent Protest March in 1917 that James Weldon Johnson helped organize, which was discussed in Chapter 3, the 2012 march saw thousands of marchers take to the street in protest against New York City's official stop-and-frisk policy. It had been revealed that a disproportionate amount – 87 percent of individuals who were stopped and frisked by the NYPD in 2011 – were black or Latino.[39] Organized by the NAACP, and supported by more than 299 rights organizations, unions, religious groups, and cultural organizations, the

---

[38] Steven Teles, *The Rise of the Conservative Legal Movement: The Battle for Control of the Law*, Princeton: Princeton University Press, 2008.

[39] New York Civil Liberties Union, "Stop-and-Frisk Report 2011," May 9, 2012, 27 pages.

protesters silently marched from 110th Street to Mayor Bloomberg's residence on 79th Street. Nevertheless, foretelling that the strategies from the past would not be enough to quell the exigencies of the current crisis, a few dozen protesters voiced their frustration with the silent strategy at the end of the march and chanted in unison: "We can't be silent! We got to fight back!"[40]

The Center for Constitutional Rights (CCR), the Legal Aid Society, the NAACP-LDF, and the ACLU were already a step ahead and had filed in federal court three separate lawsuits focused on overreaches of the NYPD's stop-and-frisk policy. The lawsuits argued that different aspects of the NYPD's stop-and-frisk policies and practices were unconstitutional and should be fundamentally changed. The ACLU lawsuit took the most narrow focus of the three, alleging that the NYPD was illegally targeting and stopping residents of public housing projects in the Bronx. In a huge win for activists, on January 8, 2013, a federal judge agreed with the ACLU and determined the NYPD "displayed deliberate indifference toward a widespread practice of unconstitutional trespass stops" and passed an injunction prohibiting unjustifiable stop-and-frisk tactics outside of certain buildings in the Bronx.[41] The lawsuit, jointly filed by the NAACP-LDF and the Legal Aid Society, is centered on the unlawful stopping and arrests of residents and guests of all public housing operated by the New York Housing Authority. The lawsuit also alleges that the NYPD's practices are based on racial discrimination against blacks and Latinos and thus violate the Fourteenth Amendment. The case captured the attention of *The New York Times* editorial board who admonished the NYPD's practices in a critical article titled "Public Housing as a 'Penal Colony.'"[42] At the time this book is going to press, the judge has rejected most of the city's challenges to the plaintiff's claims and allowed the case to move forward to trial.[43]

The case the CCR filed is the most expansive of the three lawsuits in terms of the scope of its constitutional complaint and numbers of plaintiffs. The CCR case is a class-action lawsuit against the NYPD and the City of New York on behalf of individuals aggrieved by racial profiling and stop-and-frisk policies (arguing that the NYPD's policies were a violation of individuals' Fourth and Fourteenth Amendment rights to be free from unreasonable searches and seizures, and to be free from racial discrimination).[44] The case challenges the lack of the requisite "reasonable suspicion" for conducting these searches and the blatant racial disparities in who is stopped.[45] After a ten-week trial filled with riveting testimony – including a secretly recorded conversation where a deputy

---

[40] John Leland and Colin Moynihan, "Thousands March Silently to Protest Stop-and-Frisk Policies," *The New York Times*, June 17, 2012.

[41] *Ligon v. City of New York*, 12 Civ. 2274, (S.D.N.Y. 2013).

[42] "Public Housing as a 'Penal Colony,'" *The New York Times*, April 2, 2013, p. A26.

[43] *Davis v. City of New York*, 10 Civ. 0699 (S.D.N.Y. 2013).

[44] *Floyd v. City of New York*, 283 F.R.D. 153, 159 (S.D.N.Y. 2012).

[45] In *Terry v. Ohio*, 392 U.S. 1 (1968), the Supreme Court held that even limited stops by police officers must be based on the standard of "reasonable suspicion."

inspector instructed a patrol officer to go after "male blacks [ages] 14–21" because they commit the most crimes – the judge ruled against the NYPD, calling stop-and-frisk a "policy of indirect racial profiling." The historic decision declared stop-and-frisk as practiced unconstitutional and called for the implementation of a number of remedies including a monitoring program.[46]

Notable about these different legal challenges to stop-and-frisk are the efforts made by the NAACP-LDF, ACLU, Legal Aid Society, CCR, and the Communities United for Police Reform (CPR) to raise national public awareness about the injustice. CPR is particularly interesting because it has brought together organizations, lawyers, researchers, and activists to work for change in the NYPD's policies and unites many of the litigation-centered and grassroots organizations under one umbrella. These organizations have made various reports available online for public consumption; the reports document racial disparities, debunk the claim that more stops lead to a reduction in crime, inform New Yorkers of their legal rights, and put a face to these demoralizing stops through the personal stories of innocent New Yorkers who were wrongly stopped and frisked. Organizations encouraged supporters to rally in front of the courthouse to show solidarity and generate media attention – many carried banners and stood outside in the cold for hours. Attorneys and key witnesses were seen on the morning and evening news circuit making their case directly to the public about why the NYPD's tactics were in need of reform. Organizations even utilized social media – CCR for example, told supporters to use the hashtag #NYPDonTrial to track their tweets and Facebook posts of the trial (#ChangeTheNYPD was another popular hashtag). It quickly became apparent that this was not just a litigation campaign – it also sought to change the hearts and minds of millions.

In addition, lobbying of local politicians to denounce the NYPD's stop-and-frisk policy has been useful in building up a well of public and political support. Many New York politicians donned "Stop! Stop-and-frisk" buttons at the June 2012 rally to distance themselves from the controversial policy. Further lobbying of local politicians in 2012 led to a meeting with the U.S. Justice Department where activists demanded a federal investigation into the constitutionality of the stop-and-frisk program. Recent evidence demonstrating that

---

[46] *Floyd, et al. v. City of New York*, 8 Civ. 1034, (S.D.N.Y. 2013). Judge Shira Scheindlin wrote in her first opinion, "I find that the City is liable for violating plaintiffs' Fourth and Fourteenth Amendment rights. The City acted with deliberate indifference toward the NYPD's practice of making unconstitutional stops and conducting unconstitutional frisks." And in her second opinion, Scheindlin stated: "To address the violations that I have found, I shall order various remedies including, but not limited to, an immediate change to certain policies and activities of the NYPD, a trial program requiring the use of body-worn cameras in one precinct per borough, a community-based joint remedial process to be conducted by a court-appointed facilitator, and the appointment of an independent monitor to ensure that the NYPD's conduct of stops and frisks is carried out in accordance with the Constitution and the principles enunciated in this Opinion, and to monitor the NYPD's compliance with the ordered remedies."

these various attempts at reforming stop-and-frisk are working was provided by the 2013 New York City mayoral contest, where many of the democratic candidates (most notably Bill de Blasio) made reforming the NYPD's stop-and-frisk program as a central component of their campaign platforms.

The movement to reform New York City's stop-and-frisk policies is instructive for future mass citizen mobilization and touches on central themes raised throughout this book. First, it is clear that protest for the sake of protest, untethered to one (and increasingly two) of the three branches of government, will not shift governmental structures and, at best, provide symbolic benefit. Second, coalition building between different organizations has become important in legitimizing and strengthening movements in the modern era – especially since it often takes a long time for arguments to gain widespread acceptance. The notion that beautiful posters, long marches, and emotional speeches by themselves will change the way government operates or lead to a radical transformation in society is an illusion. Dispelling this myth is crucial if we are to build a just democracy in which social movements are not simply forces – but the decisive shapers of significant reform. In making this claim, I do not mean to suggest that mass citizen protest is unimportant. On the contrary, I believe the only way our society will improve is if we mobilize and build robust and vibrant movements but that it is crucial to tie protest on the ground to protest inside political institutions. There is no doubt that the Troy Davis and Occupy movements have been useful in building up a stronger civil society and raising awareness about injustice, but both movements have also purported to demand accountability from government officials and a desire to shift governmental institutions to increase fairness – therefore, more is required. In contrast, the campaign to reform New York City's stop-and-frisk policies is an example of how social movement protest – when connected to several different political institutions – can disrupt entrenched political hierarchies.

Utopian Call to Arms

In two different books, noted chroniclers of black politics and the black freedom struggle, Michael Dawson and Robin Kelley, address the urgent question posed by Martin Luther King Jr. in what would be his final manuscript on the civil rights movement: Where do we go from here?[47] Their answers to this question are noteworthy for what they lack. Instead of a trite analysis that pits public suasion tactics against political lobbying against legal mobilization, Dawson and Kelley both stress the importance of imagination in moving forward. Emphasizing the necessity to dream outside of the box of available strategies, Dawson argues: "We need a pragmatic utopianism – one that starts where

---

[47] Robin D. G. Kelley, *Freedom Dreams: The Black Radical Imagination*, Boston: Beacon Press, 2002; Michael Dawson, *Blacks In and Out of the Left: Past, Present and Future*, Cambridge: Harvard University Press, 2013.

we are, but imagines where we want to be." According to Kelley, "The map to a new world is in the imagination, in what we see in our third eyes rather than in the desolation that surrounds us." The scholarship of Dawson and Kelley holds particularly true in thinking about some of the greatest achievements in civil rights. From the transformational bus boycott in Montgomery to American Indian fish-in protests in Washington state to the Chicano blowouts in East Los Angeles, imagination has proven to be a critical component to eventual success. The larger movements behind each of these triumphs were fueled – not through a logical evaluation of the political opportunity structure – but by a belief in an idealistic dream of a different and more just society.

A significant takeaway from the NAACP's campaign against racial violence is that the starting place for any contemporary movement must reside in a bold utopian vision of a new society. Unlike many contemporary rights–based struggles that stranglehold themselves by focusing on established movement narratives and a canon of lessons learned, the cash-strapped NAACP worked to change all three branches of government guided only by a grander vision of America than it had thus far experienced. This was a group of individuals, explicitly denied their citizenship rights, murdered in broad daylight under the auspices of the state, who chose to organize and fight back. It didn't matter to James Weldon Johnson, Walter White, or the thousands of NAACP support-ers in local branches that the federal government had refused to conclusively protect their right to live – they imagined a government that would one day listen to the voices of its most marginalized citizens. And to the extent that the Supreme Court began to respond to the most egregious miscarriages of south-ern injustice, they were at least partially correct.

Appendix

Manuscript Sources

This book is based mainly on firsthand source material and supplemented by secondhand sources. First and most important to my analysis were the Papers of the National Association for the Advancement of Colored People (NAACP), located at the National Library of Congress in Washington, DC. I conducted a small portion of the research using the microfiche film while a graduate student at Princeton University but the bulk of the research was undertaken through numerous visits to the Library of Congress. The NAACP Papers are tremendous in volume and represent the largest single collection ever acquired by the Library of Congress. The entire collection contains around 5 million items dating from 1909 to 2003. It is truly a rich resource that speaks to the careful records kept by the NAACP and the librarians who have dutifully protected and preserved the NAACP Papers over the years. Of particular importance in the NAACP Papers to the writing of this book were National Board of Director Minutes, Annual Reports, Special Correspondence file, NAACP Visual file, American Fund for Public Service file, Arkansas General file, and the Anti-Lynching file. Together, these archival materials helped me piece together a story, the important players involved, and to understand the interworkings of the NAACP.

The number of articles and books that touch on different aspects of the NAACP is considerable. But the focus on the NAACP has not been equal; much of it has underscored the organization's courageous and deliberate attack on the Jim Crow system of education. In part, owing to the significance of *Brown v. Board* to the development of civil rights law and to the civil rights imagination, researchers have focused on the formation and execution of the education desegregation campaign and such luminaries as Charles Houston and Thurgood Marshall. There has been much less research that has focused on the NAACP's campaign against lynching and mob violence, and researchers who do mention it do so only in passing, choosing instead to focus on other landmark events in describing the history of the NAACP. Researchers who have provided excellent histories of the NAACP include Patricia Sullivan's *Lift*

Every Voice, Manfred Berg's *The Ticket To Freedom*, and Charles Kellogg's *A History of the NAACP*. There are two book-length manuscripts that focus solely on different aspects of the NAACP's campaign against racial violence: Robert Zangrando's *The NAACP Crusade Against Lynching 1909–1950* centers on the organization's efforts to pass anti-lynching legislation in Congress, and Richard Cortner's *A Mob Intent on Death* focuses on the NAACP's efforts behind *Moore v. Dempsey*. Even with this existing scholarship, there is no account that documents the full extent of the NAACP's campaign against lynching and mob violence in shifting public opinion, the executive Branch, the legislative Branch, and the Supreme Court. This is an area of the NAACP's papers that has been barely mined by researchers, and much of what I document in this book are new findings as a result of delving into different parts of this collection.

Though the Library of Congress serves as the official repository for the NAACP, there is a noticeable absence of the Phillips County massacre of 1919 and the NAACP's subsequent involvement in *Moore v. Dempsey* (1923) in the NAACP Papers, which might have a connection with the erasure of the NAACP from this case in most legal studies. Fortunately, Arthur Waskow, who wrote a dissertation and then a book comparing riots during the Red Summer of 1919 to riots in the 1960s, copied verbatim typewritten transcripts of much of this material. For his book-length manuscript, see *From Race Riot to Sit-In, 1919 and the 1960s* (Garden City: Doubleday & Co., 1966). His notes were deposited in the Wisconsin State Historical Society at the University of Wisconsin in Madison and fill two note card boxes, each holding about twelve linear inches of notes on 4-inch-by-6-inch sheets of paper. Approximately half of one box relates to Arkansas.

Over the course of writing this book, the records of the American Fund for Public Service (AFPS) were used extensively. The AFPS collection is housed in the Brooke Russell Astor Reading Room in the beautiful Stephen A. Schwarzman Building at the New York Public Library on 42nd Street. Almost every progressive group active from 1922 to 1941 is represented among the fund's applicants. The collection is comprehensive and incredibly informative, detailing correspondence between the fund's committees, applications approved and denied and new policy directions. Particularly helpful in the writing of this book were Boxes 1, 2–8, 15, 23, and 28. Besides an organizational history by Gloria Samson (*The American Fund for Public Service: Charles Garland and Radical Philanthropy 1922–1941*), which focuses little on the NAACP's fight against lynching, and Mark Tushnet's book (*The NAACP's Legal Strategy Against Segregated Education, 1925–1950*), which mostly focuses on the influence of the AFPS on the development of the NAACP's litigation strategy after 1925, not that much work has examined the relationship between the NAACP and the AFPS from 1922 to 1925. The AFPS collection is an extremely valuable source for what it reveals about left-wing organizations in the first half of the twentieth century and ought to be mined further by researchers.

Individuals

In recounting the relationship between President Woodrow Wilson and the NAACP, I relied largely on the published collection (sixty-nine volumes) of Wilson correspondence, compiled by noted Wilson biographer Arthur Link, and the Woodrow Wilson Papers at the Library of Congress. The Link collection is a monumental, comprehensive, and essential account that contains a considerable amount of correspondence that is not present in Wilson's papers at the Library of Congress. Link has tracked down many of the letters Wilson wrote to others, since unlike the NAACP, he rarely kept copies of outgoing letters. As a result, a much more complete view of what was going on in Wilson's mind and his approach to issues of race is spelled out, among numerous other issues, in this collection. Chapter 3 indicates my reliance on Link's work in recounting his correspondence with others. However, while the Link collection is considered to document all the significant events in which Wilson played a major role, it does not fully encapsulate Wilson's views on the race question. In an effort to address this issue, I have utilized Wilson's correspondence with Thomas Dixon (film director and Wilson's college roommate) and Joseph Tumulty (Wilson's chief of staff) about "Birth of a Nation" in the Wilson Papers at the Library of Congress. A considerable amount of research has appropriately focused on Wilson's troubling race policies during his first term (for a political science treatment of this, please see Desmond King's *Separate and Unequal: African Americans and the US Federal Government*), and I document them in this book; much less, however, has sown together his papers with the NAACP's papers in describing how Wilson's approach to African Americans shifted – at least, in some notable ways during his second term.

Very little has been written about President Warren G. Harding that does not focus on the Tea Pot Dome scandal or how he was an ineffective president, and certainly no published work has placed him, as I do, as friendly with the NAACP. Much of the documentation I utilized in the section on Harding in Chapter 3 has never been used before. To reconstruct the relationship between Harding and the NAACP, I drew from the NAACP Special Correspondence file and the Warren G. Harding Papers, held at the Ohio Historical Society and available on microfiche. The NAACP Special Correspondence file contains much of the back-and-forth between James Weldon Johnson and Harding before and after he was sworn in as president. The Warren G. Harding Papers sheds light on his official correspondence once in office and also documents letters to and from George B. Christensen (Harding's chief of staff). In the Harding papers, I made use of Series 2 and 4, which cover a portion of Harding's years in the Senate and as president of the United States. Specifically, I used Reel 22, which includes correspondence with James Weldon Johnson during his presidential campaign; Roll 193, which includes the Negro Lynching File and correspondence on the Dyer Anti-Lynching Bill; Reel 174, which contains seven folders titled Miscellaneous Negro Matters; Reel 150, which contains the Negro Matters file; Reels 192 and 193, which contain six files titled Negro Lynching; Reel 229, which addresses the issue of "Negro rights" in Harding's administration; and Reel 232, which contains a specific file devoted to Harding's correspondence with the NAACP. Through these different sources, I was able to gain a much better sense of Harding's approach to issues of racial violence, broadly, and to the NAACP, specifically.

However, it is important to state that unlike his predecessor President Wilson, Harding's papers are not exhaustive. Unfortunately, upon Harding's death in August 1923, his wife, Florence Harding, destroyed many of their personal papers in hopes of preserving her husband's legacy in the midst of an escalating political scandal. Warren G. Harding's official senatorial and presidential papers were kept virtually intact but were safeguarded in a trust made up of the Harding's closest political confidants. In 1963, it was decided that the papers would be donated to the Ohio Historical Society, and in 1964, more than forty years after Harding's death, his papers were finally open to researchers.

The papers of the leaders of the NAACP were revealing. In particular, the Oswald Garrison Villard Papers at the Houghton Library at Harvard University proved particularly useful in sketching out the contours of the NAACP's founding and of the organization's struggle in appealing to President Woodrow Wilson. The papers of Villard, one of the NAACP's founders, are a largely untapped resource that contain much of the correspondence concerning the progressive social issues that he was involved in, relevant articles in *The Nation* and *The New York Evening Post*, and speeches. The collection of letters addressed to and from him is meticulously organized by last name. Individual folders that I consulted include: Mary White Ovington, Moorfield Storey, W. E. B. Du Bois, William Lloyd Garrison (grandfather), Francis Jackson Garrison (uncle), Fanny Garrison Villard (mom), and Woodrow Wilson. Surprisingly, a trove of useful information was hidden away in the small section categorized Uncataloged Papers in the Villard collection. In this section there are two boxes (labeled 120–120) that contain all the information concerning the NAACP in his records that could not be neatly categorized in the 4,430 folders in the main collection. Albeit a bit messy, these boxes were instructive.

Moorfield Storey was another prominent NAACP figure whose papers I examined. Storey was a leading American attorney and the first president of the NAACP. Storey's papers, comprising 2,500 items in twenty-two containers, are held at the Library of Congress. The collection has a useful index and provides insight to his relationship with NAACP leaders Mary White Ovington, Walter White, and Joel Spingarn, as well as important national politicians such as William Howard Taft and George Wickersham. The collection was revised and expanded in 1996, and the finding aid was revised for accuracy in 2008. The series that were utilized in the writing of this book were General Correspondence and Subject File. Though this collection is seen to represent only a small part of Storey's life, it was very useful to the writing of this book because a considerable portion of the collection focuses on Storey's service as NAACP president from 1910 to 1929.

Insight from other leaders in the NAACP was obtained from their published memoirs/autobiographies. These include Ida B. Wells (*Crusade For Justice*), Mary White Ovington (*The Walls Came Tumbling Down*), James Weldon Johnson (*Along This Way*), and Walter Francis White (*A Man Called White*). The four books discuss the lives of each individual and broad themes from the time, but each touches on specific aspects of the NAACP's formation and of its movement activities in its fight against lynching. These personal autobiographical accounts of important persons involved in the movement were helpful in gaining insight into the personalities and minds of the key decision makers of the NAACP.

Supreme Court Justices

To supplement the case analysis and to try to get a sense of the private motivations for the Supreme Court justices who voted in the majority, I mined the private papers of the following justices who sat on the court when *Moore v. Dempsey* was decided: Oliver Wendell Holmes, Louis Brandeis, William Howard Taft, and William Van Devanter. I examined their correspondence one year before and one year after *Moore v. Dempsey* was decided, looking for explicit mentions of the case, their reactions in private correspondence to the court's ruling, and, more broadly, any writings on lynchings and mob violence. Very little was found that was of use. However, what I did uncover was evidence that Justice Holmes was very friendly with Moorfield Storey (NAACP legal counsel in *Moore v. Dempsey*) and asked for his advice on Justice Mahlon Pitney's replacement a few months before *Moore v. Dempsey* was heard in the court and sent him a letter two months after *Moore* was decided about an unrelated matter. Also, as described in Chapter 5, Chief Justice Taft was secretly in favor of federal government intervention to halt the increase of lynchings and mob violence in southern states.

Bibliography

Manuscript Collections and Microforms

American Fund for Public Service Records, Rare Books and Manuscripts Division, Schwarzman Building, New York Public Library.

Arthur Waskow Papers, Wisconsin State Historical Society, University of Wisconsin, Madison.

Link, Arthur, ed., *The Papers of Woodrow Wilson*, Princeton: Princeton University Press, 1985.

Louis Brandeis Papers, Manuscript Division, Library of Congress, Washington, DC.

Moorfield Storey Papers. Library of Congress, Manuscript Division, Washington, DC.

National Association for the Advancement of Colored People. Annual Reports. New York, 1911–1929.

National Association for the Advancement of Colored People Records, Library of Congress, Manuscript Division, Washington, DC.

Oliver Wendell Holmes Papers, Manuscript Division, Library of Congress, Washington, DC.

Oswald Garrison Villard Papers (MS Am 1323), Houghton Library, Harvard University.

Warren G. Harding Papers, Manuscript Division, Library of Congress, Washington, DC.

Warren G. Harding Papers, Ohio Historical Society (microfilm edition).

William Howard Taft Papers, Manuscript Division, Library of Congress, Washington, DC.

William Van Devanter Papers, Manuscript Division, Library of Congress, Washington, DC.

Woodrow Wilson Papers, Manuscript Division, Library of Congress, Washington, DC.

Court Cases

Plessy v. Ferguson (1896)
Guinn v. United States (1915)

Buchanan v. Warley (1917)
Moore v. Dempsey (1923)
Brown v. Mississippi (1936)
Brown v. Board of Education of Topeka (1954)

U.S. Government Documents

Congress. Congressional Directory. 67th Congress, 2nd session, December 1921. Washington, DC: GPO, 1921.

Congress. Congressional Directory. 67th Congress, 3rd session, January 1922. Washington, DC: GPO, 1921.

Congress. Senate, Committee on the Judiciary, Report to Accompany H.R. 13, Senate Report No. 837, 67th Congress, 2nd session, December 1921. Washington, DC: GPO, 1921.

Index

Printed in the USA
CPSIA information can be obtained
at www.ICGtesting.com
LVHW021112080923
757490LV00004B/191